BOOKS BY SAM HAMILL

POETRY

Triada
Destination Zero: Poems 1970–1995
Gratitude

POETRY IN TRANSLATION

Night Traveling (from Chinese)
The Lotus Lovers (from Chinese)
The Same Sea in Us All (from the Estonian of Jaan Kaplinski)
The Art of Writing (Lu Chi's *Wen Fu*)
Catullus Redivivus (Selected Poems of Catullus)
Banished Immortal (Selected Poems of Li T'ai-po)
Facing the Snow (Selected Poems of Tu Fu)
The Wandering Border (from the Estonian of Jaan Kaplinski)
Narrow Road to the Interior (from the Japanese of Bashō)
Only Companion (Poems from the Japanese)
The Infinite Moment (Poems from Ancient Greek)
Endless River: Li Po and Tu Fu (Poems from Chinese)
Midnight Flute (Poems from Chinese)
The Sound of Water: Haiku by Bashō, Buson and Issa
River of Stars: Selected Poems of Yosano Akiko (with Keiko Matsui Gibson)
The Spring of My Life (from the Japanese of Kobayashi Issa)
The Essential Teachings of Chuang Tzu (with J.P. Seaton)

ESSAYS

At Home in the World
Bashō's Ghost
A Poet's Work: the Other Side of Poetry

EDITOR

Selected Poems of Thomas McGrath
Collected Poems of Kay Boyle
Death Song (Posthumous Poems of Thomas McGrath)
Love Poems from the Japanese by Kenneth Rexroth
The Erotic Spirit: Poems of Sensuality, Love, and Longing
The Gift of Tongues: Twenty-Five Years of Poetry from Copper Canyon Press
Sacramental Acts: The Love Poems of Kenneth Rexroth (with Elaine Laura
    Kleiner)

A POET'S WORK

Sam Hamill

A POET'S WORK

The Other Side of Poetry

Carnegie Mellon University Press

PITTSBURGH 1998

Library of Congress Catalog Number 97-76756
ISBN 0-88748-225-2
Printed and bound in the United States of America.

Earlier versions of some of these essays appeared in the *American Poetry
Review, Poets and Writers, Poetry East, Zyzzyva,* the *Literary Review,*
the *American Book Review, The Pushcart Prize* XIV, *The Selected Poems
of Thomas McGrath* (Copper Canyon Press, 1988), *What I Love* (Copper
Canyon Press, 1986), and *Bashō's Ghost* (Broken Moon Press, 1989).

First Carnegie Mellon University Press Edition, March 1998.

A Poet's Work was first published by Broken Moon Press, Seattle, in 1990.

Cover painting: *Waking, Walking, Singing in the Next Dimension* by Morris
Graves. Tempera on paper, 1979. Courtesy of Schmidt-Bingham Gallery,
New York City.

To Eron Hamill & Gray Foster
And to Morris Graves

Contents

Preface to the Second Edition

It is a great pleasure to welcome these essays back into print. Most were written for *The American Poetry Review* or *Poetry East*, and I am grateful to the editors for their encouragement. No doubt many would have remained unwritten had I not been the recipient of fellowships from the National Endowment for the Arts, the Guggenheim Foundation, and the Japan–U.S. Friendship Commission. These funds not only bought me time to dedicate to the essays, poems, and translations written during the 1980s, but also brought running water and electricity to my home and a deeper sense of obligation to my writing. I believe the primary tools of any good poet ought to include an educated ear and an operating bull-shit detector—the former to engage true passion, the latter for critical counter-balance. And I know that the writing of these essays shaped and informed my sense of commitment to the Way of Poetry, in whose service I have become a kind of *unsui*, a perpetual novice in the temple of the muse; and as Tom McGrath used to say, "You can't quit the Muse, that grand bitch."

Readers wanting a more complete history of Copper Canyon Press may be directed to *The Gift of Tongues: Twenty-five Years of Poetry from Copper Canyon Press* (1996) and my Introduction and Notes on the Books. Anyone interested in my poetry of the past twenty-five years may be directed to *Destination Zero: Poems 1970–1995* (White Pine Press, 1995) and *Gratitude* (BOA Editions, 1998).

"Some Days" was written in collaboration with my former partner and co-founder of Copper Canyon Press, Tree Swenson. The first edition of this book was published in 1990 by Broken Moon Press. Special thanks are due to my old friend Bill O'Daly, another co-founder of Copper Canyon Press and a distinguished translator of Pablo Neruda.

His advice and support over a quarter century have been indispensable, not only in the shaping of these essays, but in the shaping of the sensibility and convictions that inform them.

Sam Hamill
Kage-an, 8/97

Preface

Language—and thus knowledge—begins with listening. In the Sumerian myth of Inanna, goddess of heaven, daughter of the moon and the morning star, we find the word for "ear" being the word for "wisdom" and the word for "mind." Diane Wolkstein describes how Inanna *set* her ear: the goddess of heaven listened to the world below. In retelling the tale of Inanna—literally telling the cycle to audiences—she listened to her own telling, and, consequently, revised—that is, perceived freshly—her own telling. By listening attentively to the telling, the teller clarifies the vision.

To listen is to know. The first words were undoubtedly imitative utterances of perceived sounds: bird calls, monkey chatter. This primitive language was rooted, as our own remains, in nouns. We imitate sounds which inform, enrich, or threaten our lives; we rhyme with Nature. Whales rhyme. Coyotes rhyme. Wolves rhyme.

Sometime in ancient India, a Wise One sat and listened attentively and then set about constructing a musical notation upon which music for the gods would be fit to be played, drawing as inspiration the sounds of birds and animals from the wild. Somewhere else, a lute was being invented, its tones based upon sounds made by winds passing through the sinews of a beached whale.

"In the beginning," we intone, "was the Word." But that's not true. First we listen. And then we name. "In the beginning" was the silence of primordial ooze. Music, speech, and image are of co-dependent origination. The seer is dependent upon the seen, the speaker upon the listener. The Chinese/Japanese goddess of mercy and bodhisattva, Kuan Shih Yin (Kannon in Japanese), is named "She-who-perceives-the-world's-cries," her vision bound up in her capacity to listen. In her purest incarnation, she rejects *all* outward expressions of devotion so that she may be worshipped only by extending to others the compassion one finds in her; in order to extend the compassion one finds in Kuan Yin, one must learn to listen as Kuan Yin listens; in order to listen as she does, the listener must *become the act of listening completely.* To listen is to see.

The Talmudic tradition identifies the goddess Shekhinah as "the audible and visible manifestation of God's presence on earth." She is a temple goddess who can be heard. The whole Talmudic tradition is rooted in meditation, speaking, listening, and translating. Midrash literature claims that Shekhinah's deeply compassionate nature forces her to argue with God on behalf of suffering humanity. Jerome Rothenberg reminds us that her counterpart among the *sefirot* is Lilith, "the night wailer."

Rothenberg reinvigorates the term *poeisis,* identifying a process born in language, a "sacred action" (Breton's term) or creation. Lévi-Strauss paraphrases Rimbaud to state that metaphor can change the world. Rothenberg quotes the *Zohar:* "The Voice should never be separated from the Utterance, & [one] who separates them becomes dumb &, being bereft of speech, returns to dust." From Kung-fu Tze (Confucius) we learn that "all wisdom is rooted in learning to call things by the right name."

The essays collected here reflect a life centered in and by poetry, in and by *poeisis,* a life in which process is everything. "As a poet," Gary Snyder has said, "I hold the most archaic values on earth." But every poet is an exile, every dream of justice a threat to those who rule. Each compassionate gesture exposes the murderers among us. Everywhere we look, we find martyrs. Rothenberg identifies exile both as cosmic principle and as "Jewish fate, experienced as the alienation of group & individual, so that the myth (gnostic or orthodox) is never only symbol but history, experience, as well."

Distanced from nature and/or from "God," we turn to a *poeisis* based upon naming, and identify Shekhinah as the feminine "exiled" side of God or, in nature, an ecosphere pregnant with possibility threatened by "masculine" alienation and domination, and we speak of "feminine mystery" and the "rape" of the land. Ultimately, we are all Jews. And we are alienated from ourselves. While Jew and Palestinian alike continue to die needlessly, we are all Jews and we are all Palestinians. While a writer, whether Salman Rushdie or Dante Alighieri, remains under a death sentence, we *all* write under that sentence. A teacher without students, a student whose teachers are dead, a spiritual devotee in the garden of Zen, I begin at last to understand Marina Tsvetaeva's dictum that "All poets are Jews." Like a Shekhinah or a Kuan Yin, a poet listens.

If I should say, "Poetry saved my life," it would be true, but who would believe me? In the same way a baseball or basketball may offer a glimmer of hope to another miserable child, poetry offered me—simply put—self-definition; it gave me "something to live up to" complete with role models and an identifiable ancestry. "To have gathered from the air a live tradition/ or from a fine old eye the unconquered flame/This is not vanity." The task is at once humbling and sustaining. Listening to a Catullus or to a Tu Fu, I come into a world unchanged since the birth of the polis. I come "home." Their human suffering is our suffering, but because we share a vision of the possible world, our burden grows lighter, lighter in every sense.

I have no agenda for poetry: inasmuch as these essays constitute an *ars poetica,* at root they are simply testimony to a commitment to be at the service of poetry, to be a part of the process termed *poeisis* and which is all process, all means and no ends. I came to poetry as an abandoned child. During a miserable childhood, I survived physical and sexual abuse, drugs, homelessness, incarceration, gang rape, and innumerable other horrors and indignities of our social and judicial systems and life on the streets. Welfare and justice. I find justice and shelter and healing in poetry.

After writing my first poem with the help of adopted parents who filled my life with poetry read aloud, I never stopped reading or writing, and as the horrors and nightmares grew, I armed myself with books. I might thank the Goddess Calliope that I do not write these words from Death Row. I thank the mother of muses, Mnemosyne, that I have been unable to forget my origins and my own crimes and those directed against me.

Our burden, shared, grows lighter. These essays reflect my own engagement with poetry as a means of awakening the mind, of addressing our lovers and our neighbors and ourselves, even those whom we must despise, and being the better for it because we found a poetry which refused to lie. Poetry is therapeutic, but not therapy. For therapy, one should consult a therapist. Poetry is an outward expression of inner vision made audibly perceptible. Poetry is a form of discipline and a form of revolt. It is a gift passed on which cannot be stolen, only shared. Antonio Porchia puts it this way:

I know what gift I have given.
I do not know what you have received.

Sam Hamill
Port Townsend, 1980–89

A POET'S WORK

The Necessity to Speak

One must understand what fear means: what it implies and what it rejects. It implies and rejects the same fact: a world where murder is legitimate, and where human life is considered trifling. . . . All I ask is that, in the midst of a murderous world, we agree to reflect on murder and to make a choice. After that, we can distinguish those who accept the consequences of being murderers themselves or the accomplices of murderers, and those who refuse to do so with all their force and being. Since this terrible dividing line does actually exist, it will be a gain if it be clearly marked.

—Albert Camus, *Neither Victims Nor Executioners*

And yet we go on living closed lives, pretending we are not each personally responsible for the deaths we buy and sell. We go on living our sheltered lives among the potted plants and automobiles and advertising slogans. We don't want to know what the world is like, we can't bear very much reality.

The man in prison remembers. The man who's been in prison remembers. Cesare Pavese brings the message home most forcefully: "The lonely man, who's been in prison, goes back to prison every time he eats a piece of bread." The woman who was battered remembers. The woman who was raped will never forget. The convict and the ex-con, the rape victim, the battered child—each, reading these words, will remember.

I teach creative writing in the prisons because I have been in prison. Writing is a form of human communication expressing ideas regarding the human condition. Because writing creates emotion in the audience, the writer's responsibility is enormous. Arousing passion, exploring the grief of loss, making an other laugh, showing someone how to care—these are the concerns of the writer, and they do not come free of responsibility. But the creative writing itself is only a by-product. What I teach cannot be simply stated.

The women I have escorted to shelters where they can be protected from the rage of sick men have also been my friends and my students and my teachers. Three of every four of these victims, men and women, will return—the men will go back to prison, and the women will return to battering relationships. The battered child will grow into the child batterer.

There are presently fifteen hundred men on Death Row in the United States. There are over two hundred in Florida alone, and they are let out of their cells twice per week for a quick shower, and once per week for one hour of exercise. Ninety-two percent of these men were battered children. They have had a lengthy schooling. But they are beginning to understand how we as a society establish acceptable levels of violence. We pay the bill for murder in Nicaragua. We say the $27 million we send there this year, like the $40 million we sent last year, is for "humanitarian purposes," and we tell ourselves the money is not for murder. We weep for the battered woman, but we are stingy when it comes time to pay for groceries and bandages at the shelter. The victim of rape earns our sympathy. But we discipline our children with a belt or a stick or a fist. The battered woman learns that violence is one of the forms love takes. The battered child learns that there are two possibilities in human life: one can remain the victim, or one can seize power and become the executioner. The mother who was battered typically understands that the only condition worse than being a victim is to become an executioner.

The convict writes himself out of prison, he writes his brothers out of prison. The battered woman makes peace in the world with tender words chosen with deep care.

•

A true poet, someone once said, is often faced with the difficult task of telling people what they already know and do not want to hear. Sharon Olds, in *The Dead and the Living* (Alfred A. Knopf, 1983), writes of being a victim of domestic violence herself, and her poems are painful to read, very painful, but beautiful because they are true.

When Mother divorced you, we were glad. She took it and
took it, in silence, all those years and then
kicked you out, suddenly, and her
kids loved it.

We can't bear very much reality. When the rape victim cries out for help, we are frozen. Our emotions are mute. We are seized as though we are catatonic. We have not been taught how to properly express our feelings. We find poetry embarrassing.

A critic writing of Kenneth Rexroth's love poems in the *New York Times* declares, "Rexroth has issued a volume of breasts-and-thighs poems. What would I say, should I chance to meet his wife in public?" The poet Deena Metzger makes a beautiful, joyous poster of herself, naked, arms outstretched, following a radical mastectomy of her left breast. We are embarrassed by her naked body and by her joy, but mostly we are embarrassed because we do not know how or what to think confronted by that long ragged scar. Our vocabulary of the emotions has become critically impoverished.

.

Veterans returning from Viet Nam often found it impossible to discuss what transpired there. Delayed Stress Syndrome has probably taken as many American lives as Agent Orange. And yet, in high schools today, no one has heard of My Lai. Unless we learn to articulate our own emotions, we cannot prevent other My Lais and other Viet Nams from recurring, nor will we ever properly address the domestic violence so common in the American home.

"All wisdom," Kung-fu Tze says, "is rooted in learning to call things by the right name."

I became a conscientious objector while serving in the U.S. Marine Corps. I am proud of my decision to practice non-cooperation, and I am shamed by my complicity. In the vocabulary of human emotions, the terms "guilt" and "innocence" are insufficient. Like "right" and "wrong," they reject compassionate wisdom.

Once each month the recruiters for the business of death are permitted into our high schools to recruit more cannon fodder. There is no voice for non-violence inside those same institutions. The children who listen and enlist are being trained to become both victims and executioners. And we are all co-conspirators. Our silence grants permission to the military to establish all critical vocabulary pertaining to the armed forces. The *armed forces* are precisely what that name implies: a resort to armed force, a complete collapse of compassionate communication.

.

The battering of women and children is the most common felony committed in the United States. No one knows how often it happens because it is so rarely reported. But every cop on a beat will tell you that the most feared call of all is the domestic dispute. One never knows what to expect. It kills more cops than dope-dealers and bank robbers combined.

When James Cagney shoves half a grapefruit in a woman's face, we all laugh and applaud. Nobody likes an uppity woman. And a man who is a man, when all else fails, asserts his "masculinity." It is easy to learn to be a man. I learned to be a batterer without ever thinking about it. That's the way we learn. When I was an adolescent, it was taken for granted that real men sometimes had to slap their women around. Just like John Wayne did to Maureen O'Hara in the movies. How very often in our movies and popular fiction the assaulted woman falls in love with the assaulting "hero."

The man who slips off his belt to spank his naughty child is about to commit felony assault. If he behaves like this toward any other human being but those of his immediate family, he is locked up for the protection of society. The child is about to get a practical lesson in adult behavior when reason breaks down. This incident, repeated over the years, will help to form the growing child's sense of justice, it will inform the definition of compassion. The father will say, "I'm sorry I have to do this. It will hurt me more than it hurts you." Because this father believes himself a good man, a kind and compassionate father. But the child won't believe a word of it. The child fears the wound. The child has learned that might makes right, that parents sometimes lie, and that there are acceptable limits of violence.

If a belt is acceptable, why not a stick? If a stick acceptable, why not a baseball bat? If broken bones are unacceptable, what about cuts or welts or bruises?

•

The first duty of the writer is the rectification of names—to name things properly, for, as Kung-fu Tze said, "All wisdom is rooted in learning to call things by the right name."

"The names of things bring them closer," Robert Sund wrote. This applies to the terrible as well as to the sublime. The writer learns from the act of writing. "I write to find out what's on my mind," Gary Snyder once said. What the writer invents is its own reality.

The writer is aware that verbs show action and that precision in the use of nouns and verbs frees one from the muddiness of most modifiers. The writer accepts responsibility for every implication derived from what is stated. The writer is also eternally vulnerable.

The writer *is* the battered woman in her blossoming pain; the writer *is* the lonely face behind the steel door; the writer *is* the good man with the belt wrapped around his first. Before the first word is written, the writer is a witness who struggles not to flinch, not to look away.

We hear all around us our language being de-valued. Our president tells us that a missile with one thousand times the power of the bomb we dropped on Hiroshima is a "peacekeeper." We remember the bitter irony with which Colt named its pistol the Peacemaker. Our president tells us that $27 million is being sent to aid one side of a civil war in Nicaragua, but that the money won't be used for military purposes. The writer is in the service of the language. The writer is accountable.

.

We live in a culture in which "real men" don't often touch and often don't even like to be touched. Touch is a primary language in the discourse of emotions. There is eighteen square feet of skin on the average human being, and that skin holds about five million sensory perceptors. A University of Wisconsin study determined that denial of touch in young monkeys resulted in deformation in the cerebellum. D. H. Lawrence, in a story called "You Touched Me!," describes how simple human physical contact can restore the health of a life. Our president is a tough guy. He shakes hands, presumably with a firm grip, but he doesn't hug the foreign dignitaries. John Wayne didn't hug. Sylvester Stallone, Hollywood's male role model for our children, doesn't touch much.

We are embarrassed when the poet weeps publicly during the recitation of a poem. The physical expression of emotion makes many people uncomfortable. I was taught as a child—like most of my contemporaries—that men should not express emotion.

Men envy women their friendships with other women. Men secretly wish they, too, could have friends like that. Men have learned that ours is a lonely and insular country. We think poetry is about emotions. We are dead wrong. Poetry is not *about*. Take the rhyme out of poetry, and there is still poetry; take the rhythm out of it, and there is still poetry; take even the words themselves away, and poetry remains, as Yang Wan-li said a thousand years ago. The poet identifies a circumstance in which the poetry reveals itself. The poet is the vehicle used by poetry so that *it* can touch us. From the inside out. The words are only the frame which focuses the epiphany we name poetry. We say the poem touches us, sometimes even deeply. We often say the poet is a bit touched. Adrienne Rich dreams of a common language.

.

In the language of violence all argument is solipsistic. Those who pay tithing at the altar of violence are afraid: they fear the here-and-now and they fear the hereafter, but most of all, they fear the truth of knowledge. Knowledge is the loss of innocence. How desperately we want our innocence! How desperately we protect the innocence of our children! Our children don't know what has happened. They have never heard of Auschwitz or Treblinka, they have never heard of Canyon de Chelly. They do not know that it was their European-immigrant great-great-grandfathers who invented scalp-taking, they have never dreamed of the tortured flesh that has subtly informed our attitudes since those long-ago trials in Salem. They do not know that German death camps were modeled on U.S. camps, our own nineteenth-century Final Solution to "the Indian problem."

.

The past we name History. Out of it, today. Every day there are people who die to know. Every day, people die because they know. In El Salvador, in Chile, in the Philippines, in Korea, Nicaragua, and Lebanon. In the U.S.S.R. and in the U.S. of A.

And the murderers, the dirty little dictators who order the heads brought in upon a platter? Our money sustains their power. Just as our indifference permits gangs to run our prisons where men also die for knowing and for speaking up. Just as we continue to permit the deaths of 2500 women per year at the hands of their "lovers," one every three-and-a-half hours, and just as we permit a woman to be battered senseless every eighteen seconds of every day in this country.

And our money brings us television to distract us from what we know we are responsible for but do not want to know. It is difficult to explain things to our children. It is convenient to declare international conflict too large, too ugly, or too confusing to explain. And we likewise declare the personal too embarrassing. How else do we account for the fact that ten percent of all teenage girls get pregnant. We perform forty-five abortions per every thousand teenage girls every year, or about one out of every twenty-five girls. One in three sixteen-year-old girls is sexually active and knows almost nothing about birth control. Her seventeen-year-old lover knows nothing, typically, or doesn't care. Our silence contributes to the shame and misery of these girls and to the deaths of millions of unborn children.

We warn our daughters lest they become "loose" with their affections. We don't want them to care for the wrong people. We don't want to wound them with the knowledge that womankind has been singled out for special suffering throughout history, so we protect them from *her-story*. We persuade ourselves that perhaps, if we don't talk about sex, sexual involvement won't happen too soon. And perhaps, if we don't think about our daughters loving a batterer, that won't happen either. Our silence grants violence permission. We sacrifice our daughters to protect our own beloved innocence. In the language of violence, every speech is a solipsism and silence a conspirator.

•

The true poet gives up the self. The *I* of my poem is not *me*. It is the first person impersonal, it is permission for you to enter the experience which we name Poem.

Although the poem itself is often a "given" thing, in the justice of poetry we often earn the gift in some way. The disciplining of the self helps the poet clarify the experience so that the experience itself may be yours with as little superficial clutter as possible. The true poet asks for nothing "in return" because the poem itself is given to the poet who, in turn, gives it away and gives it away again. The poet is grateful for the opportunity to serve.

The poet wants neither fame nor money, but simply to be of use.

I am not the *I* of my poem. But I am responsible for the poem and, therefore, for that *I*. The poet invents a being, and that being, man or woman, stands before the world, naked and feeling. Thus, the poet who invents the persona of the poem is reflected similarly "undressed," and we say, "This poet takes risks," because there is neither false modesty nor the arrogance of exhibitionism, but the truth of human experience as it is, all somehow beyond the mere words of the poem.

The poet may speak for the speechless, for the suffering and the wounded. The poet may be a conscience, walking. The poet honors the humble most of all because poetry is gift-giving. The poet adores the erotic because in a world of pain there is charity and hope and because the poet aspires to a condition of perpetual vulnerability.

But there are poets who murder and poets who lie. Dante placed the corrupters of language in the seventh circle of Hell, and there are poets among them. Christopher Marlowe was an assassin.

•

I was strapped belly-down with webbing ripped from beds in a prison for the young, my face in a pillow to muffle my screams, my mouth gagged with my own socks—I was gang-raped by I-don't-know-how-many boys, ice-picked in the face, and left, presumably to die, alone all night before the guards discovered me, bloody and crazed. Fourteen years old and in the custody of the State. It has been thirty years, and I remember it like yesterday at noon. Out of my own guilt and shame over having been raped, out of my own guilt and shame over having been a batterer, out of my own silence over these terrible events, I began to articulate needs; out of defining my own needs, I discovered a necessity for believing that justice is possible; out of a commitment to a sense of justice, I found it necessary, essential, to bear witness.

•

Some of my students are women who begin writing because a writing class is permission to speak, which they do not have at home. Some of these women are battered because they have taken my class. Some have been battered when their "lovers" discovered that I talk about violence and responsibility in class. One of the kindest women I have ever known was murdered by her husband because he feared she would tell the truth. Our last conversation took place over a leisurely brunch; we discussed the origins and history of Kuan Yin, bodhisattva of compassion.

We are all impoverished by our silence.

•

There are more men in prison in the United States than there are people in South Dakota. Many of these men are eager to work, eager to learn, and dream of learning another way of life. They exist in a moment-to-moment despair that is utterly beyond the comprehension of anyone who has not been there.

The history of our prisons is a study of cruelty and stupidity so savage and so constant that almost no one wants to know a thing about it. Poor men go to prison. Men from minority races go to prison. But batterers come from every station, even from Reagan's Administration. The rich are as likely to commit sexual violence as are the poor. The batterer cannot name his fear, the thing inside that makes him strike out blindly at the very things he loves. It is his own inability to articulate his needs, his own speechlessness, that makes him crazy. Because he has been denied his language, he cannot name things clearly; because he cannot name, he cannot see what frightens him so terribly; therefore, the fear is invisible and is everywhere and consumes him.

Only when those of us who have overcome the terrible cycle of violence bear witness can we demonstrate another possibility. Because I have been both victim and executioner, I am able to speak from the bleak interior, and, perhaps, bring a little light into a vast darkness. An apology from a reformed batterer means nothing. The only conceivable good that can come from my confession is that of example for other sick men, a little hope for change amidst the agony of despair.

.

She took a class in creative writing. There was much talk of naming things correctly: objects, feelings, acts, deeds. And each time there was talk, there was also responsibility. "You will be held accountable," she was told, "just as you will be expected to hold others accountable."

And then one night it happened. She got home a little late from class. He was drunk. She tried to be especially nice, she tried to calm and soothe him. But his voice got louder and louder. He screamed. He grabbed her by the throat and shook her like a rag. And then he hit her. He hit her hard.

And then he apologized. He begged her not to leave. She was crumpled in a corner, her lip bleeding, her whole body trembling out of control. He got her a wet towel and tried to touch her face. She turned her face away and held up her hands for protection. Tears streamed down his face. He begged her not to go, he swore he'd never do that again, he swore he'd gone crazy. She knew it would happen again. It had *already* happened again.

She went that night to the shelter. She spent weeks talking to a counselor every day. She was lucky. She didn't have children. He didn't find her. She was lucky to be alive. For a while, she hated men. She hated being a victim. But she made friends in the shelter. Later, she made more friends outside. And through friendship, learned to love. True love is not without its own accountability.

.

The violence we learn at home we take with us everywhere we go. It shapes the way we look at a man or a woman, it colors our foreign policy and our tax structure. It is outright theft to pay a woman fifty-eight cents on the dollar we pay a man for doing the same job; it is economic violence.

In Viet Nam, the soldiers, those young men conscripted or enlisted from our high schools and colleges to do our killing for us, called the enemy "Gook," an epithet first used in Nicaragua in the 1920s, China in the 1930s, Japan in the 1940s, and in the Philippines since the 1940s, because that removed an element of the enemy's humanity, making it more like killing a thing than murdering a man, a woman, or a child.

.

I see them every day, the wounded women in the supermarket or in the bookstore, the children beaten to a whimper until all life has grayed in them. I've learned to recognize Fear's signature scrawled across their faces. The way one learns to recognize a man who walks with a "prison shuffle."

It is essential to make it clear that these things are personal. Our nuclear arms have 180,000 times the blast of the charge that leveled Hiroshima forty years ago. Our ability to deliver death is so unspeakably potent that it is far beyond the range of all human imagination. And we add to that arsenal every day. Nothing will change until we demolish the "we-and-they" mentality. We are human, and therefore all human concerns are ours. And those concerns are personal. "Everywhere we go," George Seferis said, "we walk on the faces of the dead."

Children in our public schools are paddled, whipped, slapped, locked in closets, lockers, and bathrooms—all quite legally. Every fourth homosexual male in a U.S. high school is the victim of a major assault during his tenure. Virtually all of them are victims of harassment. Homophobia is so rampant in our culture that it is common to see people fly into a rage over the mere sight of a gay couple holding hands in public. We excuse racism, sexism, homophobia—all the mindless violence of others—by refusing to make a *personal* issue of the problem.

We lend a helping hand to the mugger when we don't educate our children (of both sexes) about self-defense; we lend a hand to the rapist when we don't readily discuss rape. Our silence grants permission to the child molester. Because we have not learned how to name things properly, the batterer beats his child or lover in public, and we stand to one side, crippled inside, fearful and guilty.

If we really do believe that felony assault has no place in the home, we must encourage all victims to name names, to come forward and bear witness. We must find a way to save the victims. And we must find a way to save the executioners, as well.

There is a way. I know. Poetry has been a means for me, a way to find my way out of Hell. But it takes an iron will or a deeply spiritual conviction not unlike that of many poets toward poetry, the way James Wright spoke with compassion for drunkards and murderers, the way Richard Hugo testified on behalf of the dying farm towns and lonely saloons of the Northwest, or the way we might learn from Denise Levertov how to accept the loss of our mothers or to accept responsibility for our own violent realpolitik or for a marriage that was "good in its time" after that time has passed.

There *is* a third way. It begins with the end of lies and silence about violence. It begins with accepting responsibility for our own words and deeds. It begins with searching one's own heart for the compassionate justice which is located *only* there. It begins with the articulation of one's truest and deepest response to a world where, as Camus said, murder is legitimate and human life is considered trifling. Only from such a profoundly articulated *No!* can we hope to achieve a final, irrefutable affirmation of the human soul.

Orthodox, Heterodox, Paradox

We belong to the language before the language belongs to us. The new parents bend over the crib and say, "Say Ma-ma. Say Da-da." And the infant gurgles and makes a noise, "Ga-ga." The new parents are ecstatic. "He said Da-da!" the proud father proclaims without even thinking that the baby is learning mimicry. There, wrapped in its swaddling clothes, the baby begins a long march toward language. Daddy wants Baby to learn the language of law. Mamma wants Baby to learn the language of architecture or medicine.

But the child may well choose instead to learn the "language of the streets," the language of criminality. Or the child may learn the language of drug addiction, the language of the prison, or the silent language of the victimized, the oppressed. Most likely, the child will "come to terms" within several distinct vocabularies. But the language the child masters determines the child's future to a very large degree.

"In the beginning was the Word." Darwin believed that the mouth made silent gestures to accompany the language of hand-gesture before there was speech. A number of anthropologists and linguists suggest the roots of language lie in onomatopoetics, so that, as Mario Pei says in his *The Story of Language* (J. P. Lippincott, 1965), "What is 'cock-a-doodle-do' to an Englishman is 'cocorico' to a Frenchman and 'chicchirichi' to an Italian."

Still others claim that language grew out of grunts of effort, inarticulate chants, or exclamations of fear or surprise.

Pythagoras and Plato and the Stoics all simply begged the question by arguing that language "sprang from necessity." As to just *how* it sprang, they do not say, perhaps fully developed from the head of Zeus. Aristotle and Epicurus, without ever mentioning how it came about, stated that language was the product of "agreement."

Regardless of origin, we know that "Mamma" gets her name not only from the English by way of the Latin, but also from the *ma* of Chinese, the *umm* of Arabic, and so on; and that "Papa" or "Da-da" comes via the Gothic *atta,* the Latin and Greek *pater,* Gaulish *tatula,* Italian *tata,* the Chinese *fu,* the Arabic *abu,* and the Swahili *baba.* In Russian, *baba* is an old woman or grandmother, and *dyadya* is grandfather. From the first monosyllables on toward recognition of the first names, "Mamma," we cry when we stumble, or "Papa, come help!"

Gary Snyder often directs our attention to the "seed syllable" such as the meditative "O-h-m." And Wendell Berry, in his brilliant essay, "Standing by Words" (*Standing by Words,* North Point, 1983), says there are three essential criteria which must be met before a statement can be complete and comprehensible:

1. It must designate its object precisely.
2. Its speaker must stand by it: must believe it, be accountable for it, be willing to act on it.
3. This relation of speaker, word, and object must be conventional; the community must know what it is.

But even in the earliest name-learning, we are often taught wrong names for things, sometimes "for our own good," and sometimes for the convenience of those who would teach us.

We are a product of language before language becomes our tool.

.

The vocabulary learned at home often leaves us utterly ill-equipped for public "education." We need look no farther than the nearest American Indian reservation to witness what happens when the natural, integral vocabulary is suddenly replaced by the vocabulary of educators. Our attempts to "educate the Indian" are as damnable as our theft of their land. Only when teachers have sought to learn and to be of use have the white Anglo-Saxon patriarchy and multifaceted American Indian cultures coexisted productively. One by-product of our genocidal policies of the past two centuries was the loss of two hundred Native American languages. The loss of language is also the loss of articulation of emotions and values. The hopelessness of the reservation stems in part from the loss of articulation. In the economy of language, as in the language of goods, cooperation is productive and competition is counter-productive.

The new language of "education" is itself often a kind of sub-genre psycho-babble, a vocabulary designed by specialists for specialists. In order to understand how our schools fail, we must question the exact nature of our educational system, we must examine just what a public school is, and what it does, and why.

In many instances, the child is introduced to the language of violence in the home. But that violence is often confused with terms of affection. We beat the child for being bad. We love the child for being good. The beating is a clearly understood *sentence*. But what is *love?* Often love alternates between neglect and savagery. We beat the child because we love it and want it "to do good." Thus physical abuse is translated into terms of affection.

And there is a second kind of violence learned at school: the altogether acceptable violence inflicted upon the young by teachers and administrators and which is administered with our implied blessing. It is attended by yet another vocabulary of threat: the vocabulary which demands conformity. "If you don't get back in this line this minute!" the teacher screams. In our public schools children are beaten with rulers, paddles, belts, coat hangers, and hands, all quite legally. In Wisconsin, to demonstrate a point, a parent beat a principal with the same wooden paddle the principal had used on the assailant's child. The parent was convicted of second-degree assault.

The imposition of conformity from the exterior, *without accompanying insight* or self-examination, strips the child of a sense of self-worth. The ruthless conformity of regimentation is for the sake of control rather than the regimentation of disciplined introspection which becomes enlightening. Using violence to impose order in the classroom teaches children two things: obedience through fear; and when "reason" proves insufficient, violence becomes the final authority.

When I teach, I begin by making images with young children, and we always talk about clichés. One which invariably surfaces (probably because my students know I also teach in prisons) is the old "school is a prison" line, the truth of which every child intuits. But I will not let them use it because it is too easy, and because it is a dead image, but most of all because school is not a prison.

But school serves exactly the same function we would like to assign to our prisons:

1. School regiments and institutionalizes an habitual obedience to

schedules, often at the expense of reason. The first day of school, the child arrives on time, and learns to get in line. Seventeen years later, this same student, matriculating with a baccalaureate, learns to get in line. The long lines, the bell-ringing, the regimentation of humiliating and unnecessary schedules rime exactly with those of prison.

2. School teaches an absolute obedience to "authority," so much so that students most often must ask, publicly, for permission to visit a bathroom. They may not even speak without first silently raising a hand. In most schools, each day begins with a *pledge of allegiance* to—not principles, not responsibility, not decency, not even to learning—but to a flag and to "God." Never, not even once in fifteen years in public schools (except on American Indian reservations), have I seen a student question this practice in any way whatsoever. Like the penitentiary, the first rule is the rule of obedience. Orthodoxy is paramount.

3. School institutionalizes and rewards competition while punishing introversion, introspection, and general non-aggression. Despite the fact that one in three college athletes is illiterate, the collegiate athlete not only attends the finest university on scholarship, but often receives bonuses in the form of credit cards and new cars and pocket money. If there were even the slightest pretense of having standards, we would not "value" the illiterate athlete over the bookworm. Likewise, in prison there is competition for the few jobs, competition for cell block or prison farm, with the greatest rewards going to those who are most obliging.

I do not believe that regimentation and tight scheduling are inherently evil. But I do believe that, as they are imposed by public education, they are designed for no other purpose than to prepare our children for the labor market. Our schools no longer teach our children how to learn, and that the most meaningful learning truly takes place at home.

The outer discipline imposed by school and prison alike is counter-productive when it is not accompanied by inner or self-discipline. Outer discipline without introspection produced Hitler's Brownshirts. Introspection admits paradox outer discipline excludes. Para-dox is, literally, counter-opinion. Only through paradox can we come to rational understanding.

Our children are no longer exposed to the dialogues of Plato and the conversations of Kung-fu Tze. Master Kung praised the classic anthology of poetry because it kept the judicious student from arguing abstractions. Socrates taught the necessity of questioning orthodox opinion.

Wendell Berry quotes W. Ross Winterowd, author of a textbook, *The Contemporary Writer,* who articulates two astonishing false assumptions any reasonable human being would repudiate: 1) "You [the freshman student] have a more or less complete mastery of the English language." 2) The literary arts are "the highest expression of the human need to play, of the desire to escape from the world of reality into the world of fantasy."

Perhaps the author of this freshman textbook has not read Dickens. Nor J. D. Salinger. Nor Mark Twain. Nor Orwell. And even that is hardly surprising: each of the above is currently censored somewhere in our public schools.

In prison, the convict may generally read what he pleases. There are, no doubt, rules pertaining to pornography, but my prison students read Plato, the Bible, murder mysteries, *The Autobiography of Malcolm X,* and *The Communist Manifesto.*

Above all else, we wish to turn student and convict alike into productive members of the workforce. One in five high school seniors in the U.S. cannot read and write well enough to complete an employment application. Telling eighteen-year-old entering freshmen that they already have a "more or less complete mastery" of our language is utterly absurd. Neither inmate nor student is presented with an opportunity to set reasonable standards. Equality is expressed in conformity and routine. Conformity and routine (and a vocabulary) are required for entry into every employment opportunity from drug-dealing to Supreme Court Justice. Our schools are prison training centers for the job market, and the best, only the very best, of our prisons are only a last ditch effort to rehabilitate those our schools failed. Fewer than half the students presently enrolled in New York City schools will graduate high school — this despite the fact that we graduate hundreds of thousands of students from high school every year who can neither read nor write.

While Ronald Reagan continues to battle against the Constitution's deliberate separation of church and state, while he continues to argue in favor of mandatory school prayer (presumably of indecipherably Christian denomination), our schools continue to insist upon the memorization of useless information measured by meaningless tests, all concluding with a "terminal degree." The "doctors of science" who design nuclear warheads are in need of moral and cultural literacy.

"The American public," Mencken used to say, "continues, against almost overwhelming odds, to exercise its inalienable right to remain ignorant." We do indeed have an inalienable right to remain ignorant. But our public educational system has an inalienable right, an *obligation* both moral and intellectual, to uphold standards of excellence. Some of this responsibility must be returned to the family. If students with incomplete homework were returned home, much more homework would be completed.

.

The language shapes our behavior long before we begin to see beyond the mere surface of the language, indeed even before we perceive words as such. We begin with those first two nouns: Ma-ma, Pa-pa. As the vocabulary grows, we begin to perceive verbs, words that reveal actions: "Wanna go!" "Momma come!" And all the while, language is shaping our lives.

We learn that there are words we say at home which we should never say in public. There are "men's" words and there are "women's" words. Naming things out loud can be very dangerous. Ask the relatives of those who called Ferdinand Marcos a thief, a dictator, and a liar.

At school, we will learn that aesthetics have nothing to do with morality, that Art with a capital A is a kind of jigsaw puzzle which must be puzzled out. Through pedantry and rote memory, we learn how to look at Art. Our "textbooks" teach us how to look at Art, what happened in History (meaning war and commerce), and how to write. I cannot say for certain whether our current history textbook will inform us that we, as freshman, have more or less mastered History. But I do know that teachers still ask students the absurd question, "Now what was the poet trying to say?" As though our feeble paraphrase of a line of poetry could provide meaningful insight.

Despite the nonsense of academia, aesthetics and morality remain inevitably intertwined. Insistence upon specialization produces not knowledge, but isolation, exclusivity, and competition—ignorance of a sadly rarified kind. It is hardly surprising to realize just how fully academia has embraced the Poetry of Neurosis in this century.

"Teaching" the Poetry of Neurosis, the "critic" is invited into the vocabulary of psychoanalytic abstraction with the preposterous assumption that this added abstract language implies serious study or comprehension of the poem or painting itself. As soon as we understand *why* Gauguin painted those bare breasts on the platter with the melons, we will "understand" the painting. Perhaps he thought it was funny. Perhaps he painted what he saw. Perhaps what he saw was both lovely and funny. Perhaps it was neither particularly lovely nor particularly funny, only the world of Gauguin at the time he was painting island life. The painting, like a poem, is not psychoanalysis. But fads in art criticism are like fads in literary criticism and serve little purpose beyond providing academicians with more subject matter. Or, perhaps, a longer sentence.

The French critic Roland Barthes is currently a favorite subject of the critical wing of the English Department. From "radical textual criticism" to "deconstructionism," textual criticism laurels its poets and explains its explainers. Nearly all of this is rooted in preposterous assumptions. I quote from Jerôme Deshusses's *Eighth Night of Creation* (Dial, 1982):

The reaches of textual criticism can be adequately illustrated by showing how Roland Barthes, who has gone so far as to write a treatise on sociology, sees the language, which he must have pondered for twenty years. Words, he says, are exchanged for ideas, as money is for goods (a fascinating parallel between economy and ethnology). The comparison is quite fruitful, if one forgets that: (1) a word generally corresponds to a single idea, while money corresponds to an infinity of objects; (2) a sum of money does not permit identification of the goods it serves to purchase, whereas a word is the identification of the idea it expresses; (3) a sum of money divided is still money, but a word divided is no longer a word; (4) several different words can represent the same idea simultaneously, but several different sums of money cannot represent a single good simultaneously; (5) two sums of money can be compared quantitatively, but words are not quantities; (6) strictly speaking, words cannot be exchanged for ideas, since words have their place and ideas theirs—rather, ideas are exchanged by the exchange of words. No doubt Roland Barthes was thinking about Language; apparently, for him, the noun language and the verb to think tend to get exchanged for ideas that are not worthy of them.

But even here, I must quarrel with the fourth point: several different words *cannot* adequately represent the same idea simultaneously. The language of any successful politician reveals the importance of purposeful obfuscation. When either of two words will suffice, neither is adequate—at least not when language is used responsibly.

Everyone knows that Marcos is a murderer, a thief, a tyrant. When our president defends him, we are told to remember his friendship and our own best interests as a nation. But no matter how he struggles, Reagan's words reveal a tyrant, a murderer, a thief. Reagan's ideas are not adequately convincing because they cannot conceal the precise definition of words like *tyrant, murderer, thief,* words which, one by one, identify indelibly a Marcos or a Noriega, tyrants brought to power in part through the cooperation of our government. Reagan presumably uses the best words in their best order whenever he speaks. That is how we each articulate our ideas.

In a news conference (February 11, 1986), Reagan was asked by an Associated Press reporter whether the Administration would recognize the Marcos government if all the accusations of fraud and violence (including goon squads shown terrorizing voters on television and reports of murder) in the current elections proved true, as American observers appointed by the Administration have publicly stated.

"Well," the President began, "I believe ... that is, what they said was. ... What they've told me is ... that there is the appearance of fraud ... but that they have no hard evidence. ... We hope to have the same relationship with the Philippines that we've had all these historic years. There is a two-party system there as these elections show. There is a plurality. We will deal with the elected government."

Reagan cannot bring himself to state clearly that, yes, we support dictatorships and close our eyes to the murder and theft and cowardice that keeps them in office (aided by a plentiful supply of our tax dollars). So he stammers and obfuscates and simply refuses to address that part of the question pertaining to witnessed acts of terrorism. One year later, Marcos has fled Manila for the U.S., is protected—along with the billions of dollars he stole from his country—by our government.

Meanwhile, our schoolchildren go on pledging allegiance, they go on believing the American Dream, while lies and obfuscation determine our foreign and domestic policies.

Likewise, lies, fraud, and deceit inform our educational policies. Jargon replaces intelligence and common reason. And in all likelihood, our children are never presented with the undeniable truth of language and with the responsibility that attends its careful usage; they will read popular "children's literature" rather than Mark Twain or Thomas Jefferson; and year after year they will "advance" through the grades whether or not they have learned any of the essentials of language usage.

Albert Camus stated shortly before his death that his writing was no more than "a long journey to recover through the detours of art the two or three simple and great images which first gained access to [his] heart."

Ronald Reagan's language reveals even that which he struggles to obfuscate: his stammering reveals a human being who can no longer identify (to say nothing of recover) the two or three simple and great images which first gained access to his heart. Clearly, the President of the United States, speaking on behalf of those people who elected him, sees that our military bases, particularly the huge navy base at Subic Bay (with all its attendant dope-dealers, prostitutes, whorehouses, pawn shops, bars, tattoo parlors, saloons, strip-joints, gambling casinos, massage parlors, and pornography palaces) are more important to U.S. interests than is a free and democratically elected government in the Philippines. If there are any true images to be regained for Reagan, they are the "simple" images of greed and might; his language, like his policies, degrades humanity.

We are products of our language, so much so that most of the world around us suffers as a direct consequence of the way in which we permit our elected representatives to degrade and abuse that language.

Meanwhile, Lt. Col. Oliver North of the U.S. Marine Corps lies to his superiors, lies to Congress, and lies to the people of the United States, pockets (apparently) millions of dollars in profit from his gun-running on behalf of the president, and is declared a hero. Just whether he is a chronic and compulsive liar or whether he lies only for profit or only as a result of his supreme patriotism remains unclear. But North's lies — and his dedication to an official policy of lies — lead directly and irrevocably to crimes against humanity.

.

Things, events, and ideas enter our culture (that is, our lives) only through their names and attributes. Deliberate misnaming may delay the realization, but sooner or later someone will undoubtedly revise our official dishonesty. When an army general in Viet Nam declares, "We had to destroy the village in order to save it," the high brass at the Pentagon and in the White House applaud. But the photographs from such instances as My Lai bring home the proper language. It may be difficult and complex to understand how we commit murder with language, but how we commit murder with guns is so elementary that a second-rate actor elected president of the country can't possibly conceal our complicity.

Although our nation was founded in part on the practice of genocide as surely as on the practice of slavery, we do not teach our children about the smallpox-infected blankets we sold to the Sioux, to the Cherokee, to the Nez Perce, and others. Our children do not know what happened at Sand Creek, at Canyon de Chelly, or at Little Big Horn. They do not know what happened at the trials in Salem. They believe that slavery brought about the Civil War. They do not know that we supported both Hitler and Mussolini before World War II. No one in public schools questions the morality of the genocide committed with the dropping of atomic bombs on Hiroshima *and* Nagasaki, the victims of which were mostly women, children, the elderly, and animals. Even today, our elementary, junior high, and high school teachers rarely address the rights of women. Our revision of history leads our children into a fairytale "America" — as though there could be but *one* America — in which the U.S. can do no wrong, indeed, into a U.S. which has done no wrong. But the "America" of a young woman on the Blackfeet Reservation is a far cry from the "America" of Ronald Reagan or Oliver North. The "America" of a ten-year-old black boy addicted to drugs on the streets of New York City is not the "America" which provides sanctuary for a Marcos.

But if what we pass on to our children as "history" fills them with false security and unrealistic dreams, our neglect of language usage not only underwrites false history, but undermines as well every moment of their waking lives. Because they do not comprehend what language accomplishes and how simple nouns and verbs define experience, they do not properly respect language; because they do not respect language, they use language carelessly; language used without care is imprecise; because their language is imprecise, their thoughts and feelings are never clearly defined; because their thoughts and feelings remain muddled, they proceed from day to day in perpetual confusion.

Through our acceptance of violence against the language, we invite violence against ourselves. Our inarticulate children are stupefied with a plethora of fantastic dreams about a life of leisure and plenty. But the world makes no such promise. The future we are presently inventing promises, at best, a bleak existence of filth and poison and starvation and debris, and, at worst, nuclear winter.

A couple of hundred years ago, no one thought it the least unusual for a child to sit down and compose a sonata. And if the child happened to be Mozart and the sonata a particularly good one, everyone applauded. But they did not have separate standards for judging a good sonata by a child and one by an old man or woman. There was a standard for judging sonatas.

Today, many of our "educators" would be appalled at the idea of a child working at a serious composition. I can no longer expect my junior high and high school students to be able to define a noun or a verb. I can no longer expect them to be able to write a simple declarative sentence.

Our word *sentence* comes from the Latin *sententia* (opinion), from which we also derive *sententious* (terse, pithy, energetic); its other taproot is *sentire* (to feel). The noun *names* (persons, places, things, or ideas); the verb *shows* the action, even when that action is "passive" or is a non-action. The *sentence* (which is a *term*) is a completely realized unit of thought (including incumbent emotion).

Our children are sturdy. They are capable. I have said nothing here that is beyond the grasp of a junior high school student, and little that can't be taught at elementary level. Our children quickly perceive that our language and our fate are inextricable.

Understanding how the study of grammar, or language, or rhetoric (in the fullest sense of the latter term) clarifies one's thinking goes back at least as far as the early Greeks. Egyptian education was based upon composition. Chinese education began with the study of the *Book of Songs* and calligraphy. All cultures begin with *naming*.

Grammar is no more than a logical organization for the presentation of thoughts and feelings. "Structure," Berry says, "is intelligibility." And, "A sentence is both the opportunity and the limit of thought—what we have to think with, and what we have to think in. It is, moreover, a feelable thought, a thought that impresses its sense not just on our understanding, but on our hearing, our sense of rhythm and proportion. It is a pattern of felt sense."

To permit our schools to neglect the study of grammar is to deny our children the opportunity to explore the limits of their own thoughts and feelings.

"Be ye perfite in ane mynd & in ane sentence."

The Degradation of Money

I could face all this, the hell with it, if I had the means (that is, only the daily bread for my wife and me) to devote myself to the work I want and know I can do—so that I wouldn't be working like a crippled man. The degradation of money. Yesterday I had the most humiliating idea I may ever have had in my life: to stop writing for a period of time—five or ten years, I don't know—to find a job that would allow me to save a little money, and then do what I want. A ridiculous thought; for living things there is no deferment.

—George Seferis, *A Poet's Journal* (Harvard University, 1974)

But there is not a single poet in the United States who makes a living as a poet. The open marketplace envisioned by the founders encourages economic discrimination against women and minorities. It values the "worth" of a good baseball player to the tune of millions of dollars per year. It may make a millionaire of an adolescent with a guitar. It may make a mediocre journalist rich and turn a romance novelist into an international celebrity. But there is not a single poet in the United States who makes a living as a poet.

I recently placed a poem with a respectable literary magazine. I worked on that poem for thirteen months. Not daily, of course, but with regularity. And I'd spent forty-odd years preparing for it. I was lucky to have placed it where I did: it will appear in a magazine which actually pays for poetry. I received, gratefully, a check in the amount of five dollars for, perhaps, one-hundred-fifty hours of actual writing time, or something less than three cents per hour for my labor.

Why does one write poems? Why, although they are such secret things (for one who writes them), does one consider them more important than anything else in life? This vital need.

—George Seferis, *A Poet's Journal*

When I get a little money, I buy books; and if any is left, I buy food and clothes.

—Desiderius Erasmus

Evidence of the degradation of poverty is everywhere evident in poetry. One finds it in the poetry of Richard Hugo, who worked on an assembly line at Boeing Aircraft for nearly twenty years, during which time he wrote some of his greatest poetry, poems paying homage to the poor, the degraded, the oppressed, and the misbegotten. The poverty Hugo experienced as an assembly-line worker was not simply financial, but rather a poverty of spirit which contributed to chronic depression and a sense of alienation he never overcame. One finds it in the poetry of Muriel Rukeyser, in her cotton dress and burly compassion, in her commitment to redefining social priorities. One finds it in the intelligence of W.S. Merwin's drunk banging in an old abandoned furnace, in the poetry of Thomas McGrath and Kenneth Rexroth and Denise Levertov, in every poet of the working (and unemployed) classes.

Tu Fu was so poor during the An Lu-shan Rebellion that his young son starved to death. The greatest poets of ancient China lived either by patronage or by their begging bowls.

Ezra Pound conspired with everyone who would listen to sell subscriptions to buy Eliot's way out of his bank-clerk position, to buy him time to write.

Old Mrs. Melville wrote a friend, "Poor Herman! First he wrote a book about fish which no one wants to publish, now he's gone back to writing poetry again."

Orwell wrote from firsthand experience of catching and eating rats in *Down and Out in Paris and London* (Berkeley, 1959). We remember Kafka, and the old blind beggar, Homer. We remember the parable of the rich man and the camel and the eye of the needle. We remember that Kung-fu Tze, Socrates, Jesus, Mohammed, Gandhi, Lincoln, and King all were poor.

Neruda and Vallejo were poor. Theodore Roethke was finally undone by bitter memories of his humble origin—poor Roethke! More than the money, he envied the status of the rich. We remember how often we have been taught that being poor and honest has a dignity that no other way of living can ever earn.

Nazim Hikmet and Yannis Ritsos and Mahmoud Darweesh spent years in prison for what they said in their poems. We remember Pound in his cage, sleeping on newspapers and wrapped in a single blanket; or the poverty of Osip and Nadezhda Mandelshtam, of Brendan Behan, of Albert Camus, who as a child loathed the bannisters of his tenements out of fear of rats. And we remember the poverty of Berthold Brecht.

Everywhere we look, there are models.

I have been asked to be one of the evaluators for several small literary grants to be made by a state arts agency. The money for these three $1000 and one $3000 grants comes from the city, the state, and from matching funds from the National Endowment for the Arts. The young woman who administers the program apologizes profusely because she cannot pay me for reading and evaluating ninety-seven manuscripts. The arts agency pays her a salary sufficient to save her from the humiliation of food stamps, but she must live in a cheap apartment and live frugally. The agency reimburses me for the mileage for my trip, two hours each way, to and from the city. But the time I spend, both in meetings and in evaluating the ninety-seven manuscripts, I must donate.

Writers are expected to make these sacrifices. Doctors and lawyers and grocers and psychiatrists make similar sacrifices for the good of the community, but with one paramount difference: they earn a decent living from their primary work.

The degradation of money. I teach in prisons and public schools and universities not simply for the money I earn, although I cannot survive without it, but because I love the subject and my students.

A typical poet in North America finds it necessary to relocate every year for the first few years after college, and every several years for a couple of decades after that. The poet becomes disconnected, never developing a true sense of place or of community outside the community of the printed page. The typical poet teaches, partly because teaching leaves the summer free to write, partly because the subject is a passion. But teaching drains. The writer-in-residence is rarely a candidate for tenure because it is far less expensive to make that position temporary, keeping the resident artist on the lowest rung of the pay-scale. Even within the confines of the artificial community of would-be scholars, the poet is heretic. And the poet outside academia? That poet is a scholar-out-of-office, a professor of desire.

The young writer is in college. At some point, he or she writes home, "I think maybe I will dedicate my life to poetry."

The family soon writes back, "That's nice. But what will you do?" Meaning, "to make a living," or to save the family embarrassment.

I have a friend, a poet about as well known as an American poet can be, whose wife told me this about their marriage: after meeting and approving the union with the poet, her family took her aside. Would it be all right, they wanted to know, if they introduced the poet to their friends not as a poet, but as a professor. After all, it is so much more dignified.

Our public life is a jungle where everyone is out to slaughter the other with guile, slander, cowardice, shamelessness. These people make you feel as though you were chewing fog.

—George Seferis, *A Poet's Journal*

At this writing, I am approaching fifty years old and am "employed" about four to five months per year at a salary that approaches ten dollars per hour. I have six years of university education, read several languages, and research a dozen more. I have been lucky enough to have been honored by several grants and awards. But I have no health insurance, no retirement fund, minimal insurance on my home, and no money in the bank. For the past twenty years (with two significant exceptions), I have survived from week to week. But I have enjoyed far greater wealth than I ever dreamed possible.

The general public distrusts art. A 1985 Associated Press article pointed out that fifty-seven percent of the public disliked abstract art, while a whopping seventy percent visited an art museum less than once a year. "Thirty-five percent said they never visited art museums, twenty-seven percent never attended concerts, and thirty-nine percent never went to the theater." The article broke down groups by education, by income, and by region. Less than half of all college graduates support subsidies for the arts. Fewer than one in three high school graduates supports subsidies for the arts. Our federal budget designates more money for military marching bands than for art.

Nowhere in the article was literature even mentioned.

Because money for literature is scarce, and because the general public measures quality by money, the poet is constantly faced with the prospect of being expected to "play poet" as though it were an amateur competitive sport. Private and university presses regularly run contests with the first prize being publication of the "best" book. Which leaves literally hundreds of poets sending out manuscripts with cover letters explaining how they have been "runner-up" in contest after contest. It would be all too easy (and probably just) to dismiss these poor careerists as victims of poetic justice, except that contests degrade not only the naive participants, but poetry as well.

Robert Graves stated that he wrote for "a few friends" rather than for a public. The poet's chief loyalty, he said, "is to the Goddess Calliope, not to his publisher, or to the booksellers on his publisher's mailing list." And certainly not, I would add, to the judges of a poetry contest.

Poetry is not a contest. Anyone believing contests show anything but trends should have a look at the Yale Younger Poets list. Does anyone read Howard Buck? He was the first. John Chipman Farrar, David Osborne Hamilton, Alfred Raymond Bellinger, Thomas Caldecot Chubb, Daryl Boyle, Theodore H. Banks, Jr., or Viola White? Marion Boyd, Beatrice E. Harmon, or Elizabeth Jessup Blake? Eleanor Slater, Lindley Williams Hubbell, Mildred Bowers, Ted Olson, Francis Claiborne Mason, or Frances Frost? Louise Owen, Dorothy Belle Flanagan, Shirley Barker, or Henri Faust? Each is a poet, each wrote, presumably, good poetry.

Careerists scramble over token university positions. Many of these writers see a position in a university as a step toward national recognition, which it often is. But the attitude built into contests inclines them to disregard their critics while embracing easy flattery.

Contests chart the calm blue seas of fads. Back in the days when poets served severe apprenticeships under the stern gaze of elder poets, it may have meant something to have "studied under" so-and-so. But we have too often chosen the democracy of the Writing Program with its composition by committee rather than enduring the tyranny of genius. "Genius," Blake said, "is not lawless." Nor is it expressed by committee. MFAs, a "terminal" degree, produce more MFAs. Universities certify hundreds of new American poets every year, far, far more poets being "drafted" into semi-official poetry societies than football players drafted into the pros. Many of them have been winners or runners-up in contests sponsored by The Associated Writing Programs, by literary magazines, university English departments, private presses, and/or nefarious vanity publishers.

In recent years, there has been a new wrinkle: the invention of the "literary lottery," a contest in which the participant pays to enter, then prays to be among the anointed. I'm told a decent publication can get two or three thousand entrants. Charging a five dollar "reading fee," one has a budget of, say, eight thousand dollars from reading fees alone. Since one can put out a pretty well-made book in an edition of a thousand for approximately three to five thousand dollars, even after postage and advertising, our "editor" has raised several grand. The losers may then be among the "runners-up" who are cordially invited to enter again next year.

What really dissatisfies in American civilization is the want of the interesting.

—Matthew Arnold

When Scott Walker decided to move Graywolf Press from Port Townsend to St. Paul, our local newspaper ran a sympathetic story. Walker told of his love for the Northwest, and of Port Townsend in particular, but, he said, he simply couldn't raise funds here. In Minnesota, he explained, there would be more grants, there would be corporate and private funds to help. Our local paper was very sympathetic; losing Graywolf Press, it said, would be a loss to us all. But our paper never reviewed his books. When Graywolf was struggling to find funds, neither our local paper nor the major dailies in Seattle, among the worst in the country (the *Seattle Post-Intelligencer*, a Hearst paper, doesn't even have a book page), came to his aid. But they all mourned his moving.

What does the economic situation of the poet have to do with the art of letters? Simply this: the poet's marginal position within the community, the lack of a permanent position, and the lack of future economic stability constantly undermine the poet's sense of self-worth. We are told in many ways that our most valued work has no "value" to the culture at large. When the poet, in order to have the all-important time to write and to study, works for a pittance and lives in motels or moves from college to college, one of the most important connections in culture is severed, and the poet becomes a low-grade highbrow entertainer, a fly-by-night gadfly to be used and passed on by institutions.

Poets have no right to expect to be paid for their labors. They have no right to expect enthusiastic audiences. They have, in fact, no right to expect any material return of any kind for their work, work which is correctly defined as the economy of the gift. But if the other arts are valued by the culture at large, the calling, the *vocation* of the poet, like that of painter or composer, should be honored; the poet, like the painter or composer, needs money to buy time in order to work.

Poetry is not perceived as a vocation. When universities certify young poets, they degrade both the poets and the poets' work. It is an honor to teach a child how to listen and how to speak in rime; it is honorable and useful work to teach at all (just as I, sitting here at my desk in the early morning, thinking, drinking coffee, am now involved in a discourse, am setting up a dialectic, am both teaching and learning, engaging my life with yours, Imagined Reader, in the shared hope that the realizations resulting from this discourse will be mutually beneficial). But the work of teaching is another vocation.

Nevertheless, we are belittled by the arrogance of ignorance in others, just as the farmer is degraded by the ignorant assumptions of those who never learn to read a water table or to understand an animal or to make a simple piece of furniture with their hands. Just as the "women's work" of the past was belittled by men too self-important to learn how to darn a sock or to bake a loaf of bread.

In point of fact, the American economic system is degrading to all artists and to art itself. The true artist is faced with perpetual adolescence in the American economic reality, and often lives from hand-to-mouth, embarrassed and frustrated by poverty, frequently insulted by public perceptions and misconceptions about what art is and is not, always on the lookout for the handout, for the patron, a spiritual pagan in the Church of the Almighty Dollar. This condition has existed since the early *polis*.

But the poet stands outside even the community of artists, for the musician, the painter, the actor, the sculptor, the clown—all these may hold out hope that someday it will become possible to eke out a livelihood from the various crafts of their respective disciplines, while the call to poetry more closely resembles the vows of poverty one takes in order to enter a religious community. No poet in this country can realistically expect to ever enjoy a regular income as a result of mastering the craft of composition. Removed to the margins of culture, poets remain in economic shadows.

What is the "comparable worth" of a poet compared to a local minister? And compared to a cop? Who shall "police" our grammar? The poet labors many years, preparing for the gift of inspiration; from this inspiration, the poet makes a gift. But neither poet nor poem is divorced from the morality of the marketplace. There is, as Seferis said, no deferment for the living.

Perhaps this complex problem has no solution; certainly, it has no simple and obvious one other than the re-education of the general public. The entirely necessary and honorable work of the National Endowment for the Arts and various state arts agencies is not sufficient; they are under-funded and provide convenient targets for the likes of Jesse Helms and his ilk. But pouring more tax dollars into state and federal coffers will not, of itself, solve the problem. There are more arts bureaucracies than ever before. The problem will be solved by Boeing Aircraft contributing to the welfare—not charity, but *welfare*—of the poet as it already does the painter. The situation will be resolved when it is defined in the high school and college classroom, when it becomes a suitable subject for "home economics."

Poetry exists as a gift economy, interdependent with the shadow work of the artist, and with the "hard economy" of the greater culture. No one can survive by the economy of the gift alone in capitalist society. No one can live by the hard economy alone. Everyone, at one level or another, is engaged in shadow work.

"In the economy of the spirit," Valéry said, "thrift is ruinous."

Shadow Work

Plato, who despised and distrusted poets, believed that love (in its largest sense) was *gnosis,* the binding (*re-ligio*) which transforms opposites into a unity. For Plotinus, love was the result of "strenuous contemplation in the soul." Kenneth Rexroth, in his beautiful "Letter to William Carlos Williams," defines a poet as one "who creates sacramental relationships that last always." And in the *Timaeus,* Plato says, "It is impossible for the determination or arrangement of two of anything, so long as there are only two, to be beautiful without a third. There must come between them, in the middle, a bond which brings them into union."

Horace wrote, "By right means, if possible, but by any means, make money." Dr. Johnson wrote, on April 5, 1776, working on his "own time" and without remuneration for his thinking, "No man but a blockhead ever wrote, except for money." And Nigel Dennis exclaimed, "One is always excited by descriptions of money changing hands—it's much more fundamental than sex!"

A poet's work was defined by Dr. Williams in *Spring and All:* "To refine, to clarify, to intensify that eternal moment in which we alone live." Williams sought a poetry which would not control energy, but would release it. A re-invigoration of the spirit.

A poet's work is shadow work. I borrow the term, altering it slightly, from Ivan Illich's 1981 *Shadow Work* (Marion Boyars), and it would be improper not to permit him the initial definition:

I do not mean badly paid work, nor unemployment; I mean unpaid work. The unpaid work which is unique to the industrial economy is my theme. In most societies men and women together have maintained and regenerated the subsistence of their households by unpaid activities. The household itself created most of what it needed to exist. These so-called subsistence activities are not my subject.

My interest is in that entirely different form of unpaid work which an industrial society demands as a necessary complement to the production of goods and services. This kind of unpaid servitude does not contribute to subsistence. I call this complement to wage labor "shadow work." It comprises most housework . . . shopping . . . the homework of students, the toil expended commuting to and from the job . . . compliance with bureaucrats . . . and the activities usually labeled "family life."

A poet's work is shadow work, it is work performed without regard for remuneration of any kind, most often without consideration for even the *possibility* of remuneration. The major difference between the shadow work of the poet and that of all of us lies in the fact that a poet's work contributes virtually nothing to the formal economy. Nor is the poet's work (except in certain "chairs" of certain universities) an unpaid condition of employment. Poetry has nothing to do with "employment" except in its most Latinate sense: *implicare*—to enfold or involve. The poet's involvement is most likely to be through the employment of contemplation, a sublime activity which is not an action.

The poet, contemplating the experience of love, creates an expression of the irrefutable unity of opposites; that is, the poet seeks to discover the third thing, the bond that binds, the "sacramental relationship" that can, through the poem, be rediscovered again and again. When Buson writes his poem,

> By white chrysanthemums
> scissors hesitate
> only an instant

his poem is not "about" scissors and chrysanthemums. It is an essay on birth and life and death and the rhythm of days and seasons, and it suggests profound unity. He balances action against perfect stillness, life against death, beauty against emptiness. But he excludes none of them. Against the death of chrysanthemums, he places the human hand with all its implications of beauty and life in flowers which the human mind holds dear. Against the cutting, he places the moment's hesitation, a perfect stillness. And in that perfect stillness, we glimpse the great void of which we are a part. Through the poem, we are invited into the reality of the "other" life.

Poetry is not commerce. It is not something to be exchanged or traded. It is a gift to the poet, a gift for which the poet, eternally grateful, spends a lifetime in preparation, and which the poet, in turn, gives away and gives away again. The actual work of preparation is shadow work: it must be performed without thought of money, and it is "essential" work in that it enables the poet to recognize and accept the gift and, in giving the gift away, do so with a great accompanying energy. But that energy, that experience we name poem, cannot be traded in the marketplace because it cannot be subverted. It won't light a lightbulb, run a heater or an air conditioner or a microwave oven. It is only a poem — necessary, and inviolable, an articulation of a world beyond the possibilities of money.

As the audience for poetry shrank, as social awareness even of the existence of poetry evaporated, poetry turned more and more toward the inner, other world. Poetic language has always been confused with religious language. Since World War II, poetry has spoken almost as a religion, but as a religion without a bureaucracy and with an almost complete absence of dogma. As Heidegger said, "We were too late for the gods, and too early for being, whose poem, already begun, is being."

"All the new thinking," Robert Hass writes, "is about loss. / In this it resembles all the old thinking."

·

Illich has some illuminating observations on the nature of what we call work: "Both 'work' and 'job' are key words today. Neither had its present prominence three hundred years ago. Both are still untranslatable from European languages into many others. Most languages never had one single word to designate all activities that are considered useful. Some languages happen to have a word for activities demanding pay. This word usually connotes graft, bribery, tax or extortion of interest payments. None of these words would comprehend what we call 'work.'"

To the Greek mind, handwork was anti-aristocratic and best left for servants. St. Paul's declaration that "who does not work does not eat" was generally ignored by the Christian hierarchy. The Rinzai Buddhists had their own version, "No work, no food," which they generally honored. Yet throughout these cultures, as throughout most others, there has been a consistent shadow work that provided, necessarily, for the health of the spirit or soul. It is *gnosis,* the work of knowing. It is not the same as "scientific" work, which is often more the exercise of technology than the labor after knowledge and which is subsidized. The poet's work cannot be subsidized except that subsidies can "purchase time" for a poet. And that "purchased time" is used almost in its entirety for shadow work.

But before examining the poet's shadow work, it might be helpful to understand just when and how the economic division of labor into "productive" and "non-productive" types came about. Illich claims that it was "pioneered and first enforced through the domestic enclosure of women." And while its roots pre-date the Industrial Revolution, it was indeed our faith in technology combined with our insatiable lust for "goods" that divided the home and that removed the hearth from the center of production, transforming it into a center of consumption only. "An unprecedented economic division of the sexes," Illich says, "an unprecedented economic conception of the family, an unprecedented antagonism between domestic and public spheres made wage work into a necessary adjunct of life. All this was accomplished by making working men into the wardens of their domestic women, one by one, and making this guardianship into a burdensome duty."

While men were encouraged to pursue new vocations beyond the home (and beyond "mere" subsistence), women were being redefined through the lenses of biology and philosophy. This newly defined "nature of woman" has been amply explored in Susan Griffin's magnificent *Woman and Nature* (Harper and Row, 1978). Woman was thought to be the matrix of society, one for whom common economics should have no meaning, one for whom the keeping of the household and the overseeing of children would be reward enough. "This new conception of her 'nature' destined her," Illich says, "for activities in a kind of home which discriminated against her wage labor as effectively as it precluded any real contribution to the household's subsistence. In practice, the labor theory of value made man's work into the catalyst of gold, and degraded the homebody into a housewife economically dependent and, as never before, unproductive. She was now man's beautiful property and faithful support needing the shelter of home for her labor of love."

But in materialist culture, what is the "value" of "labors of love"? Man began to perceive himself as utterly dependent upon wage work, he began to perceive himself as sole arbiter of society's problems, and he began to see the "requirements" of woman and wife and family as a kind of extortion. Suddenly, man and woman were completely estranged from subsistence work. The family cow disappeared. The family garden went fallow or turned into a small flower garden.

"Capital gains" replaced the family's customary re-investment in the *means* of family production, and the family-as-means-of-production disappeared.

Womankind became mystified. "Woman's work" was born simultaneously with the devaluation of shadow work and subsistence labor. The sexes became increasingly divided, with man perceived as the "provider" and woman as the "consumer." We consoled woman, whose work was perceived as "non-productive," by further mystifying her "re-productive" capacities. In practical terms, sex became the paradigm for the economics of "women's work" at the direct expense of all notions of partnership and communion and true cohabitation.

The soap-making, weaving, sewing, broom-making, quilting, canning, planting and harvesting, rug-making, animal husbandry, and household repairs at which woman excelled were taken over by technology. When women did begin to re-emerge from the domicile, and as they entered the marketplace, they found that, because their work was mystified and devalued, they would find employment only as menial assistants to production—at sewing machines, then at typewriters and telephones—for which they were paid second-class wages, and at which they labored without benefit of union or insurance or retirement benefits—a position which was not in fact greatly different from that position now occupied by the poet or by the free-lance "literary" writer except that woman had little or no hope for advancement.

Shadow work was born with the invention of wage labor, and, as Illich says, both alienate equally. Both become forms of bondage—wage labor through the issuing of long-term credit, shadow work through its devalued "non-productive" and non-capitalist characteristics. Industrial society produces victims as surely, and proportionately, as it produces "wealth" in the form of consumable goods. Just as South African apartheid supplies the white economy with "prosperity," Hitler expected his victims to "produce" while waiting for their inevitable extinction. It is the ultimate exclamation of the Work Ethic: *Arbeit macht frei.*

.

For the poet, whose work is a "labor of love," whose labor is to "refine, to clarify, to intensify that eternal moment," the real work becomes "feminized" and mystified in the eyes of the public. Poetry is perceived as something rarefied, semi-precious, and non-productive (to say nothing of counterproductive). Alienated from all forms of subsistence, from virtually all personal productivity, isolated on the assembly line of manufacturing or in the sterile executive suite in which no real product is actually produced, the contemporary male has relegated care of the culture, social work, family lay ministry, education, and all form of housework to the shadow economy. Divorced from the foundation of immaterial good, he struggles to make sense of his life, a life dictated to by forces entirely outside the self, outside partnership with spouse, and outside the domicile. He neither understands nor values gift labor.

To clarify the difference between "gift labor" (the work the poet invests in making the poem which will then be given away) and what I have termed "shadow work" (that work performed by the poet in preparation for the gift of inspiration), let me quote Lewis Hyde's remarkable study, *The Gift: Imagination and the Erotic Life of Property* (Random House, 1983): "The costs and benefits of tasks whose procedures are adversarial and whose ends are easily quantified can be expressed through a market system. The costs and rewards of gift labors cannot. The cleric's larder will always be filled with gifts; artists will never 'make' money."

The poet's necessity to speak is bound to society's need for cultural, social, and spiritual livelihood. There is no "price" for a great painting or poem or musical composition. A true "bardic" tradition in which a poet is paid to sing the praises of the king produces less real poetry than does the shotgun granting we now see under the auspices of the National Endowment for the Arts. The poet can neither buy nor sell the poem just completed. There is no marketplace for poetry. But, to quote from Hyde again,

There is a place for volunteer labor, for mutual aid, for in-house work, for healings that require sympathetic contact or a cohesive support group, for strengthening the bonds of kinship, for intellectual community, for creative idleness, for the slow maturation of talent, for the creation and preservation and dissemination of culture, and so on. To quit the confines of our current system of gender means not to introduce market value into these labors but to recognize that they are not "female" but human tasks. And to break the system that oppresses women, we need not convert all gift labor [and all shadow work] to cash work; we need, rather, to admit women to the "male" moneymaking jobs while at the same time including supposedly "female" tasks and forms of exchange in our sense of possible masculinity.

May Sarton has written that the greatest deprivation is that of being unable to give one's gift to those one loves. Then, she says, "the gift turned inward, unable to be given, becomes a heavy burden, even sometimes a kind of poison."

Without the shadow work, without the years of study and contemplation and self-searching, without the mastering of discipline from within, and without the years of trial and error, the years of work to know language and to gain a sense of craft in language, how can the abstract inspiration be transformed (through the appropriate infusion and release of human energy) into something worthy of being given? The "product" of love's labor. The quality of the economy in gift-economics is determined in part by the quality of the shadow work which attends it.

.

A man I shall call Joe has a family. He is in his thirties. He has a dull office job in the city. Having been born and raised in the heart of the U.S.A., he rarely attends a church or a civic function, but has a deep abiding faith in God and Country. He loves his wife. He loves his three children. But his life is hard. He has very little vocabulary for his emotions. He often drinks too much in order to avoid his emotions, in order to obliterate them. He produces nothing with his own hands and knows of no one in whom he can comfortably and intimately confide. His closest friend is a man almost identical to himself. They work together, they play together, they drink to obliterate their feelings together and sometimes in order to gain courage to discuss what they cannot, when they are sober, comfortably discuss.

But Joe is afraid. He fears the blank gray future with its office dust and telephone and file drawers. He fears the twenty-three years left on his mortgage. He fears the two years left on his automobile loan and the loan he took last year to pay for the birth of his youngest.

He cannot give the quality of love to his family which he would like to give. He is overcome, almost daily, by a dreadful ennui. His nightly entertainment consists almost entirely of televised violence, and he often fantasizes himself as one who is physically inviolable, able to overcome all problems by sheer physical will.

It is one of the most common portraits in twentieth-century literature. From "The Hollow Men" to Willie Loman, from Tennessee Williams to Ernest Hemingway, modern man is filled with existential dread which can be relieved only in shadow work and gift economics, those two "other" kinds of economics for which our families and schools leave us totally unprepared.

Joe needs and wants to give his family an enormous gift, but in order for that gift to be understood, it must be articulated in such a manner as to preclude any possibility of misunderstanding. He would also like to share his sense of frustration and, indeed, grief. The greatest gift he might receive from his family is the gift of understanding. His habitual drinking to escape reality may well turn to drunken expressions of rage that take the form of physical violence because he remains unable to articulate either his deepest love or his enormous frustration and his personal agony. Neither his home life nor his education has prepared him to meet the responsibilities that are concomitant with emotional health.

The poet's gift to Joe is the gift of articulation, the gift of good words. But the poet is also left to his or her own resources, for the shadow work of language has no place in public education, and even the language itself resists a poet's use. The actual working material of language, of poetics especially, was articulated by Paul Valéry in his essay "Pure Poetry" (*The Art of Poetry*, Bollingen, 1958):

Language falls successively under the jurisdiction of *phonetics, metrics,* and *rhythmics;* it has a *logical* and a *semantic* aspect; it includes *rhetoric* and *syntax.* One knows that all these different disciplines study the same text in many different ways.... Here, then, is the poet at grips with this diverse and too rich collection of primal qualities—too rich, in fact, not to be confused; it is from this that he must draw his *objet d'art,* his machine for producing the poetic emotion, which means that he must compel the practical instrument, the clumsy instrument created by everyone, the everyday instrument used for immediate needs and constantly modified by the living, to become—for the duration that his attention assigns to the poem—the substance of a chosen emotive state, quite distinct from all the accidental states of unforeseen duration which make up the ordinary sensitive or psychic life. One may say without exaggeration that common language is the fruit of the disorder of life in common, since beings of every nature, subjected to an innumerable quantity of conditions and needs, receive it and use it to further their desires and their interests, to set up communications among themselves; whereas the poet's language, although he necessarily uses the elements provided by this statistical disorder, constitutes, on the contrary, *an effort by one man* to create an artificial and ideal order by means of a material of vulgar origin.

In order for the poet to be in a position to give a gift that is useful, the poet must master the use of a material which is itself created and used every day by people who have no conscious use for nor faith in poetry. The poem exists in a condition of gift economics. But the work that precedes the poem, the years and years of preparation, come under the category of shadow work, just as the true poet continues to be dependent on shadow work in the form of reading, note-taking, researching, as well as furthering one's self-discipline, one's shamanistic practices, and one's spiritual life.

Poetry subverts materialistic economics because there is no "product" in the marketplace sense of the term, and because poetry teaches us to participate in the economy of the gift and in the economy of shadow work. For Joe, who suffers as a result of his inability to articulate both his needs and his gifts of true emotion, life in the material economy alone is supremely dangerous—it leaves him "emotionally bankrupt"—and he is left with a television serving as a substitute for friendship, as a substitute for partnership, and, ultimately, with himself alone with his loneliness. The loves and hopes and fears that threaten to overcome Joe may well also overcome his family, taking domestic violence (which is, after all, an inarticulate expression of self-hatred) as their form. Not only does Joe require emergency help, but his family is similarly endangered. Unless the necessary shadow work is done, the exchange of true gifts (the gift of one's self, the gift of giving) cannot take place in any comprehensible way.

The quality of time and attention invested in the shadow work contributes directly to the *quality* of transformation of the gift (inspiration) in the hands of the maker (poet). The hunter says, "If you want to catch fish, think like a fish; if you want to catch bear, think like a bear." Wanting to speak for the voiceless, the poet must spend time with those for whom the articulation of complex ideas and emotions is an enormous (and, often, losing) struggle. Wanting to participate fully in the economy of gift-giving, in the economy of love and hope, the shadow work must be attended to, and attended to with all due care and commitment.

The blockhead who writes nothing except for remuneration remains isolated in the material economy alone. The holistic life, the life of health, requires finding a balance within the boundaries of all three separate but interlocking economies; all three are bound together in a sacramental relationship that lasts always.

The Long Apprenticeship

All truths wait in all things.   —Walt Whitman

A single stroke of the early prayer-bell wakes me. Does it also waken my soul?

—Tu Fu

The poet's calling insists upon a lifelong apprenticeship. The writer is called a "younger poet" until the age of forty. A good editor approaches the poet the way a wise old woman approaches a frightened child. "How do you edit someone's feelings?" someone asks.

Easily. Because the feeling is most often what's wrong with the poem. The poem is a gift, but it is also a shape of order, a work of knowing, and of learning. Ezra Pound spent forty-four years working on *The Cantos*. He talked of cutting them by one-third. In making his songs, he learned from his songs. He learned of a terrible beauty, he learned of monumental error. He drank from a river of pride, and died with dignity, with humility.

"More poets fail from lack of character," he said, "than from lack of talent." To feel is not enough unless the feeling itself is disciplined and knowing.

Like the athlete, the poet has certain "natural talents," but without discipline and rigorous training, the simplest movement looks awkward and the runner stumbles. The poet learns to fall. Every poem is a failure of one kind or another.

There are many times more great athletes than great poets. Emily Dickinson sits at her desk in her white dress with a long, balanced quill in her hand. She does not write in silence. Her own voices slip between the robin's song and the breeze that rattles the leaves. And then it's gone. She shows her poems to no one. Writing is its own reward. She sits properly at the altar of the Unknown, waiting for discovery. And she discovers, over the course of a lifetime, common things, that "Leaves like Women inter-change / Exclusive Confidence— / Somewhat of nods and somewhat / Por-tentous inference . . ." She discovers the sacred interrelatedness of things.

History is severe with athletes and poets alike, for almost none will be remembered. But we remember old blind Homer before we remember the man who ran from Marathon. Still, the poet has good reason to be humble. The poet kneels at the altar of the Unattainable where neither poem nor audience achieves perfection, grateful for the least crumb given—the in-exorable flesh of the poem. The athlete has an audience; the poet speaks to poets. It took thirty-eight years to sell the 200-copy first edition of Emily Dickinson's poems.

The poet addresses later generations. But who listens?

·

The poet, like one who has taken vows, is "in training" all the time. In blessed moments, the poet inspires (inhales) the *anemos,* the breath of the muses, and becomes "inspired," but without discipline, the Mind refuses to speak. If frogs had wings, they could fly.

Alone in cloisters, the Mind is perfectly at rest, looking neither in upon itself nor out upon the world. The poet breathes.

·

The poet would make a pure, living language at perfect pitch, a language sung, spoken, chanted, incanted, whispered, and as boldly naked as a prayer. But there is no dream of heaven.

The Work is the Way. Until work itself disappears, and the words disappear from the page, and all desire vanishes—and only *then,* the sudden paying of attention, the Mind aroused, aware. After long silence and after prayer, the poet listens: street sounds, a radio in the mountains, the drone of a distant car, birdsong, windsong, the soft *thunk-thunk* of the heart.

Desire dreams of remedies for conditions which cannot be cured. The physician addresses the symptom, the poet goes to the source. But the poet who thinks he knows more of mortality than a farmer is a fool.

Let the poor novitiate attend to chores. Keep them simple and clean. One can milk and feed while the Enlightened One shovels manure.

·

In the hands of a poet, a book is holy writ. It is a text. But the book does not contain the poem. The poem is in the self.

She opens Denise Levertov's *The Sorrow Dance* (New Directions, 1970) and turns to a given page. There is a title in bold, "The Mutes," and a page and a half of narrow ragged lines of words. It is a poem she first heard before she went to the shelter. In the few brief moments before the poem takes place, she remembers. But the man who beat her is unclear, and it is strange to remember when she thought she'd live like that forever, that terror. And a voice that is her voice and is not her voice, the voice of a poet begins to fill her . . . "Those groans men use / passing a woman on the street / or on the steps of the subway

to tell her she is a female
and their flesh knows it,

are they a sort of tune,

an ugly enough song, sung
by a bird with a slit tongue

but meant for music?

Or are they the muffled roaring
of deafmutes trapped in a building that is
slowly filling with smoke?

Perhaps both.

Such men most often
look as if groan were all they could do,
yet a woman, in spite of herself,

knows it's a tribute:
if she were lacking all grace
they'd pass her in silence:

so it's not only to say she's
a warm hole. It's a word

in grief-language, nothing to do with
primitive, not an ur-language;
language stricken, sickened, cast down

in decrepitude. She wants to
throw the tribute away, dis-
gusted, and can't,

it goes on buzzing in her ear,
it changes the pace of her walk,
the torn posters in echoing corridors

spell it out, it
quakes and gnashes as the train comes in.
Her pulse sullenly

had picked up speed,
but the cars slow down and
jar to a stop while her understanding

keeps on translating:
'Life after life after life goes by

without poetry,
without seemliness,
without love.'

.

She loves the way the line-breaks insist upon certain ways of saying. She
thinks she has almost learned the music. The page is only a reference. A
sutra is not religion.

Each time she gives her own voice to the music of the poem, she is
humbled. She learns from it. The image of the smoky building sometimes
makes her almost weep.

When she remembers now, there is not so much bitterness, only the
sorrow. She knows that bitterness is a thief without dignity. And she
knows that sorrow can sometimes be a habitat for majesty.

.

The poet dedicates a life to poetry. The poetry has other lives to address.
But no one will be saved. The poem is a door leading to an interior
landscape, it defines that which is in the heart and mind, realizing the unity
of the one with the other. In making the poem, the poet learns from the

poem; in learning to "read" the poem, the reader re-visions the experience, likewise learning.

•

She looks at the lines on the page, settling on the line that reads:

yet a woman, in spite of herself

and she sees that the line is made of breath and sound and intention; it is not made by strict syllabic count nor by image nor by haphazard visual stimulation. "In spite of," she thinks. She remembers how often people say "in spite of" when what they actually mean is "despite." But this "in spite of" is pure and clear in its intent. The poem articulates our respect for language, but the language itself is only a frame through which we may experience the poetry.

And she realizes that this poem has taught men and women alike an enormous lesson. The poem never ends. But the final notes of the song end in an act of supreme tenderness and compassion. A beginning.

In a savage time, no act of tenderness or compassion goes unnoticed.

•

Poetry is not a religion. It is not precious. It is not sanctimonious. Nor is it fragile.

It is difficult in the same way it is difficult to be both serious and funny. "Beauty is difficult, said Yeats," said Pound. A good teacher knows when to make things difficult.

President Ronald Reagan of the United States of America sees a movie in which one U.S. G.I. destroys thousands of Vietnamese in order to save a few American lives. The next day he declares, "Now I know how to deal with terrorists and their like." Our president has a knack for simplifying things. As was once said of Ezra Pound's Chinese, "He knows when to dumb it down." Talking with Russian students in Moscow, Reagan stated his belief that "The United States humored the Indians by putting them on reservations. Maybe," he observed, "we made a mistake in trying to maintain [American] Indian cultures, maybe we should not have humored them in that kind of primitive lifestyle. Maybe we should have said, 'No, come join us. Be citizens along with the rest of us.'"

The president of the United States no doubt believes that the thousands of people who died along the Trail of Tears were simply being humored. Perhaps he even believes that the smallpox-infected blankets we traded to many tribal nations were a blessing to "primitive culture."

Our president is dis-eased—a fatal and highly contagious fever called megalo-mania compounded by delusions of grandeur. The press has given him the salacious epithet, The Great Communicator. He is loved by the public. He explains to us how certain boys and men in Central America who murder women and children in the night and who torture and slaughter civilians and animals and casual witnesses alike are really freedom fighters who need and deserve our money. He tells us the rich pay taxes enough already. He explains how nuclear power is safe. He dumbs things down just right.

John F. Kennedy had Robert Frost. Jimmy Carter had James Dickey. Nixon didn't have a poet. Carter had an evening with a hundred poets in the White House. Carter and Kennedy were both eloquent and both struggled for civil rights. Under Nixon and Reagan, civil rights declined. Adlai Stevenson wasn't elected president because the public thought he was too smart.

Poets are not the unacknowledged legislators of the world. A poet would rather agitate than legislate. One speech of Ronald Reagan reveals a stammering of the mind, an eye incapable of delineating detail, an intellect which has learned its history from Hollywood movies, its ethics from political slogans. Exactly when must one call a lie a lie?

.

When William Stafford tells us sheepishly, "Anything can be a line," we know that isn't true. We also know that Stafford doesn't want to exclude any possibilities. We find him at his table at 5 A.M. waiting "to see if anything happens," knowing he'll be there every day, "just in case."

The struggle begins each day—to embrace a greater and greater discipline, and to so fully integrate that discipline that all evidence of discipline itself finally disappears—to "lighten up" in every sense.

.

She finds in Denise Levertov's poem the Terrible transformed into the Sublime. There are lines of awful tragedy, and lines of tragic comedy:

Such men most often
look as if groan were all they could do

where she recognizes characters out of Samuel Beckett, crippled by their own inarticulate desires, but suddenly threatening. But they have somehow simultaneously re-invigorated her own sense of grace—she is unafraid, and therefore is compassionate.

Perhaps what the poem "teaches" is a didactic lesson, but the poem neither preaches nor argues. It is a permission—for anyone willing to speak or to listen, to experience a way of being. Each time one repeats the words, the poem is a different poem. The breath changes it, the heartbeat changes it, familiarity changes it, and yet it continues to deliver its message.

The poet wants to "learn" the poem by making it. Wanting the poetry of others as well, the poet memorizes, taking the words and rhythms and images into memory, into sleep and dream, and recalls the poem by way of the voice in order to give the gift away again.

Reading "The Mutes" again, she realizes Levertov has spoken for the desperate men as well, and that the poet, also, would reach out whenever a way can be found. The poet would make of this "strickened, sickened" language a poultice to help heal the soul's deepest wounds, as even their feeble grunts have strengthened her. And these three things so often lacking in all our lives—poetry, seemliness, and love—she gives as she passes.

.

Every writer has false emotions at one time or another. Everyone is sometimes self-deceived. Reading a new poem, we do not respond, "So-and-so certainly expresses herself well!" Rather, we say, "So-and-so has touched me deeply." Reading great writing, we do not marvel at the writing, but think, "I wish I'd said that," or "I've often seen that myself," or "That's the way *I* feel."

The poet speaks for universal understanding, lending voice to feelings we all have, illuminating those feelings so that we come to understand them more deeply and more clearly.

Passion can be distilled. The poet waits cautiously for the air to clear, for the passion of the moment to grow into the passion of the year or of a lifetime. Not just to record the experience recollected (re-gathered) in tranquility, but to give voice to memory and its revision, and to discovery, all the while accepting fully responsibility for everything that is said.

One learns slowly to question the sincerity of one's own emotions. The poet searches for the best possible editor, for tough-minded critics, because even when the craft and shape of the poem feels right, one's emotions sometimes lie.

.

Giving up pride, giving up ambition, giving up the self, the poet moves closer to the Universal *I* of the poem. The events of the poet's day only superficially influence the poem itself. One need not have been to Kicking Horse Reservoir in order to have drowned a former lover there. Richard Hugo's poem provides an outlet for every failed lover, a moment of catharsis. Galway Kinnell's nightmares may be nightmares from the sleep of heightened wakefulness, but they are the nightmares of us all. Kenneth Rexroth used to say he wrote poems "to overthrow the Capitalist system and to seduce women ... in that order." But Rexroth's poetry reveals a poet who reads to his lover, not his own poems, but the poetry of the world, poetry in French and Japanese and Greek and Latin, and it is precisely *from* those other languages and poets that his own inspiration comes; through *them* his own life and work become clarified.

.

Like Adrienne Rich, I dream of a common language. I do so knowing the first lesson of biology tells us that only diversity breeds health. I learn my lessons from women who aid battered women, from men in prisons for serious or for innocuous "victimless" crimes. When a man behind bars or a woman from a shelter responds to a poem, I suffer the sin of pride. I am grateful when a few lines I have written help another clarify significant perceptions. But the pride of authorship is a wall between the poet and the poem at hand.

I am a member of a tribe. I speak a particular regional dialect of a particular language. My inflections and my cadences are a signature as unique as any I ever signed on a check.

The self asserts itself sometimes, and at other times recedes. Making the poem, I suddenly remember Master Dōgen: "We study the self to lose the self. Only when you forget yourself can you become one with all things."

A Poet's Place

Condemned to live in the substratum of history, the modern poet is defined by loneliness.

—Octavio Paz, *The Bow and the Lyre* (University of Texas, 1973)

In his *On Method,* Samuel Taylor Coleridge declares that poetry is "a form of Being," and is moreover "the only Knowledge that truly is, and all other Science is real only as it is symbolical of this." And in the *Biographia Literaria,* he suggests that the work of the poet is to strip religion of its sectarian opinion in order to arrive at the revelation of divine powers.

William Blake believed "The Religions of all Nations are derived from each Nation's different reception of the Poetic Genius," and that the Jewish and Christian testaments were indeed an original "derivation from the Poetic Genius" of their respective cultures. He also recognized that "Prisons are built with stones of Law; Brothels, with the bricks of Religion."

But as Paz suggests, "Lyric poetry sings of passions and experiences that cannot be reduced to analysis and that constitute a waste and an extravagance. To exalt love," he says, "is a provocation, a challenge to the modern world...." Love and poetry know no price but that price which is paid again and again in the service of love and poetry. Love and poetry exist outside the laws of materialist culture. When Marx declares "the bourgeoisie has turned the doctor, the lawyer, the priest, the poet, and the man of science into paid servants," he is wrong only in regard to the true poet. Even in Marx's lifetime, the patronization of poetry on any significant level was nonexistent. Even then, poets existed outside the comfortable drawing rooms of the bourgeoisie. By the Age of Marx, the poet has become a religious heretic, one who believes in divine inspiration and its revelatory powers, one who believes, indeed, that all religions are one, and that the revelations which serve as the roots of religion are in fact expressions of the poetic experience. Or, as Paz says, that "religion is the poetry of mankind."

In the twentieth century, we see such poets as Rilke, Yeats, Eliot, and H. D. becoming immersed in hermetic studies, in explorations of comparative religions; we find Rexroth schooling himself deeply in all the world's major religions, and especially in Buddhism and Gnosticism; we find Robert Duncan's explorations of the Talmudic tradition and Gary Snyder's search for the continuous thread that leads from primitive shamanism up through the ages into materialist culture.

This search for origins, for ancestry, is the search for a sense of place in a culture which has no means for justification of the spiritual exercise of divine revelation. The poet returns to tribal culture and gathers a few initiates into the spiritual community, into the secret society of poetry.

.

Poetry does not exist in polite society. As Paz says, although the poet is not obliged to move away, the poet lives in exile. And although a great many poets do leave their families, their homes, their territories and cities and countries, they most often carry those places with them, just as Dante took Florence everywhere he went, just as Pound continued to be "the Idaho kid," just as Tu Fu, driven from Ch'ang-an by the An Lu-Shan rebellion, continued to be a scholar-out-of-office even in his thatch-roofed hut in the mountains.

In Western culture, the poet does not exist. Most often, poetry is looked upon as a sort of hobby indulged in by the overly sentimental, the naive, and/or the highbrow bent upon demonstrating wit. No one any longer is aware of a need for poetry.

Once again, Octavio Paz:

The modern poet has no place in society because, indeed, he is "no one." This is not a metaphor: poetry does not exist for the bourgeoisie or for the masses of our time. The practice of poetry can be a distraction or a disease, never a profession: the poet does not work or produce. Therefore poems have no value: they are not products susceptible to commercial exchange. The effort expended on their creation cannot be reduced to work value. Commercial circulation is the most active and total form of exchange our society knows and the only one that produces value. As poetry is not a thing that can enter into the exchange of mercantile goods, it is not really a value. And if it is not a value, it has no real existence in the world. The volatilization operates in two directions: the thing the poet speaks of is not real—and it is not real, primordially, because it cannot be reduced to a commodity—and also poetic creation is not an occupation, a task, or a definite activity, since it cannot be remunerated. That is why the poet has no social status. . . . When the world was reduced to the data of consciousness and all works of art were reduced to merchandise-work value, the poet and his creations were automatically expelled from the sphere of reality.

.

The current status of the poet is, historically, a recent development. Tracing the Judeo-Christian tradition, one might well begin with the Mosaic code in the era of the First Temple (ca. 1000–600 B.C.) when Jewish culture was bound by a body of laws bestowed upon them by divine revelation. The written law of the time, *Torah she-bi-khtav,* was accompanied by oral law, *Torah she-be-al-peh,* contained in the *Talmud* and which evolved as a complementary explication of written legislation. This oral law was a necessity for the preservation of the understanding of written laws during a time in which the language rapidly evolved. Oral laws defined the meanings of words in the written laws, as when, in Leviticus 23:40, the *Torah* refers to the "boughs of thick trees" without naming the particular tree. Those schooled in the oral tradition could explain to the novitiate that the tree in question is a myrtle.

Moreover, the *Talmud* contains, in addition to law, legends, history, exercises in logic, science, anecdotes, and humor. But it is an oral tradition which explicates law without being a citable authority *on* law. The name itself, *Talmud,* means *study* or *learning,* and is the product of belief in *mitzvat talmud Torah,* the religious duty to study and learn, not in order to gain access to some future Paradise, but for the sake of learning itself. As it says, "the true scholar is a living example by way of life."

The *Talmud* (and the Talmudic tradition) is not simply an exercise in legalities. Rather, it treats in *halakhah,* or biblical verses handed down from generation to generation, all its subjects, in the words of Adin Steinsaltz, as "Natural phenomena, components of objective reality."

Composed by many mouths, it is made up of "conversations" or debates much as Socrates had with his contemporaries in Greece. But because the views expressed are anonymous, the individuality of each is sacrificed to a grander, more general spirit. The ancient Talmudic scholar believed that time or history could be best understood as a living thing, present and future being logical outgrowths of the developing past, and that the proper student might attain true knowledge only through active participation in Talmudic conversation and thereby becoming a creator of the tradition as it is studied.

When the first identifiable sage, Ezra the Scribe, read aloud from the *Torah* during the Second Temple, "interpreters" accompanied him in order to explicate and expound on the significance of his text. Following Ezra the Scribe, Jewish history entered the period of the *Knesset Gedolah*, or Great Assembly, when the sages (*sofrim,* meaning both writer and counter) "counted all the letters in the *Torah*," meaning they completed the Bible, selecting texts for canonization and giving the Bible its final form. All of this work was done in verse form, but for the conversations or debates themselves. The Great Assembly also created a regular liturgy, the *Shemoneh Esreh* (with its eighteen benedictions), the primary Jewish liturgy even today.

.

By the time of the rule of Herod, Jewish culture had entered the period known as *tannaim* (from *tanna:* one who studies, passing on through repetition what one has learned from the sages and teachers), during which oral laws were organized by subject or by mnemonic association. Pre-tannaitic scholarship had been almost entirely collective and anonymous. But by the period of *tannaim,* the sages were clearly identifiable and carried with them personal traits as part of their reputation: "Rabbi Hyrcanus is a cemented cistern that never loses a drop; Rabbi Erekh is an inexhaustible spring."

Rabbi Hillel was asked to define the entire *Torah* in a single sentence. "Do not do unto others that which you would not have them do unto you. All the rest is commentary."

In studying the *Talmud* and the Talmudic tradition, everything which is not *halakhah* (verses handed down by the sages) or explication of *halakhah,* is *aggadah,* or explanation of verses from which practical *halakhic* conclusions cannot be derived, as well as anecdotes regarding the great sages. There are also proverbs, travel stories, philological explanations, and history.

Piyyutim, or liturgical poems, were appended to the *Shemoneh Esreh,* some of which survived generation after generation, and some of which

lost relevance and vanished. Talmudic scholars, being occupied by common daily work as well, never lost contact with their communities, even
though there is much evidence to suggest their labors in studying foreign
languages and customs. They were, in practice, living evidence that each
related subject itself becomes *Torah.*

It might well be said that our critical as well as poetic tradition takes
its cue from Talmudic studies beginning three thousand years ago.

•

At about the time of the end of the First Temple, we find among the Greeks
the rise of the pre-Socratics. Like the Jewish sages, the pre-Socratics make
no distinction between the philosophical and the scientific, and there is
evidence to suggest that Pythagoras and other early thinkers schooled
themselves in shamanic traditions, probably via Scythia and Thrace, and
began the tradition in Greece of personal revelation. The Ionians were the
first to embrace the teaching of Zoroaster, who reinterpreted traditional
Iranian religion through his own personal revelation to found monotheism. He came only about two hundred years after the Greek alphabet
was brought in and adapted from the Phoenicians (ca. 800 B.C.).

Probably, the *Theogony* of Hesiod is the earliest Greek book to survive.
Hesiod's genealogy of the gods includes the great Succession Myth adapted
from the Near Eastern cultures, as well as a great many "gods" invented
by Hesiod himself, the latter including Earth, Night, Sleep, Strife, and
others.

During the first half of the sixth century B.C. three Milesians gained
notoriety: Thales the teacher, and his pupils, Anaximander and Anaximenes. Thales *wrote* nothing. They supposed that the universe was controlled by a supreme divinity who set up a system of divine order. What
they sought to establish was the relation between the "Divine" and the
empirical world about them. They saw in the cycles of the seasons and the
predictable changes evidence of an all-controlling law in the universe. And
beyond that, they saw the Unbounded (*to apeiron*), or supreme divinity.
Etymologically, *to apeiron* may also be said to mean that which cannot
be completed, so that they saw a divinity which exists beyond the bounds
of time and space.

Thales, the eldest of the Milesian trio, held that water was the origin of
all things and that there is water both below the earth and above the
firmament. Aristotle quotes him as saying "All things are full of gods," an

observation not the least at odds with his notion of watery origins.

But for his pupil, Anaximander, not water, but opposites were the primary forces for change in the world. He believed that in the separation of opposites was the perpetual movement of the Unbounded. Aristotle credits him with the idea that a vortex (*diné*) was used to explain both the separation of the kosmos into heavy and light components and the circling of heavenly bodies. As the kosmos developed, the opposite worked against its twin.

Anaximenes added to this the concept of the *psuche,* or "breath-of-life" which escapes the body upon death.

By the time of Xenophanes, monotheism was spreading not only among the Greeks and Jews, but among the Iranians as well. Xenophanes argued that since it is contrary to divine law for gods to have masters, there must be but one god. Xenophanes was "both a poet and reciter of poetry" who wandered the Greek countryside and who believed that in human experience there could be no certainty.

A contemporary of Xenophanes, Herakleitos, composed terse, memorable, rhythmic prose full of allusions, puns, and deliberate ambiguities. (It should be noted that our word *rhythm* comes from the Greek *rhein:* to flow—so that rhythmic contrasts are to be understood as contrasts of flow.) The prose style of Herakleitos is inseparable from his meaning. He believed that most people were capable of seeing only the illusory exterior of things and experiences. In this, he echoes the sentiments of Xenophanes: "Even if a man were to spread the most complete truth, he himself could not recognize it—all things are cloaked in appearances."

"The nature of things," Herakleitos says, "is in the habit of concealing itself. Latent structure is master of obvious structure." And in Fragment 79 (and elsewhere) he uses the term *daimon* for "god"—*daimon* being "one who knows." And Herakleitos struggles against the obvious tools of the writer, searching for something deeper, when he says, "Eyes and ears are bad witnesses for men, for they belong to men whose souls cannot understand their language."

And, "Other men are unaware of what they do awake, just as they are unaware of what they forget about in sleep." But Herakleitos had no prescription for enlightenment, only the ability to transmit what his own insights had taught him. His faith resided in the *logos*—which during his time variously meant word, story, reckoning, and proportion. In all probability, he chose *logos* in all its cloaks of meaning and implication. "Having never heard me, but the logos, it is wise to concur that all is one."

It is well to remember that Herakleitos had no abstract vocabulary at his command. "A road is, upwards and downwards, one and the same." And he apparently observed that opposites not merely coexisted, but were indeed identical in many respects. "Hesiod did not know what day and night are: they are one."

And out of his thinking and speaking, one idea came to hold notions of poetic understanding above all others: "They do not understand how what is at variance is in agreement with itself: a back-turning structure (*palintropos harmonie*) like that of the bow and the lyre." The noun used, *harmonie*, comes from *harmozein* — "to fit together." Herakleitos saw that two or more different parts could be fitted together to make a structure which is more than the sum of its parts. It is one of the most profound observations in the history of poetics.

"One thing, that alone is wisdom: to be skilled in the plan upon which all things are controlled throughout the universe." (Fr. 40)

"One must know that war is universal, and that justice is strife." (Fr. 80)

.

By the time of Demokritos, the doubts Herakleitos expressed regarding our ability to understand sensory data had been developed into doubts about sensory data itself: "There are two forms of knowledge, one legitimate and one bastard; to the bastard belong sight, hearing, smell, taste, and touch. The other kind is legitimate and is distinct in nature from the former." (Fr. 11)

It was during the time of the Sophists that the teaching of writing and speaking became part of the *techne*, or science, of education, so that it might be said that they, along with Talmudic scholars, were the first teachers of creative writing. These "professors of speaking" reduced language and insight to a marketable "science" and offered their wisdom in exchange for money. To their way of thinking, mental culture was an acceptable end in itself.

They are the foundation upon which our notion of "classical education" is constructed. Theirs was a training "for life," not for science or industry per se, for they believed, like Socrates after them, that "the unexamined life is not worth living."

.

For us, as for the pre-Socratics, as for the early Talmudic scholars, "learning" begins with proper naming. "All learning," Paz says, "begins as the teaching of the true names of things and ends with the revelation of the key word that will open the doors of wisdom for us."

Our culture draws its attitude toward poetry (indeed toward all that is "Art" with a capital A) from the nineteenth-century notion that "primitive cultures," that is, all cultures preceding this one, were simpler, some so much so that they retained an innocence of which we are incapable. But nothing could be further from the truth. When Kung-fu Tze was asked, some 2500 years ago, what would be his first act should he administer the empire, the Master replied, "The rectification of names."

The battered woman, before she can even begin to heal the soul's wounds, must learn to say, "I have been a battered woman," and to thereby properly identify her previous condition. Only after she has named what *is* can she begin to name what may be.

Victorian sensibilities delighted in preposterous misnomer. Victorian culture perceived itself (as we now perceive "American" culture) as a product of manifest destiny, a triumph of divine will over primitive innocence, of technological advancement over primitive ceremony. Hence, in late nineteenth-century literature we find strict adherence to the notion that a poem is a kind of formula, and that, if the poet is properly trained, the author need only "fill in the blanks" in order to arrive at true poesy. It was a time of the triumph of rhyme and meter over "content" in poetry.

The Modernist revolution was, in large part, a common-sense response to the almost absolute frivolity of the generation of poets preceding Pound, Yeats, Eliot, H.D., et al. Ornament is not art.

But it was also these same poets who, turning back to the truth of "primitive" complexities, turned away society at large. The reading public simply could not understand the difference between the artifice of the troubadours of Provence and the artifice of, say, Tennyson. But in point of fact, the difference was enormous: the troubadours were singing their lyrics to an audience fluent in Latin and Greek, an audience which could readily trace traditions back to pre-Socratics. Tennyson provided entertainment to materialist drawing-room audiences whose primary interest was, indeed, entertainment, and who perceived a classical Greece free of complexity. Most of what we think of as "high-brow" attitudes toward the arts originated in Victorian culture. The troubadours sang to an audience which participated in the experience of the poem. The Victorian audience experienced the poem in a manner which in effect prescribed our experience of television—passive non-engagement, studied aloofness.

After Tennyson was applauded for telling us to "Cleave ever to the sunnier side of doubt," the Modernists remembered the dictum of Publilius Syrus, "*Necessitas non habet legem*," that necessity knows no law.

True poetry has always, as Paz says, been "a food that the bourgeoisie—as a class—have been incapable of digesting." Poetry has always been the food of exiles and dissidents. Poetry knows no class. But poetry, especially in early civilizations such as China and Greece, was very much a necessity. It taught the proper names of things, it elucidated a code of responsibility and defined taboos, it lent a completely human voice to personal joy and grief, and, most important of all, gave living depth to myth (which comes from the Greek *muthos:* word of mouth).

The Place of the poet is in the service of the language. When, in post-industrial revolutionary America, the language began a decline at the hands of technocrats and fell into psychobabble and dessicated jargon and was filled with deliberate misnomer by bureaucrats and politicians, the poet became priest and priestess in secret sects and learned to speak only to smaller and smaller audiences of the initiated. Where once the poet insisted upon the necessity of calling things by the right name, where once the poet insisted upon the necessity of adding to and passing on the mythos of the culture, bureaucracies began trading in commodities known under the euphemism of "mass culture."

Again, Octavio Paz: "Many contemporary poets, wishing to cross the barrier of emptiness that the modern world puts before them, have tried to seek out the lost audience: to go to the people. But now there are no people: there are organized masses. And so, 'to go to the people' means to occupy a place among the 'organizers' of the masses. The poet becomes a functionary. . . . The poet has a 'place' in society today. But does poetry?"

John Haines and the Place of Sense

LIVING OFF THE COUNTRY

"As a poet I was born in a particular place, a hillside overlooking the Tanana River in central Alaska, where I built a house and lived for the better part of twenty-two years. It was there, in the winter of 1947–48, that I began writing poems seriously, and there many years later that I wrote my first mature poems." But nearly twenty more years would pass before John Haines's first book, *Winter News* (Wesleyan University, 1966), would present his strong, clear, direct poetry to the reading public. And now, more than thirty years after those first "serious" poems, comes *Living Off the Country* (1981), the thirteenth volume in the University of Michigan series of "Poets on Poetry."

The earliest of these "essays on poetry and place" dates back as far as 1969, when Haines wrote a controversial review of the Paul Carroll anthology, *The Young American Poets*. Haines has not been the least bit reluctant to view recent North American poetry with a critical eye.

"There is," he says, "no adequate substitute for ideas. Having ideas doesn't guarantee anything, either, but lack of them has contributed to the demise of a number of poets in our time." He then offers Theodore Roethke as an example of the prototype: "full of energies directed all over the place, but relying in the end, perhaps, too much on personality, making of private life and the fantasies of childhood and adolescence a small world of his own to replace the greater one he could neither feel at home in nor find adequate terms to describe. These limitations have since come to typify a mode made prominent by much of Lowell, Plath, Sexton, and Berryman. . . ."

The cults of personality and neurosis are all-too-much with us and have been at least since Pound, Yeats, and Eliot. This is self-evident, as Haines points out in an interview, in the recent application of show-business

63

techniques in the presentation of poetry to the reading public: it is not unusual to see the photograph of the poet in the *American Poetry Review* take up more space than the text of the poet's poem. We are consequently, however subconsciously, invited to judge the poet by his or her appearance before we ever even get to the poem. One cannot help but wonder, thinking back over the centuries, whether the public might not have been put off by the rather harsh, uninviting countenance of Dante, or, more recently, by the indelicate appearance of Amy Lowell.

And, coincidentally, Haines puts out the intractable fact that fewer and fewer of our younger poets seem to have read the literature of the past. It is hardly surprising that one finds almost no sense of tradition in so much poetry of the last quarter-century. There is only the monotonously re-peated first person pronoun with its steady repetition of "*Look at me! Look at me! I'm so sensitive!*" The best seem to write descriptive prose; the worst, a flat reflexive prose of a rather low order.

Our poetry stripped of ideas corresponds perfectly to the cult of person-ality. One remembers the early Ezra Pound at his unbearable worst: the costumes, the ceaseless posturing, the invitations he extended to have his own photograph taken with the literati, and all the while writing precious imitations of the troubadours he so earnestly romanticized. But Pound had at least learned his languages; he was above all else a student; he read positively everything, searching for tradition. William Carlos Williams observed of Pound that by the age of twenty-one he knew more poetry than anyone else in the country, maybe even in the world. And even when he was busy promoting himself, he wrote good hard-nosed criticism rooted in common sense and practical wisdom, criticism of a kind we almost never encounter in our current crop of younger poets.

Our world is much more complex than the pre–World War I society Pound inhabited. Even the forms of poetry, Haines insists, have been commandeered by advertising, and subsequently corrupted. "Inflation of content and style and reputation, a continual crying in the streets by publishers and reviewers, even those otherwise well-meaning, until the wonder is that anything at all can be saved from the general damnation. And yet somehow writing persists, and now and then a good poem gets written."

Another recurring complaint is the absence of a sense of history in our poetry. In the best commentary yet on the poetry of the Swedish poet Tomas Tranströmer, Haines justifiably praises the poet's strong historical sense which binds him to the modern European tradition. "It is not a thing we find frequently in North American poetry," Haines says, "though something like it can be found now and then in the poems of Philip Levine, Robert Bly, Denise Levertov, and Hayden Carruth. . . ."

And while one may leap to include Gary Snyder, Wendell Berry, or Kenneth Rexroth on this brief list of exceptions (or even one or two others one suddenly remembers), the exceptions remain proof of the general observation. That generation of poets now in its mid-thirties to mid-forties appears to be completely untouched by World War II, unaware of war in Korea or Laos, and indifferent toward the issues which made U.S. involvement in Viet Nam a certainty. This same generation seems totally unaware of its own history during the past century.

"It may be," Haines suggests, "that, in spite of wars and other emergencies, the events of modern history have not touched us here as deeply as they have others elsewhere; we are oddly impoverished in our safety. We have hardly faced our own history as anything but dream and fairytale, or are only now beginning to. Then again it sometimes seems as if something were growing among us, a deafness and interior silence, born perhaps of a suspicion that history has no meaning."

Czeslaw Milosz has stated that only at moments of cataclysm and upheaval does poetry become the popular expression of people's hope and identity. Poetry, he has said, "is the most expressive voice of freedom." But the general public, in times of plenty especially, views poetry as a harmless hobby; the younger generation of poets seems to view it as a form of self-identity, a piety which can be placed between ourselves and the future, which we often perceive in its most nihilistic, threatening aspect. For a poet, as for all active intelligence, the way to find meaning and thus engagement lies in establishing connections with the drift of human history.

In an essay, "Homage to the Chinese," Haines places himself on the Tanana River in the late 1950s and begins to reveal some very important, but unlikely, influences. He says he felt "disengaged," isolated from the mainstream of current literature. And then he got a copy of Kenneth Rexroth's *One Hundred Poems from the Chinese* (New Directions, 1956) and "began reading the Chinese poems in the evenings in time spared from fishing and cutting wood. The poems seemed to speak for something in my own life, as I sat reading late by lamp or candle in the small cabin I kept on Tenderfoot Creek, an old, reclaimed camp with a dirt floor and mossy roof-poles." Thus Haines's by now well-known sense of place and history began to take root in his reading of ancient Chinese poems.

Rexroth's translations from the Chinese, along with those of Robert Payne and Ezra Pound, filled Haines with a sense of "renewal and rediscovery." He wrote poems again, "direct (and weak) imitations of Chinese poems" that he would eventually see as "trials." Later, he would add the powerful influences of Machado and Trakl—the Spanish Machado with his elegant simplicity and lyricism, the German expressionist Trakl with his dense, nearly impenetrable, darkness and sense of temporality.

Finally, we begin to glimpse how years and years of deliberation preceded the calm, easy grace of the Haines style of *Winter News* and *The Stone Harp* (Wesleyan University, 1971), and how this style is no longer disengaged, how this style (in the largest possible sense) connects directly with that of Tu Fu, Trakl, Machado, William Carlos Williams, Pound, Tranströmer, and Milosz. And we can see that Haines's unique voice brings with it the reverberations of poetry *and its necessity* from the beginnings of time, connecting the poet to a living tradition with all its incumbent responsibilities. "Genius," Blake declared, "is not lawless." Haines, isolated in the expansive wilderness of central Alaska where everywhere *not* Alaska is referred to as "Outside," finds connections everywhere—in classical Chinese lyrics, in painting, in music, in native cultures, in the land and weather and work. He calls to mind the famous remark of Gary Snyder: "As a poet, I hold the most archaic values on earth." Haines, taking up those same values, recognizes a far superior "law" than that of most of our poets—the law of continuity found in perpetual transformation. His "ideas" are not unrelated to those of Tu Fu or Machado; his work has been a revitalization of our basic need to remain a part.

Haines's essays on poetry are, like his own poems, superb. His is a very serious sensibility, but one which manages not to become overly weighty or burdensome, and one that refuses intractable formulae. His essay on Robert Bly is a small masterpiece. "It is hard to stay awake inside America," he says, "hard to stay alive. The soul feels empty there. After the sleep of ice, the buffalo hunt, the big plow, and the house on the plains, we walk around our yards, survey our fences. The soul comforts itself with work, with business, with crop production, with money, and alcohol; it falls asleep at night before a dream, paid for and stale." Responding to Bly's first and most readable poems, *Silence in the Snowy Fields* (Wesleyan

University, 1962), Haines says, "I have been grateful for them. Driving through that country, the names and places have come back to me, still fresh, given life by the grace of a poet. It is a gift, perhaps the finest a writer can make to his country."

But when he gets to later poems, beginning with *The Light Around the Body* (Harper and Row, 1967), Haines is devastatingly accurate: "In many of the poems Robert Bly has written after his first book, the images seem stalled and static. Much weight of meaning is put upon them, and the denunciatory tone, the moral fervor spoken into the silence, is too much. The images clash, withdraw from each other, come back for another try. Forced, the language refuses to move, and the lines lie about on the page like stuck rocks. . . ." Haines's critical vocabulary is not that of the high-minded tastemaking of a Helen Vendler, nor that of Criticism with a capital C—rather, it is the vocabulary of sincerity, of a thoughtful man speaking with due care.

The years Haines spent in Alaska have become, like Alaska itself, almost mythical. In the first of four sections of *Living Off the Country,* "Alaska and the Wilderness," he debunks the myth of Alaska as it is relished and perpetuated by its city-dwelling residents, while instilling in the reader a greater sense of the real place, an Alaska freed from Romantic wilderness-watching. He does not neglect the immense struggle of that country within itself: "A sometimes fateful configuration—the enmities: Anchorage against Fairbanks and Juneau, the bush against the city, southeastern versus southcentral, white conflict with native, and the state against peoples. Who profits from these polarities? It seems to me that we are all diminished by them, they are part of the sad psychology of our time, in many ways shaming and wasteful."

He finds in John McPhee's best-selling *Coming Into the Country,* a book many "outside" think of as *the* Alaska book, a humor undercut by an all-pervasive sadness, by a suspicion that the antagonisms may turn out to be "a big and painful joke." Speaking of "place" and poetry and the development of a sensibility, Haines reverses the cliché to say, "a place of sense." A true sense of place is a rarity in contemporary poetry. Most often, what passes for that sense is a shopping list of *things* inserted into a brief lyric by a shallow imagination; it is the poet's version of the traveler's postcard from a literary cruise through the country.

The imagination, Haines says, connects with the "real world," and thereby leads toward an ever-expanding "sense of place." Much of our personal vocabulary is drawn from place, from region, just as the human voice carries with it certain tones and cadences and pronunciations that imply landscape and weather pattern. "The forms to be found there, various and unique, yield their meaning to one who lives by the ocean, among the mountains, or beside a river," he says. "We are penetrated by these things, intruded upon, and made into what we are or can be. Much of the best of what I have written has been saturated with landscape. I have been led by this and other realizations to feel that there are always two places, dream and actual life. When the two are brought together by an act of imagination there occur those sometimes brief moments of compelling clarity and completeness. And these moments are, or ought to be, part of the real life of humankind: place and image, reality and dream made one."

Living Off the Country is compelling in ways that most of the others in the "Poets on Poetry" series are not. There is, for instance, but a single interview with the poet. So we are left with the precise prose of one of our best poets only to find that his prose, his critical faculties, and his perceptions of the *use* of poetry are all as finely tuned as his impeccable ear for the line in speech. "There is nothing so useful in art," Haines writes, "as a vital form." Haines finds that vitality of form in prose as well as poetry — *Living Off the Country* is cold and crisp and clear like the air after a week of winter snow.

THE STARS, THE SNOW, THE FIRE

Few of us at the end of this noisy, bloody, treacherous century will have been fortunate enough to have lived for a time completely within ourselves, freed from the frenzied distractions of mass media and popular culture, alone with the elements and the seasons and the empty heavens. Hunting, trapping, repairing clothes and shelter, or simply learning to read the falling snow as a book of time, one comes to inhabit a form of patience only solitude can define.

In the busy world of civilization, a world of city-states run by technocracy and greed, we learn of the "greenhouse effect" and of the clear-cutting of rain forests and of acid rain and poisoned air and water only in sound-bytes and photo-ops, and our attention span shrinks to the size of a tap-dancing California raisin, and global ecocide is "covered" in two televised minutes sandwiched between commercials for beer posed in a dying wilderness—"It doesn't get any better than this!"—and ads for four-wheel-drive off-road vehicles which destroy the very watersheds they enter.

Generally, we have two kinds of writing about Nature: from those who travel, and from those who have deep roots in a specific place. The walking tour was, of course, a well-established European genre two or three centuries ago, and Thoreau might serve as a model deliberate tourist. He enjoyed his walk from the pond into town almost every day. Melville, on the other hand, wrote of the sea from years of experience at sea. Either, to become truly accomplished, must master a way of life. Robinson Jeffers's landscape is his "meaning."

More recently, Wendell Berry has chronicled the complex struggle of the rural family farm, its economics and its ethical reasoning. But homesteading in central Alaska is another matter, a vanishing possibility with the deadly encroachment of civilization. The vast solitude is most often silent, a world without human neighbors and almost without women.

John Haines has spent twenty-five of the last forty years living in a small cabin on a hillside above the Tanana River, sixty miles out of Fairbanks in central Alaska, referring to it as a "place of sense." And for most of the other fifteen years, he was working to hold on to his remote homestead where, he has said, he was born as a poet. His own books of poetry and his marvelous essays on poetry (*Living Off the Country*) are a testament to his thoughtfulness and attention to craft.

His basic tools in *The Stars, the Snow, the Fire* (Graywolf, 1989) are traps, snares, axe, gloves, rifle, and imagination. The landscape is beautiful and severe, a country of extremes: at mid-winter, night lasts all day; at summer solstice, daylight never completely ends. Living in such an environment makes one's own life seem very, very small, and time is measured not by hours or days or weeks, but by seasons. Attention to daily details becomes paramount—food, firewood, and water must be thought about in advance. There's no minute-mart down the road. But these immediate differences from life in the contiguous forty-eight states is not Haines's point at all. He is attuned to shadows, to dawns and dusks, to simple tasks undertaken and journeys completed.

Haines captures the introspection long winters bring on, and with it, the responsibilities of listening in one of earth's most quiet places:

"I have said little, sitting across the table from Allison. I am silent because I am young, and because I have almost nothing to tell; it is my place to listen now, watching the faces and gestures of these two men long past their youths. . . .

"Who comes here, to this whiteness, this far and frozen place, in search of something he cannot name? Not wealth, it may be, but a fortune of the spirit, a freshness denied him in the place he came from. The North glitters and brightens; the land grows dark again, and the fugitive glow from a gas mantle lights the shadows." Listening, Haines feels included in a company of vanishing men who pass, "knotted and dispersed, in a solitude without women."

The quality of his listening might best be reflected by the fact that he has waited forty years for this memoir to take shape. Moreover, he tells us, most of the writing of *The Stars, the Snow, the Fire* took place away from his homestead. Through the filter of memory, Haines achieves a prose style centered by attention to telling detail and an overall tone of contemplation that approaches the sacred, a moral imagination which is virtually free of the ego.

If, as Gary Snyder has suggested, the experience of "the sacred" is rooted in "mindfulness" or attentiveness, what John Haines has held in mind through four decades is a quality of life which is reduced to the sacred and elemental, a simplicity connected to ancient wisdom. "Before knowledge," he says, "there was wisdom, grounded in the shadows of a dimly lit age. We ourselves have been night creatures, and once the human soul left its sleeping body, to soar and feed nightlong in the shape of a bat or exotic bird, returning to the sleeper at daybreak."

To live observantly over many years in one place is to become intimate with trees and grasses, birds, insects, animals, geography; to become a conscious citizen of one's watershed community, to participate in its rites and trials. Only through time and engagement can we come to an understanding of the real names of things. Commenting on the phenomenon of finding bats so far north, Haines says, "We misread these images if we think of them as horrible and frightening only, for the harm they seem to threaten. For behind that immediate and apparent violence they are as well, and perhaps above all, images of a lost and intenser being. Standing erect in polished bronze, Yamakanda, a many-armed Tibetan god, clutches his consort in what appears to be a ferocious and devouring embrace. But that embrace can be understood as an expression of devotion and love, and the terrible, wrinkling smile that accompanies it is formed with the only face the beast-god has to wear."

During a three-day journey to check and reset his traps, Haines ruminates on a life of trapping and hunting:

"I have learned to do these things, and do them well, as if I'd come into something for which I had a native gift. And a troubling thought will return sometimes: having done so much, would I kill a man? I do not know. I might if I had to, in anger, perhaps, passion of defense or revenge. But not, I think, in the cold, judging light of the law. I have seen a war, a dead man floating in the sea off a Pacific island, and I was there. By my presence alone, I took part in many deaths. I cannot pretend that I am free and guiltless. Justice evades us; the forest with all its ancient scarcity and peril is still within us, and it may be that we will never know a world not haunted in some way by a return to that night of the spirit where the hangman adjusts his noose and the executioner hones his axe to perfection."

Being comfortable with those animal intelligences most of us hide away under a false blanket of complacency, Haines comes into a deeper awareness:

"I leave some part of my mankindness behind me for a while and become part tree, a creature of the snow. It is a long way back, and mostly in shadow. I see a little there, not much, but what I see will never be destroyed.

"I may not always be here in these woods. The trails I have made will last a long time; this cabin will stand twenty years at least before it falls. I can imagine a greater silence, a deeper shadow where I am standing, but what I have loved will always be here."

"What one loves," Odysseas Elytis has said, "is always being born." Alienated from and terrified by the wildness within, twentieth-century humanity continues its struggle to dominate the left brain with the right, to value the material over the spiritual, the destination over the journey. We would civilize our own animal wisdom; alienated from the very ground we walk, from our parents and our children, we turn to the "cold, judging light of the law" for power and revenge. In the Age of Exxon, all our furnaces are burning, but a chill remains. John Haines locates a solution only within each of us, a way which can be found only through insight and contemplation. His memoir is an act of love for one of earth's shadowy, remote corners, a little warmth during a long, cold season. Meanwhile, our own future lurks out there in half-defined shadows, patiently waiting, becoming exactly what we make of it.

Living with Strangers

Nothing in the world is so rare as a person one can always put up with.

—Giacomo Leopardi (*Pensieri,* tr. by W.S. Di Piero, Oxford, 1984)

The charter of PEN International states, "Literature, national though it may be in origin, knows no frontiers, and should remain common currency between nations in spite of political or international upheavals." While the sentiment and the ideal present noble attitudes and aspirations, the statement is rooted in an entirely false assumption. Literature is not, by nature, "national" in origin.

If the French claim Albert Camus for one of their own because he wrote in French, could we not respond by proclaiming him Algerian? And as an "Algerian," is his nation the Algeria of blacks? Of the French colonialists? Of the Arabic Algeria? Camus, like Madame Bovary, speaks French. But his experience as a human being, as an artist, is, like Ms. Bovary's, located in the articulation of minute particulars. Both the fictional Bovary and the real-life Camus are driven by a need to connect with another human soul. This drive to connect contributes more to the demolition of national boundaries than to their definition. It is the root of all art.

Literature is a "currency" between nations only in the sense of "electrical currency" which "charges" the spirit. As recently as the 1930s, U.S. customs agents searched baggage and traveler alike, not for drugs, but for copies of Henry Miller's novels, for contraband like *Ulysses* or *Lady Chatterley's Lover,* for translations of the *Kama Sutra* or the Marquis de Sade. And by the late 1940s, one's bookshelf could land one in front of the House Committee on Un-American Activities, and from there to the blacklist. Great literature enervates bad government by exposing it while uplifting the human spirit. It is not "national" in origin, but humane.

73

For those who write American English, the very paint upon the palette is an amalgam of international minutiae—from our alphabet (a Greek term) which arrives mostly from Egyptian hieroglyphs via classical Greek (and thus is pictographic) to our vocabulary with its wonderful blend of Latin and Germanic roots. For style and cadence, our poets draw from the Hebrew and the Aramaic, and, for form and meter, from the Greek and Latin and from Northern European oral epic. Our translators draw from the tradition that goes back to the Babylonian *amoraim* (from the verb *amar,* to speak or interpret) who translated the scholars' *halakhic* teachings from the original Hebrew to Aramaic. Even our national ethic, Judeo-Christian, is an amalgam of other languages and cultures. And none of this would have been possible without the translator's art.

For every Gregory Rabassa who receives a tiny royalty for each of the millions of copies of his translation of *One Hundred Years of Solitude,* there are dozens of translators who will be rewarded for years of labor and study only by knowing a few hundred or a few thousand copies of their works may reach the hands of interested readers. And for the translator of poetry, the poetry is the only reward.

In his remarkable "How To Read," Ezra Pound perceives three distinct aspects of poetry:

Melopoeia, wherein the words are charged, over and above their plain meaning, with some musical property, which directs the bearing or trend of that meaning.

Phanopoeia, which is a casting of images upon the visual imagination.

Logopoeia, "the dance of the intellect among words," that is to say, it employs words not only for their direct meaning, but it takes count in a special way of habits of usage, of the context we expect to find with the word, its usual concomitants, of its known acceptances, and of ironical play. It holds the aesthetic content which is peculiarly the domain of verbal manifestation, and cannot possibly be contained in plastic or in music. It is the latest come, and perhaps most tricky and undependable mode.

Pound goes on to say that a foreigner may appreciate the melopoeia without comprehending either of the other two aspects of the poem, but the translator faces insurmountable problems in bringing over such a quality from one language into another. "Phanopoeia," he says, "can, on the other hand, be translated almost, or wholly, intact." And, in conclusion, "Logopoeia does not translate; though the attitude of mind it expresses may pass through a paraphrase."

Living with poetry in translation is like living with strangers: what often begins in beautifully romantic exoticism concludes in misunderstanding, impatience, and, sometimes, hostility. It is true these qualities also define the experience of living with family, but in the case of strangers from distant cultures they are frequently magnified. After a few weeks of eating in Greek tavernas, one longs for a cup of real coffee; after a month of sashimi, pasta sounds like Paradise.

One's relationship with poetry in translation is indeed often uneasy, but it is vital to one's spiritual health. The situation is not unlike the situation of Cavafy's great poem, "Waiting for the Barbarians":

> What are we waiting for, assembled in the forum?
>
> The barbarians are due here today.
>
> Why isn't anything going on in the senate?
> Why are the senators sitting there without legislating?
>
> Because the barbarians are coming today.
> What's the point of senators making laws now?
> Once the barbarians are here, they'll do the legislating.
>
> .   .   .   .
>
> Why don't our distinguished orators turn up as usual
> to make their speeches, say what they have to say?
>
> Because the barbarians are coming today
> and they're bored by rhetoric and public speaking.
>
> Why this sudden bewilderment, this confusion?
> (How serious people's faces have become.)
> Why are streets and squares emptying so rapidly,
> everyone going home lost in thought?
>
> Because night has fallen and the barbarians haven't come.
> And some of our men just in from the border say
> there are no barbarians any longer.
>
> Now what's going to happen to us without barbarians?
> Those people were a kind of solution.

In this context, it doesn't matter whether we imagine the translator as barbarian, or whether we consider the original language a barbaric yawp. The two, mutually resistive, tools of culture combine to frame an epiphany, a moment of recognition. The poem achieves universality in part through its compassionate tone and in part through its narrative structure which invites broad interpretation.

Cavafy's poem in English translation has served as a model for dozens of purely North American poems over the last decade or so, most notably Richard Hugo's "Plans for Altering the River."

This is a poem I gave at the beginning of each workshop I taught in our prisons, a poem I've given to the wives and husbands of chronic drug abusers and of abusive partners, a poem of force and intelligence capable of making a real difference in a reader's life. It speaks of hope and failed expectation, of yin and yang and mutual interdependency.

Ugolino, recounting his suffering, tells Dante, "*Io no piangeva; si dentro impietrai. / Piangevan elli . . .*" ("I wailed not, so became a stone inside. / *They* wailed . . ."). Through addressing the phanopoeic aspects of the poem, along with the logopoeic "attitude" of the original, the translator struggles to achieve a melopoeic equivalent. Through this equivalency, the reader experiences sympathetic harmonies or resonances. Ugolino's silence turns his inner self to stone. His inability to translate his terror into sound betrays his own heart's interests. This inability to articulate one's experience was a common theme of poetry in the 1960s when almost every workshop poem had stones, darkness, and silence as three principal components. During the 1960s and early 1970s there was a conscious attempt on the part of many poets to achieve what was then called "the international style." The movement was, unsurprisingly, a bust.

But for the translator, the truth of the experience lies somewhere inside the words—the sounds and rhythms and silences—of the original poet. To translate the experience of the poem, one must often move away from the original language in order to achieve a melopoeia or a logopoeia somehow equivalent. In the best translations, the poetry (not simply the "translation" or words, but the *poetry)* entirely obliterates any sense of the translator's presence.

George Seferis, in his great poem, "An Old Man on the River Bank," says, "I want no more than to speak simply, to be granted that grace. / Because we've loaded even our songs with so much music that they're slowly sinking / and we've decorated our art so much that its features have been eaten away by gold / and it's time to say our few words because tomorrow the soul sets sail." Seferis, composing his few words in modern Greek, follows on the heels of Cavafy in bridging the older, literary Greek (*katharevousa*) and modern, spoken Greek (*demotic*); his line has its roots in *dekapentasyllavos,* a fifteen-syllable line with a strong caesura and two main accents, but has been re-visioned through the poet's study and translation of Eliot and Pound. The "Englishing" of his poems is a collaboration between the English Philip Sherrard and the American Edmund Keeley, who previously collaborated on *C. P. Cavafy, Collected Poems* (Princeton University, 1975), quoted above.

The result of this collaboration is one of the supreme accomplishments of the translator's art in our time. Some of the individual poems — "A Word for Summer," "Mathios Paskalis Among the Roses," "Last Stop," and others — are among the finest poems of our time in our language. The translators, like the poem, move toward what Matthew Arnold called The Grand Style in his *On Translating Homer,* wherein he demolishes Tennyson not for literal shortcomings but for refusing to address Homer's plain, direct style. "Homer," Arnold says, "presents his thought to you just as it wells from the source of his mind: Mr. Tennyson carefully distills his thought before he will part from it. Hence comes, in the expression of the thought, a heightened and elaborate air. In Homer's poetry it is all natural thoughts in natural words; in Mr. Tennyson's poetry it is all distilled thoughts in distilled words."

If "distilled thoughts in distilled words" could express Seferis's "simplicity" adequately, anyone with a dictionary could perform the task. Matthew Arnold uses two French terms to make his point: "The real quality it calls *simplicité,* the semblance *simplesse*. The one is natural simplicity, the other is artificial simplicity. . . . The two are distinguishable from one another the moment they appear in company."

After serving Ezra Pound as authority on all matters Chinese for many years, Willis Hawley (incorrectly identified as "William Hawley" on the title page of Pound's *Confucius*) was asked to evaluate Pound's translations from the Chinese. "Well," he said, "Pound knew when to dumb it down."

Keeley and Sherrard present an English equivalent of Seferis's complex simplicity without "dumbing down" the poem. The result, like the original, fills one with a grand sense of being in the presence not only of a great and complex mind capable of beautiful simplicity, but also of great nobility. Much of the poetry of Seferis lies in his tone and rhythm, especially his almost boundless compassion, a feeling for humanity which surely must rank with that of Tu Fu and precious few others. While he was not immune to the sickness of the soul which so obviously identifies the poetry of this century, his dis-ease produced a depth of knowledge and feeling, a breadth of understanding only a few in our isolated culture are capable of fully grasping.

Another Mediterranean poet deeply influenced by translating American authors—this time into Italian—Cesare Pavese was as obsessive about his love affairs as he was about his art. As a poet, his masterwork, *Lavorare Stanca* (*Hard Labor*) (Viking, 1976) should be familiar territory thanks to William Arrowsmith's seamless translation. Pavese served three years of confinement ("detention, not imprisonment") for "anti-Fascist activities" in the late 1930s, spending that time in the village of Brancaleone in Calabria completing the poems.

Pavese's poetry is rarely overtly political. But he summons up his personal demons and confronts them in harrowing poems offering, head-on, visions of life in perpetual oppressive silence where "The night is the same as always. / You pass the fields, and you smell the smell of grass. / The men in prison are the same men. And the women / are still women, still making babies and saying nothing."

In another poem, "Discipline," Pavese says,

Drudgery begins at dawn.

. . . .

Nothing can disturb the morning. Anything
can happen, we have only to lift our heads
from work and watch. Boys skipping school,
who do no work at all, are roaming the streets,
two or three are even running. Along the avenues the leaves
throw shadows on the street, and nothing but grass is missing
between the houses which watch, unmoving. In the sunlight
along the river where they swim, kids are undressing.
The city lets us lift our heads and think
of these things, knowing we'll lower them later.

The phanopoeic aspects of the poem, its images, are not those usually associated with enormous tragedy, but with joy and youthful fervor: boys skipping school to go swimming, shadows over a street. But in the last line they culminate in subjective social melancholy and deep wisdom. The "dance of the intellect," or logopoeia, is profoundly ironic in this poem as in many others. And the American rhythms, whether one insists upon audible line-breaks or whether one reads "by punctuation alone," are somehow just right.

In "Motherhood," Pavese describes a man, "big, heavy / body, his own man, self-sufficient," and his three sons, reflecting on the absence of the mother who "died young" giving birth to the third child. "The three sons have a way of shrugging their shoulders, / a way the man remembers. . . . The three young men / have grown up arrogant and vain, and one of them, by accident, / has fathered a boy of his own, who only has a mother."

Pavese's ironic twists are not the learned ironies of the writing workshop, but the felt ironies of truthful perception. They are as different from one another as *simplicité* from *simplesse*. Pavese, like the dark German expressionist Georg Trakl, was driven by a terrible vision of the world which located "reality" in the hard implications of juxtaposed images. Writing of the poems in an Afterword to *Lavorare Stanca,* Pavese says, "I moved abruptly from a lyricism combining explosive personal feeling and self-analysis (wretched introspection which led to self-indulgent outbursts of feeling, which in turn always ended in a pathological scream) to the narrative clarity and serenity of 'South Seas.' I could explain this change only by recalling that it did not, in fact, happen suddenly." Indeed, the poems of *Hard Labor* are utterly free of "self-indulgent outbursts of feeling." They are poems of personal and social tragedy, poems in which the poet doesn't often matter.

Arrowsmith, editor of *The Greek Tragedy in New Translation,* is no stranger to translation. Having brought us impeccable versions of a half dozen of Euripedes' plays and two of Aristophanes' plays, he brings Pavese's vision and attitude into beautifully direct poetry as much deeply felt as thought. More recently, Arrowsmith has been translating the complete poems of another, more difficult, Italian poet, Eugenio Montale, the 1975 Nobel Poet. The first two volumes, *The Storm and Other Things* (Norton, 1985) and *The Occasions* (Norton, 1987), have already appeared and have received universal recognition as a monumental accomplishment.

Cavafy, Seferis, Pavese, and Montale are four of the knottiest trunks of hardwood any carpenter could labor over. They are poets of ideas and events as well as of emotions and ideals. Aristotle tells us in the *Poetics,*

"Everything depends upon the subject; choose a fitting action, penetrate yourself with the feeling of its situation; this done, everything else will follow." It is good advice for the translator, too, especially when underscored by Cicero's advice: "Translate not the words, but the meaning." Lao Tzu believed truth resides not in words, but in the heart; the heart may, through the light of words, reveal or dis-cover truth. Plato says in *Cratylus,* "Name; the word seems to be a compressed sentence, signifying being for which there is a search."

The translator faces a signified "being for which there is a search." But it is not simply a process of naming. It demands what the body knows as well as what the brain has learned; it demands a whole psychology rather than a simple strategy; it needs a breath and a heart as much as a voice or a definition. Otherwise the reader receives only the phanopoeia, none of the poetry.

The relationship is mutually interdependent, like that of lovers. "The beloved," Antonio Machado says, "is one with the lover, not at the end of the erotic process, but at its beginning." The poetic process itself is one of binding being or consciousness to religion/love. The act of writing, the act of translating, reveals itself as an act of communion. Just as the image in a great poem explains only itself, Octavio Paz says, "Meaning and image are the same thing. A poem has no meaning other than its images." The translator is caught up by images and rhythms, seduced by them, and becomes a lover of the process we identify as poetry. Enchanted, seduced, the translator adapts the poet's psychic powers and spiritual vision to new cultural conditions of being which grow out of differing but sympathetic harmonies.

Paz is wrong in his insistence upon the image as the only "meaning" of a poem. Image is not necessarily metaphor. Metonymy is not always synecdoche. How can the rhythms of perception be divorced from qualities of perception?

Dudley Fitts, in his Foreword to Mary Barnard's brilliant versions of Sappho, points directly to her logopoeia and her melopoeia rather than to her phanopoeia as he explains his praise: "What I chiefly admire in Miss Barnard's translations and reconstructions is the direct purity of diction and versification. There are perilous guesses, audacious twists, and inevitable flights to the authority of intuition alone. . . . What Miss Barnard perceives, and what no one would ever have guessed from the general run of talk about Sappho, is the pungent downright plain style. . . . Like the Greek, it is stripped and hard, awkward with the fine awkwardness of truth. . . . It is exact translation; but in its composition, the spacing, the arrangement of stresses, it is also high art."

Just how can Mary Barnard's "perilous guesses, audacious twists, and inevitable flights to the authority of intuition alone" produce "exact" translation? They carry an emotional equivalency in their prosody, in their attention to detail, and in their understated eloquence. To better understand Barnard's contribution to the "grand style" we should be familiar with Sappho's most famous and most often translated poem, "*phainetai moi kenos isos theoisin*," in some of its sturdier English garments.

First, a literal prose rendering: "That man is like a god who sits in your presence and hears close by your sweet speech and lovely laughter. It brings my heart to flutter. When I may only rarely see you, words fail, my tongue breaks down, and soon a subtle fire runs under my skin; my eyes lose their vision, my ears ring, sweat pours over me, and trembling seizes my body. I grow paler than dry grass, and growing madder, seem little better than dead. But I must dare, since one so poor . . ."

The most famous translation is not a translation at all, but a free adaptation by Catullus, "*Ille mi par esse deo videtur . . .*" which actually begins another whole tradition, one revitalized by Pound's *Homage to Sextus Propertius* (from *Personae,* New Directions, 1971) and more recently called everything from trans-adaptations to translitics. And there is of course a whole history of Catullus translations, some of which miss the Latin poet's versions of Callimachus as completely as his Sapphic.

Smollett's translation of 1741 was primary in its time:

Thy fatal shafts unerring move,
I bow before thine altar, Love.
I feel thy soft resistless flame
Glide swift through all my vital frame.

For while I gaze my bosom glows,
My blood in tides impetuous flows,
Hope, fear, and joy alternate roll,
And floods of transports whelm my soul.

My faltering tongue attempts in vain
In soothing murmurs to complain;
Thy tongue some secret magic ties,
Thy murmurs sink in broken sighs.

Condemned to nurse eternal care,
And ever drop the silent tear,
Unheard I mourn, unknown I sigh,
Unfriended live, unpitied die.

Smollett's iambics impede rather than propel the reader. In order to achieve his rhymes, he distorts meaning to the point of incredulity replete with glowing bosom and silent tears. Some of what Sappho says may indeed sound awfully clichéd after a couple of thousand years, but one must get at the core of the experience, which is never clichéd regardless of the particulars of a given situation. Clichés do not build good poems *or* translations.

A hundred years later, Tennyson has a version in his *Eleanor* beginning, "I watch thy grace; and in its place / My heart a charmed slumber keeps, / While I muse upon thy face; / And a languid fire creeps . . ." but, like Catullus, veers in other directions.

Sappho, known to the Greek and Latin poets as the "Tenth Muse," is by now turning over in her grave. About 55 A.D., Plutarch informs us that this ode was "mixed with fire." Longinus, about 250 A.D., reminds us that Sappho's poetic is "not one passion, but a congress of passions."

The iambics of Smollett and Tennyson and many others completely miss the sonic stress and audial definition of the original. Thus they miss not only melopoeic equivalents, but the logopoeic as well. And because they have committed themselves to a verbal Procrustean bed, they also misrepresent the phanopoeic juxtapositions of the original, failing simultaneously in all three aspects of the poem. Neither Smollett nor Tennyson seems to comprehend the simplicity of Sappho's style, her direct treatment of her subject. One can, in fact, sing "the sweet-voiced song of healing love" without falling into drivel.

C. M. Bowra locates Sappho at the center of a *thiasos,* a religious cult which excluded men and which was in perpetual conflict with other, similar cults throughout Lesbos. "The sense of her poems goes naturally," he says, "with the meter and seems to fall into it, so that it looks like ordinary speech raised to the highest level of expressiveness." Denys L. Page strenuously objects to Bowra's treatment, finding the poems to represent the personal loves and jealousies and pleasures of Sappho and her friends. Scholars will continue to argue over Sappho's personal circumstances as long as we have history, but all apparently are in complete agreement regarding her prosody.

Mary Barnard looked closely at Sappho's trimeter variations of ionic *a majore meter,* preferring to condense rather than expand at places where the manuscripts are fragmentary. She scrupulously rejected any inclination to "fill out" the text to "make a poem." We are left with a poem in hard, clear language:

He is more than a hero

He is a god in my eyes—
the man who is allowed
to sit beside you—he

who listens intimately
to the sweet murmur of
your voice, the enticing

laughter that makes my own
heart beat fast. If I meet
you suddenly, I can't

speak—my tongue is broken;
a thin flame runs under
my skin; seeing nothing,

hearing only my own ears
drumming, I drip with sweat;
trembling shakes my body

and I turn paler than
dry grass. At such times
death isn't far from me

This is Sappho raw, in her toga rather than in Victorian evening gown and jewels; this is a harder, a saner poet, one prepared to recite to the accompaniment of a simple lyre, a poet of uncluttered emotional response. It is far closer to the original both in its directness and in its melopoeia—which was meant for a spoken voice—bringing us closer to the logopoeia, bringing us closer to the emotional elegance of Sappho's great simplicity. The inversions and banging rhythms of previous translations detracted from the essential truth of the poetry by "distilling" her thoughts and dressing them up for society.

T. S. Eliot complained that Gilbert Murray's translations erected an impediment between reader and original text. Barnard's memoir, *Assault on Mount Helicon* (University of California, 1984), gives the following account of her struggle to get at the heart of Sappho:

"I found here in Sappho's Greek ... the style I had been groping toward, or perhaps merely hungering for, when I ceased to write poetry a number of years before. It was spare but musical, and had, besides, the sound of the speaking voice making a simple but emotionally loaded statement. It is never 'tinkling' as Bill Williams's friend A. P. characterized it. Neither is it 'strident' as Rexroth described it. It is resonant although unmistakably in the female register."

She sent a draft of the poem to her correspondent, Ezra Pound, who praised her efforts and asked for further revision. "The JOB of the writer of verse," he said, "is to get the LIVE language AND the prosody simultaneously. Prosody: articulation of the total sound of a poem (not bits of certain shapes gummed together)."

Barnard turned to the hundred or so poems once again. "I made no attempt to translate into the original meter. Greek normally has more syllables than English. I have never been able to see any way of rendering a Greek stanza in the equivalent number of English syllables without padding. The padding may take several forms: the embroidering of an image, repetition, or the introduction of unnecessary words ... all of which contribute to make the poem lax, to use Pound's word for the effect. One may also use a great many words of Latin derivation, or follow the Greek syntax slavishly; either of these dodges might work for Pindar ... but they are out of place in translations of Homer and Sappho. Underlying the stanzaic form there is, I swear (in the teeth of those who have said otherwise) a cadence that belongs to the speaking voice. That underlying cadence is what I tried to find an equivalent for, because, so far as I knew, no English translation had yet conveyed it."

Indeed, no one had. But a second American poet, William Carlos Williams, takes the same poem as the opening passage in Book V, Part II, of *Paterson* (New Directions), published the same year as Barnard's *Sappho*, 1958. The Williams version is so very close to Barnard's, one must assume that since the two were in correspondence, Williams must have used her version at least in part. Book V, Part II, of *Paterson* concludes with a series of questions-and-answers in the form of a self-interview:

"Q. But shouldn't a word mean something when you see it?

"A. In prose, an English word means what it says. In poetry, you're listening to two things . . . you're listening to the sense, the common sense of what it says. But it says more. That is the difficulty."

And that is exactly why Barnard's *Sappho* (University of California, 1958) is far superior to that of, say, a Smollett or a Tennyson: she says more with fewer words, she offers more and demands greater attention. Her commitment to poetry outweighs her commitment to words. She articulates a structure which contributes to the understanding of the poetry far more than it obscures. It is good poetry in American idiom.

In the seventh century, the poet Marvan distinguished a difference between the fitful inspirational music of the Aeolian harp which developed, he believed, from the sound of wind over the sinews of a beached whale's skeleton, and the purposeful rhythmic clatter of the smithy's anvil. Robert Graves distinguishes the two by directing one's attention to the slow pull and push of the oar in Anglo-Saxon poetry which, he says, remained unrhymed because "the noise of the oarlocks does not suggest rhyme." Iambic measure, Graves says, grew out of Helladic totem dances, perhaps from hobbling Iambe's attempts to coax a smile from Demeter at Eleusis. The early English "Two Sisters of Binnorie" tells us that the first harp strings were simply a drowned girl's hair. Chaucer's hendecasyllabic line comes from the five alternating hammers ringing the five stations of the Celtic year.

Shakespeare's favorite form was Italian in origin—the sonnet—but he of course changed its structure to accommodate his own language, his own rhythm of perception. And later still, Milton added a "tail."

Buried somewhere at the bottom of "poetic reality" where mythology and history merge, the original impetus toward measure is lost forever to us all. And yet it lies at the heart of ever-renewable poetry of all ages and languages.

Barnard's *Sappho* would not be possible without Tennyson's fustian which is itself indebted to, among many, Catullus's adaptation. Add to this the very necessary scholarship of a couple of thousand years, a good serviceable translation into modern Italian which inspired Barnard, a hard-headed editor like Pound, and the perseverance of a saint, and the contemporary reader has a slim volume of mostly brief poems in a living and lively language.

One who has not read the songs of Dowland and Campion may not always recognize the music in a line of poetry by Thomas McGrath or H. D. or Ezra Pound, but may indeed hear "music." Melopoeia for its own sake is mere ornament and detraction, the heavy gold that eats away the features of art. But when, in the hands of a good maker, we get great poetry from other times and cultures brought freshly into our own realms of comprehension, the direct result is a broadening of our own perspectives, the enrichment of all our lives.

"Know the root," Confucius says, "and find an orderly mode of procedure." Living with strangers isn't often easy. One must remain vulnerable, one must be willing to be seduced. Blessings on the Barbarians we call translators. Those people are a kind of solution.

After Elytis

If there is a humanistic view about the mission of Art, this, I believe, is the only way it can be understood: like an invisible operation, which is a facsimile of the mechanism we call Justice—and naturally I am not talking about the Justice of the courts but about the other Justice, which is consummated slowly and equally painfully in the teachings of the great magistrates of mankind, in the political struggles for social liberation and in the loftiest poetic accomplishments. From such a great effort, the drops of light fall slowly every now and then into the vast night of the soul like lemon drops into polluted water.

—Odysseas Elytis, *Open Book*

For one who has read as much of the work of Odysseas Elytis as has been brought into English from the original Greek, the mere mention of his name brings certain words and images leaping to mind: justice, liquidity and liquid light, Beauty with a capital B, and perhaps most of all the notion of otherness and glimpses of the perpetual "other side" of experiences and things.

But for those among us who have not looked closely at the poems of Elytis, he remains a slightly aloof Nobel Laureate often mentioned as a "surrealist poet" as though he were a functionary of some mysterious European literary cartel. It is an unfortunate position, both for the poet and for the North American reading public, but one that will soon no doubt be corrected. The surrealism (the "super-realism") of Elytis should not be confused with the more programmatic surrealism of French poets of the middle decades of this century. Elytis's poetry, I suggest, draws not so much from modern artistic movements as from the deepest wells of practical classicism. In attitude, he often resembles Anaximander, the pre-Socratic who found in the perpetual struggle of opposites the supreme movement of the Unbounded. Like the pre-Socratics, Elytis is far more interested in the origins and sources of mythology (in the mechanism, to use his own term), than in the figures themselves. Like Hesiod, he draws on antiquity, adding his own gods and goddesses to an ever-changing pantheon.

His earliest poems explore nature and metamorphoses and are primarily responsible for his categorization as a surrealist. In his second period, during which he wrote one of the great long poems of this century, *The Axion Esti,* he searched for newer forms and methods while struggling with an ever-greater "historical and moral awareness." In recent years, his work is best exemplified by *Maria Nephele (Maria Clouds)*, a long poem consisting of "parallel monologues" between Maria, a punk bête noire filled with the ennui of disillusionment, and the older male "Antiphonist." But defining these three periods in his work is also self-defeating: his career has been one of singular development.

Although associated with René Char while he was in Paris, Elytis actually resembles Camus, both in tone and in stance, more than he does any of the French poets. In Greece, his name is often mentioned in conjunction with that of George Seferis. But while Seferis, influenced by the neoclassical Modernists Pound and Eliot whom he translated, felt altogether at home with the figures of Antigone, Oedipus, et al., Elytis prefers characters entirely his own, but characters which nonetheless are the embodiment of mythological figures. In this, he would probably prefer Seferis's Stratis the Mariner to his Antigone. Like Seferis, and like Cavafy before him, Elytis makes use of both the old, "pure" *katharevousa*, and *demotic* Greek, bringing the whole of the language to bear fruit. But in Elytis, the archaic word is rare, and when used, it is used with great precision. He also evokes a powerful sense of place through the use of many regional dialects.

In Elytis's poetry, the major elements are air and water (yet another pre-Socratic connection). And like the poets of the classical Orient, he struggles in a search for a Paradise—not the eternal innocence of dogma, but a Paradise within. "When I say 'paradise,' I do not conceive of it in the Christian sense. It is another world which is incorporated into our own, and it is our fault that we are unable to grasp it." Our inability to realize the Paradise within creates a sense of tragedy of enormous proportion, one that is itself the "other side" of Camus's sense of the absurd. Just as Camus was not an existentialist, Elytis is not a surrealist. Both are Mediterranean pre-classicist sensibilities, and each represents a deep humanitas. And while Elytis adores innocence for what it is, his is a search for enlightenment, for the "drop of light in the vast night of the soul." He struggles to achieve not the French sense of *la belle clarté,* not clarity for its own sake, but for "limpidity." He says of this struggle, "What I mean by limpidity is that behind a given thing something different can be seen and behind that still something else, and so on and so on. This kind of transparency is what I have attempted to achieve. It seems to me something essentially Greek."

Not the figures of mythology, but the *mechanism*—a search for the psyche, for the breath of life, for light, for air, in a dark, drowning world. So that Maria of the Clouds can become Mary and Helen and Antigone, but alive among the statuary which represents (and mocks) them. "If you move from what is to what may be," Elytis says, "you pass over a bridge which takes you from Hell to Paradise. And the strangest thing: a Paradise made of precisely the same material of which Hell is made. It is only the perception of the order of the materials that differs. . . ."

In Elytis, one is always entering another life. Unlike Seferis, who spent a lifetime struggling against melancholy, Elytis finds hope even in tragedy and heroism in the Beautiful. In his *Open Book,* he speaks of Matisse painting "the most juicy and ripe, the most charming flowers and fruits which were ever made" during the years of Auschwitz and Buchenwald, "as if the very miracle of life had found a way to coil within them for good." Just as we often disregard the prophet who shows us the realpolitik of our afternoon reverie, we are startled by the prophet capable of dreaming the Beautiful in the face of enormous tragedy. Elytis is a poet deeply engaged with his time.

Imagination and reality are not separate, mutually antagonistic things, but are in fact the two faces of one being. Rather than attempting to answer mysterious riddles, Elytis reveals the Mystery. Just as we can glimpse the Then in the Now, we see the possible through the impossible, the dream in the wakeful deliberate act. The apparent detachment of Elytis is not unlike the seeming remoteness of the Zen master—we must surrender the self before we can bathe in radiance. "The light of the sun and the blood of man are one." Like the Zen master and the Taoist ascetic, he approaches religion with an open heart and a skeptical eye because, after all, "Man is drawn to god like a shark to blood." For Elytis, the metaphor is a means of transcendence, a glimpse of satori. But there is always that "other" or "other side" beyond.

Like Herakleitos, he understands that "war is universal, and that justice is strife." Unlike Herakleitos, he does not disregard all sensory data; eroticism in Elytis is not just a metaphor.

And if these notes after the poems of Odysseas Elytis make the poet sound difficult, I might quote Yeats (or Ezra Pound quoting Yeats) to the effect that beauty is difficult. But after the difficulty comes the ease. Justice is strife, but through Justice, we may arrive at Paradise. Only through the eyes of wisdom can the poet perceive the true power of innocence. "Let them call me crazy / that out of nothing is born our Paradise."

And is it not the power of innocence which declares during the Nazi occupation of Greece in 1943, "What I love is at its beginning always"? He says elsewhere (in the *Open Book*), "I do not speak about myself. I speak for anyone who feels like myself but does not have enough naiveté to confess it. If there is, I think, for each one of us a different, a personal Paradise, mine should irreparably be inhabited by trees of words that the wind dresses in silver, like poplars, by men who see the rights of which they have been deprived returning to them, and by birds that even in the midst of the truth of death insist on singing in Greek and on saying 'eros, eros, eros!'"

Elytis is, finally, a poet of enormous charity and hope. I went with my partner and our daughter to visit him in his apartment in Athens in 1983. I knew that he spoke very little English and that we would have to converse with the aid of an interpreter. He seated the three of us on a couch and poured us bourbon. Wanting to get business out of the way, I explained that a book published in North America would not bring him much in the way of royalties. I asked about his Greek publisher, having found everyone we met in Greece knew his poems well enough to recite passages or whole poems.

"My publisher," he said, "prints about 25,000 copies. And then, after a few weeks, when they're sold, they bring it out in paper."

I explained how Americans do not read poetry.

"That doesn't matter," he said with a wave of the hand. "A real poet needs an audience of three. And since any poet worth his salt has two intelligent friends, he spends his whole life searching for the third reader."

His personal fastidiousness and his personal charm are not in the least at odds with the charm and care of his poems. A Greek poet with a Nobel Prize in literature is a national figure. The flood of requests for his time never slows. And yet he retains his propensity for generosity, and his utter lack of pride.

"The poet must be generous," he wrote in the *Open Book*. "Not wishing to lose even a moment from your supposed talent is like not wishing to lose even a drachma from the interest of the small capital donated to you. But Poetry is not a bank. On the contrary, it is the conception which actually opposes the bank. If it becomes a written text communicable to others, so much the better. If not, it does not matter. That which must happen and happen uninterruptedly, endlessly, without the slightest irregularity, is anti-servility, irreconcilability, independence. Poetry is the other face of Pride."

The Shadow and the Light

When Joseph Brodsky was named recipient of the 1987 Nobel Prize in Literature, the North American press made much of the poet's initial encounter with a Soviet judge who asked, "By what right do you call yourself a poet?" It is a question no judge has a right to ask, to be sure, but a question any conscious reader poses in the course of investing attention in any book of poetry.

Brodsky recently resigned from the American Academy and Institute of Arts and Letters over a dispute involving Yevgeny Yevtushenko, whom the former views as a Soviet apologist. Brodsky left the Soviet Union in 1972 to settle in New York City, where, as a more-or-less "official" exile, he enjoys a good deal of celebrity. Both Brodsky and Yevtushenko have, at various times, been called "Russia's greatest living poet."

That Brodsky is taken seriously as a writer is beyond dispute. His selected essays, *Less Than One* (Farrar, Straus, Giroux, 1986), includes commentary on Cavafy, Akhmatova, and Tsvetaeva, and others; it is also full of statements which are simply goofy, preposterous assertions which would be ignored had they not issued from the mouth of a Nobel Laureate. Brodsky turns literary meditation into high polemics, wrestling with angels, feeling alternately hot and cold breath on his neck as he writes — if he is to be taken at his word. He takes his relationships with the Classics to be almost terminal, struggling to turn them toward his own ends. Where a poet like Octavio Paz finds nourishment, Brodsky encounters only an enormous obstacle which must be overcome in order to assert self at the expense of tradition, immediate self-gratification at the expense of the long view, mere personality at the expense of community.

At the beginning of an essay on Eugenio Montale, Brodsky says, "A significant part, therefore, of *every* [my emphasis] poet's endeavor involves polemics with these shadows [the Classics] whose hot or cold breath he

senses on his neck, or is led to sense by the industry of literary criticism."
In Brodsky's declared view, the Classics do not represent clarity and resonance, but murky shadows. "'Classics' exert such tremendous pressure
that at times verbal paralysis is the result. And since the mind is more able
to produce a negative view of the future than to handle such a prospect,
the tendency is to perceive the situation as terminal. In such cases natural
ignorance or even bogus innocence seems blessed, because it permits one
to dismiss all such specters as nonexistent and to 'sing' (in vers libre,
preferably) merely out of a sense of one's own physical stage presence.

"To consider any such situation terminal, however, usually reveals not
so much lack of courage as poverty of imagination. If a poet lives long
enough, he learns how to handle such dry spells (regardless of their origins),
using them for his own ends. The unbearableness of the future is easier to
face than that of the present if only because human foresight is much more
destructive than anything that the future can bring about. . . ."

Since only one of these essays is listed as a translation, Brodsky may—
indeed *should*—be held to account in a very strict way for his prose. His
language is invariably sexist: in every instance, unless referred to by name,
the poet is a "he." Nor is his cheap remark regarding *vers libre* further
explained. Presumably, his is simply an expression of post-Victorian contempt for the "organic" line in prosody. The baggage he carries is that of
the old literary establishment, that of the professional exile loaded with
esteemed awards for his every utterance, that of a political reactionary
who has made a "career in letters." Much of this is no more than the
fustian and bluster of a man who takes himself all too seriously, who
persists against all odds to insist upon his right to perceive the role of the
poet in society in Shelley's Romantic vision of the poet as unacknowledged
legislator.

"Classics exert such tremendous pressure that at times verbal paralysis
is the result." In Brodsky's view, the mind is "more *able* to produce a
negative view of the future" and therefore "natural ignorance or even
bogus innocence seems blessed." But every poet attempting every poem is
evidence to the contrary of Brodsky's assertions. Perhaps there are indeed
poets who "sing" out of a mere sense of stage presence. But since few poets
have a stage, it must be assumed that most poets compose out of a deep
need to *connect* not only to the Classics and the tradition, but with present
reality as well. Nothing could be more hopeful, and it is this very hope
and need which lies at the impulse of every poet.

Even in the essays themselves, Brodsky offers little that could be considered original. There are no major reassessments, and no major discoveries. On Cavafy, for example, he is far less insightful than was Marguerite Yourcenar some twenty years ago in her little-known masterpiece in *The Dark Brain of Piranesi* (translation, Farrar, Straus, Giroux, 1980), "A Critical Introduction to Cavafy." Reading Brodsky's essay, one wonders just how closely the Nobel Laureate read the best book-length study on the Greek Modernist, Edmund Keeley's brilliant book, *Cavafy's Alexandria* (Harvard University, 1976). In any case, Brodsky's assertions in this essay run from the preposterous to the outrageous. "Ninety percent of the best lyric poetry," Brodsky says, "is written post-coitum." This declaration will be news to the "classical" poets of China and Japan, it will be news to those who enjoy Catullus and Wordsworth, and to the poets of the Greek Anthology, including Sappho. It is not coitus which has produced the most and the best lyric poetry, but the longing *for* profound intimacy. In addition to the above, Brodsky might brush up on his Dante since the latter often puts in cameo appearances in Brodsky's verse. Or is Dante no longer considered lyrical? "The beloved is one with the lover," Machado says, "not at the end of the erotic process, *but at its beginning.*"

Brodsky's own poetry is another matter. A neoformalist by tradition as well as inclination, the English versions rarely rise above a sort of intellectual doggerel. In *A Part of Speech* (Farrar, Straus, Giroux, 1980), one finds "A Song to No Music," translated by the author and David Rigsbee:

Scholastics, you may utter. Yes,
scholastics, and a shameless hide-and-
seek game with grief. But look and guess:
a star above the horizon,

what is it but (permit this turn
so that you won't detect a surplus
of elevated style) a corn
rubbed by the light on space's surface?

Scholastics? Almost. Just as well.
God knows. Take any for a spastic
consent. For after all, pray tell,
what in this world is not scholastic?

Alternating eight- and nine-syllable lines, writing rhymed quatrains, Brodsky indeed produces verse; but as to whether he produces *poetry,* perhaps only those who read the Russian originals may capably know. His verse, insomuch as it appears in American English, does not compare favorably with Stanley Kunitz's passionate musicality nor with Richard Wilbur's refined intelligence.

It would appear that Brodsky is more concerned with syllabic count and rhyme-scheme than with quality of image or accuracy of metaphor. "A shameless hide-and-seek game with grief" is followed by "a star above the horizon" which is "a corn rubbed by the light on space's surface." A *corn?* What one gets from wearing tight shoes? Or is this star a *kernel* of corn rubbed by light? Perhaps an *ear* of corn? The meaning, the image, remains ill-defined, more bizarre than revealing, far more perplexing than illuminating. What, exactly, *is* a spastic consent? And when was the last time anyone actually said "Pray tell"? The interjection exists only to fill out the count and to rhyme; it was a cliché in the past century.

Kenneth Rexroth once observed, "Wallace Stevens writes exactly like an insurance executive." Joseph Brodsky writes like a Russian exile enjoying enormous celebrity in a profoundly anti-Soviet atmosphere. The results are often unintentionally funny, as in the opening poem from *A Part of Speech:*

> So long had life together been that now
> the second of January fell again
> on Tuesday, making her astonished brow
> lift like a windshield wiper in the rain,
>> so that her misty sadness cleared, and showed
>> a cloudless distance waiting up the road.

Is this a parody of the *New Yorker* poem of middle-class ennui? Even in the hands of a formalist of Richard Wilbur's formidable resources, this poem is a syntactical nightmare: "So long had life together been . . . " and the reader asks, "Been what?" The inversion is baffling. Eyebrows like "a windshield wiper in the rain" — *really.* Later on in the same poem, we are treated to "her lips, fluttering from my shoulder" and other utterly confounding images.

Formality of structure invites formality of diction. One of the things that makes bad verse bad is the same thing that makes parodies and satires humorous: clunking formal rhythm combined with ridiculous imagery and casual diction. Brodsky's attempts to combine colloquial diction, wit, and formal structure oftens produce unintentionally hilarious results.

At the end of "The Funeral of Bobo," Brodsky writes, "Now Thursday. I believe in emptiness. / There it's like hell, but shittier, I've heard. / And the new Dante, pregnant with his message, / bends to the empty page and writes a word." Chatty, self-consciously arty, for the most part he is a curious cause célèbre, a capitalist counterpart to Yevtushenko, a speaker from the "international" stage as it exists only in New York City. His iambics are no fresher than the slack vers libre he seems to scorn. His lines are often brittle, the rhymes leaden. In his first collection of poetry since winning the Nobel Prize, *To Urania* (Farrar, Straus, Giroux, 1988), he offers a poem—a love poem of sorts—

Cafe Trieste
  to L.G.

To this corner of Grant and Vallejo
I've returned like an echo
to the lips that preferred
then a kiss to a word.

. . . .

Cold, through the large steamed windows
I watch the gesturing weirdos,
the bloated breams that warm
up their aquarium.

Evolving backward, a river
becomes a tear, the real
becomes memory which
can, like fingertips, pinch

just the tail of a lizard
vanishing in the desert
which was eager to fix
a traveler with a sphinx.

Your golden mane! Your riddle!
The lilac skirt, the brittle
ankles! The perfect ear
rendering "read" as "dear."

Under what cloud's pallor
now throbs the tricolor

.   .   .   .

saints and the ain'ts take five,
where I was first to arrive.

The poem opens on an inversion: "To this corner I've returned." The image made in that stanza is striking, as are the images drawn in the following two stanzas. But the opening line of the fourth stanza brings the reader up short: "Evolving backward"? The opposite of *evolve* is *devolve*. When the "fingertips" in the fourth line of the stanza pinch "just the tail of the lizard" in the desert which is "eager to fix a traveler with a sphinx," the leap from cafe to desert is simply too great to be made without a gloriously willed suspension of disbelief.

When "the perfect ear" renders "read" as "dear," one cannot but wonder at the desperate struggle to achieve mere charm. Coming upon another tinny inversion, one reads, "Under what cloud's pallor / now throbs..." and the reader perhaps leaps toward an image the poet certainly never intended. Is there another poet writing American English who would dare to write of "linen waters" and "afterlife's sweet parlor" where the saints "take five"? Of course Brodsky is not writing English, is not thinking in English. But he is credited as co-translator along with several others.

Reviewing *To Urania* in the *New York Times Book Review,* John Bayley, "the Thomas Wharton Professor of English at the University of Oxford," compares Brodsky to "Auden, Browning and Catullus, set in a serene domestic landscape painted by Pierre Bonnard or Edouard Vuillard, for Mr. Brodsky has extraordinary synesthetic powers and often seems as much a painter as a poet.... Mr. Brodsky's frivolity, like Auden's, is itself infinite and benign.... Mr. Brodsky uses English rhymes with a recklessness no contemporary native poet would care to try."

An odd choice: an Oxford don to assess the work of an exiled Russian poet translated into American English. Setting aside Prof. Bayley's qualifications of the above statements, I shall address these statements directly, for they represent the depths to which critical judgment sinks when personality and an impressive list of awards overcomes common sense. While Brodsky would, at a glance, appear to follow Auden's lineage, the former has none of the delicacy of ear for vowel sounds so common in the latter; the former's "reckless" use of rhyme remains tinny, the result of overreaching, while Auden often balances end-rhymes with interior and slant rhyme, ever attentive to pitch and nuance. Brodsky exhibits neither Browning's narrative power nor his melopoeia. And Catullus? *Catullus?* What has Brodsky produced with a bite equal to the fury of Catullus in numbers XXXIX, XLI, or with the self-revealing passion of numbers LXXI or LXXV? He simply hasn't the *grit* of a Catullus. *Quid est, Catulle? quid moraris emori?* And exactly when did frivolity become benign, or an asset to a poet? And of all artists whose primary working matter is language, poets should be least reckless. Perhaps in an age when James Merrill can establish himself as a major American poet on the basis of a three-volume Ouija board epic, the reckless and the frivolous set standards by which all poetry shall henceforth be judged.

Literary fame in the United States has far more to do with mass media than with literary art. Perhaps the media recognizes Brodsky as a poet because routine iambics and predictable rhymes are themselves immediately recognizable as verse. His prosody, lacking the sophistication of an Ezra Pound, say, or a Rilke, is perfectly discernable on the page even to a relatively naive eye. There is an oddly Victorian quality about much of Brodsky's poetry. Despite its post-modern stance, despite a very contemporary decor, one sniffs the air for the faint musky odor of mothballs among velvet dresses and stiff gowns. One feels behind the poems the movement of an intelligent but otherwise rather conventional mind. Brodsky is poorly suited to the task of speaking from an international stage. As a spokesman for literature with a capital L, Joseph Brodsky is often at odds with common sense.

Writing thirty years ago in *The Bow and the Lyre* (University of Texas, 1973), certainly among the most eloquent books on the subject of poetry ever written, Octavio Paz said, "Modern poetry has become the food of the dissidents and exiles of the bourgeois world. . . . The poet's language is that of his community, whatever the latter may be. The poem feeds on the living language of a community, on its myths, its dreams and its passions, that is, its strongest and most secret tendencies. The poem establishes the people because the poet retraces the course of language and drinks from the original source."

While Brodsky, celebrated Soviet dissident, defines the poet's experience with the Classics as "polemics with these *shadows*," shadows defined in part by "the industry of literary criticism" (what an astonishing and ambiguous term!)—while Brodsky struggles against a situation he defines as nearly "terminal," Paz locates the poet within a living community of people; while Brodsky wrestles not with angels, but with shadows, and becomes enervated and sterile, Paz "drinks from the original source," and finds nourishment, sustenance. In a recent collection of essays, *Convergences* (Harcourt Brace Jovanovich, 1987), Paz seeks a "literature of convergence born long ago in the sacred legitimacy" of the translator whose task it was to bring from one culture into another a universal and eternal truth. While Brodsky remains hyper-aware of the "industry of literary criticism," Paz seeks the poets and their translators in order to partake of the "universal communion of poetry."

In the text of the poem, Paz locates holy ritual and passionate adventure leading to universal truth-in-experience. There is no hot or cold breath on Paz's neck as he writes. Rather than struggling *against* the immense impenetrable shadows of literary history, Paz enters a community of shared experience. Against Brodsky's recklessness and frivolity, Paz returns, in *The Bow and the Lyre,* to the origins of learning: "All learning begins as the teaching of the true names of things and ends with the revelation of the key word that will open the doors of wisdom for us. Or with the confession of ignorance: silence. And even silence says something, for it is pregnant with signs. We cannot escape from language.... The nets for catching words are made of words.... The poet's language is that of his community, whatever the latter may be."

Paz has written some of the greatest poetry of our time. "Nocturno de San Ildefonso" and "Pasado en claro" are large, complex lyrical meditations, the poet's sweeping intelligence buoyed by a discipline well-suited to fitting a wonderful homage to Bashō into six haiku or expanding a world created in a window as night "invents another night." His "Nocturno" opens on a surreal nightmare scene suggesting almost post-holocaust conditions:

Empty streets, squinting lights.
                    On a corner,
the ghost of a dog
                    searches the garbage
for a spectral bone.
                    Uproar in a nearby patio:
cacophonous cockpit.
                    Mexico, circa 1931.
Loitering sparrows,
                    a flock of children
builds a nest
          of unsold newspapers.
In the desolation
               the streetlights invent
unreal pools of yellowish light.
                         Apparitions:
time splits open:
                a lugubrious, lascivious clatter of heels,
beneath *a sky of soot*
                 the flash of a skirt.
C'est la mort—ou la morte

.   .   .   .

                    The indifferent wind
rips posters from the walls.
At this hour,
          the red walls of San Ildefonso
are black, and they breathe:

Paz is describing the National Preparatory School at the old college of San Ildefonso, built by Jesuits in the mid-seventeenth century in Mexico City. The "sky of soot" alludes to Ramon Lopez Velarde's "Dia 13," and the "*C'est la mort*" comes from Gerard de Nerval's "Artemis" poem. In the third section of the poem, Paz says,

The boy who walks through this poem,
between San Ildefonso and the Zocalo,
is the man who writes it:
                    this page too

is a ramble through the night.
                          Here the friendly ghosts
become flesh, ideas dissolve.

Good, we wanted good:
to set the world right.
We didn't lack integrity:
                          we lacked humility.
What we wanted was not innocently wanted.
Precepts and concepts,
                          the arrogance of theologians,
to beat with a cross,
                          to institute with blood,
to build the house with bricks of crime,
to declare obligatory communion.

                          Some
became secretaries to the secretary
to the General Secretary of the Inferno.
                                    Rage
became philosophy,
                          its drivel covered the planet.

"We didn't lack integrity," the poet says, "we lacked humility." And out
of this "history of an error," the poet chose "the act of words: / to make
them, to inhabit them, / to give eyes to the language."

                     Poetry is not truth:
   it is the resurrection of presences,
                                    history
transfigured in the truth of undated time.
Poetry,
        like history, is made:
                               poetry,
      like truth, is seen.
                     Poetry:
                          incarnation
of the-sun-on-the-stones in a name,
                                    dissolution
of the name in a beyond of stones.

Poetry,
>> suspension bridge between history and truth,
is not a path toward this or that:
the stillness in motion,
>>> change
in stillness.
>> History is the path:
it goes nowhere,
>>> we all walk it,
truth is to walk it.
>>> We neither go nor come:
we are in the hands of time.
>>> Truth:
to know ourselves,
>> from the beginning,
>>> hung.
Brotherhood over the void.

Paz's humility is expressed in the "we" of the poem, in his gentle insistence upon "brotherhood" and "communion" and passionate philosophy until we become bound up in the poem itself, a part of the experience, a part of being, of almost transcending the void. At the end, the poet turns in the night to his sleeping wife: "She too is a moon," he says, "a clarity that travels / not between the reefs and clouds, but between the rocks and wracks of dreams: / she too is a soul." He locates truth in the swell of a breath, "the palpable mystery of the person," and listening, he is "bound to her quiet flowing."

"Nocturno de San Ildefonso" opens on a surreal nightmare, but by its closure, a calm catharsis has taken place. There is "quiet" and "flowing" between the poet and his wife, between the observing reader and the silent moon. It is a powerful, wise, and beautiful work.

If Brodsky's verse is marked by strict inflexible meter and rhyme, Paz is recognizable in part by his openness of form, by a line that draws from the Modernist Poundian lineage rather than the Victorian. If Brodsky is a bourgeois poet, Paz is a proletarian intellectual. In "As One Listens to the Rain," Paz says,

Listen to me as one listens to the rain,
not attentive, not distracted,
light footsteps, thin drizzle,
water that is air, air that is time,
the day is still leaving,
the night has yet to arrive,
figurations of mist
at the turn of the corner,
figurations of time
at the bend in this pause,
listen to me as one listens to the rain,
without listening, hear what I say
with eyes open inward, asleep
with all five senses awake,
it's raining, light footsteps, a murmur of syllables,
air and water, words with no weight:

and his lines fall weightlessly like rain gathering into rivulets of sound and meaning, the experience of the poem rooted in musicality, every image appropriate, precise ambiguities reinforcing each careful gesture, the feeling of the poem identified by its sound and rhythm. Paz eschews the intellectual exercise in favor of the search for felt wisdom, and the structure of each poem is far more than mere scaffolding—it is the *beingness* of the poem *in* sound, it is poetry from the oral tradition.

Octavio Paz is one of the few absolutely essential poets of our time, a passionate, fearlessly unflinching witness and commentator on poetry and culture. His essays and poems form a great body of work which should be lived with, should be studied, like that of a Rexroth, a Pound, or a Williams. If more of our younger poets went to school on Paz rather than on their Creative Writing instructors, they'd be not only better poets, but better and wiser people. Paz has built a mountain. It's beautiful there, even at a glance from a long way off, but you won't know what it means until you inhabit the terrain.

The Collected Poems (New Directions, 1989) is doubly valuable because it is bilingual and because Eliot Weinberger's translations are both accurate and beautiful. More than half the poems appear in English for the first time, and Weinberger has brought over not only a durable equivalent for Paz's richly complex ear, but his grand sense of time as well. It is a profound accomplishment.

The amply awarded Paz may never receive a Nobel Prize. Prizes reflect surfaces while the true poet, ever the exile, carries a little light into vast depths. The ever-industrious Paz would appear to be far less interested in "industry" as "business" than in the appropriate technology of human and humane vision. He would be eyes for the rain. He ranges through cultures, languages, and civilizations only to hear himself murmur, "Theory is gray, green the tree of life." Lorca sang, "*Verde que te quiero verde. / Verde viento. Verdes ramas.*" And his eyes were open wide to the dream.

More than two millenia have passed since Aristotle wrote, "Although writing and the spoken word are not the same for everyone, the states of the soul and the things that these signs designate are the same." Paz is a great poet not merely because he often writes an "organic" line any more than Brodsky is called great as a result of composing by strict meter. In a culture which supports no living poets *as* poets, asked by what right I call myself a poet, I might reply, "By rites of communion perfectly articulated by Octavio Paz."

On the Making of
Ezra Pound's *Cathay*

More than seven decades have passed since the notebooks of Ernest Fenollosa were brought to Ezra Pound by Fenollosa's widow, Mary. Included in the notebooks were versions of Noh dramas, an almost completed essay on "The Chinese Written Character as a Medium for Poetry," and notes for some one-hundred-fifty poems, a scant fourteen of which would make the bulk of *Cathay*. During the ensuing seventy years, these "translations" have been the subject of scurrilous attacks by pedants and sinologists, praised by poets as diverse as T.S. Eliot, Kenneth Rexroth, and Yvor Winters, and grist for an ever-growing mill of thesis-writing. With the 1915 edition of *Cathay* long out of print, today's reader comes to the poems only in the context of Pound's *Personae,* his collected poems, and often at the expense of historical perspective. It is not my intention to speculate on Pound's *forma mentis* (that I leave to the wizardry of Hugh Kenner, who is suited to the task), nor to explicate his errors (nor those of Fenollosa), but to place the work in its proper historical milieu, so that the uninitiated reader may better understand the origins of a most influential, albeit tiny, volume of poetry in English.

Ernest Fenollosa was born in Salem, Massachusetts, in 1853. Drawn early to the study of philosophy, he was graduated from Harvard and continued in post-graduate studies there in philosophy and theology before turning to the study of art at the Boston Museum of Fine Arts. During this time, he was offered a position teaching philosophy at Tokyo University through his friend Edward Morse. Fenollosa married and sailed with his bride in 1878.

Fenollosa arrived in a "new Japan" that was undertaking a national program in "modernization" that was not drastically different from that which China has undergone since the Revolution. With the patronage of the shogunates lost, Noh drama had disappeared; painters who worked in the classical tradition were starving; the Buddhist temples were forced to sell off their centuries-old treasures as souvenirs. True "modernization" was, indeed, under way.

Fenollosa began collecting traditional Japanese art. And through collecting and studying, he, almost single-handedly, resurrected interest in Japanese art. He became so influential that the Japanese government named him Imperial Commissioner of Fine Arts for the Imperial Museum as well as for the Tokyo Fine Arts Academy. He lectured widely to enthusiastic audiences. The poet Yone Noguchi declared, "Ernest Fenollosa is the discoverer of Japanese art for Japan."

He returned to the United States in 1890, prepared to teach "the significance of Japanese art to the West," as he had been asked to do by the emperor. He presented lectures on the history of Japanese art and served on the arts jury for the 1893 Chicago World's Fair; and he established one of the world's great Japanese art collections at the Boston Museum.

In September, 1896, he returned to Japan. It was during this second visit that he began to study Chinese philosophy under the direction of Michiaki Nemoto, a renowned *I Ching* scholar, and Chinese poetry under the tutelage of Kainan Mori, also a well-known scholar, and his former student, Nagao Ariga. There were also sessions with a Mr. Shida and a Mr. Hirai.

Fenollosa was almost vehemently anti-Confucian. He viewed the neo-Confucian government of China as a "government of corrupt Puritans," and credited the shogunates and their samurai with saving Japanese art from "the mad storm of Confucianism." Only the Zen art of the Ashikaga period, he claimed, achieved the high sophistication of the Sung dynasty.

Besides his *Certain Noble Plays of Japan,* only his *Epochs of Chinese and Japanese Art* remains purely his own. The former was edited by Pound, the latter edited by Mary Fenollosa. His notes on the Chinese poems would remain locked away for five years following his death. In truth, his study of Noh drama was far more intense (and far more accurate) than his studies in Chinese poetry—and that is hardly surprising, as he spent more than twenty years studying the Noh. And thirty studying Oriental art.

At the time of his death in 1908, Fenollosa was in London to research his theory of the Pacific School of Art, a theory which held that the Orient and the Pacific West were of a single origin in pre-history. He supported his thesis with examples drawn from Eskimo and Athabaskan drawings and ivory carvings. He was one of the first to lend credence to the "Pacific land-bridge" theory.

Pound's interest in Oriental literature may be dated from a lecture March 15, 1909 by Laurence Binyon, who discussed Oriental and European Art, a lecture Pound said was "intensely interesting." Later that same year, Pound was introduced to T. E. Hulme and F. S. Flint who had joined to promote a group of writers interested in a program to modernize poetry by emphasizing "free verse, visual images, and Japanese haiku." A year and a half later, Pound composed a poem reflecting on his arrival by train at La Concord in Paris. He had been deeply touched by the faces emerging from the sudden darkness of the station. Pound would later say of the experience, "There came an equation, not in speech, but in little splotches of color . . . [and] I realized that if I were a painter . . . I might found a new school of non-representative painting that would speak only by arrangements in color."

The original poem of thirty lines was later destroyed, it being "of secondary intensity." Six or eight months later, he composed another draft, but one of "half that length." But this one also lacked "that proper emotion." Thinking on his poem, Pound remembered the haiku he'd been introduced to, and tried to find "some theory of haiku" that might intensify the emotions. And he suddenly realized that two images, when "superimposed," both "clarified and amplified one another" with a resultant feeling of having closely seen a single emerging image. Remembering years later, he wrote in *Gaudier-Brzeska*, "I found it useful in getting out of the impasse in which I had been left by my metro emotion." And finally, through his meditations on the theory of haiku, he found his "splotches of color" by producing a poem consisting of title and two lines, the only colors being transparent white and black:

In a Station of the Metro

The apparition of those faces in the crowd;
Petals on a wet, black bough.

By then, it was 1912, and Pound came into contact with the Bengali poet/translator Rabindranath Tagore, and persuaded Harriet Monroe to publish six of his poems in *Poetry* along with his (Pound's) introductory essay in which he states: "There is a deeper calm and a deeper conviction in this eastern expression than we have yet attained. It is by the arts alone that one people learns to meet another far distant people in friendship and respect."

Pound then set out, with the assistance of a student of Tagore's, to translate some poems of the fifteenth-century Hindi poet, Kabir. And in 1913, Tagore became the first Asian poet to receive the Nobel Prize in Literature. Pound also reworked several poems from H. A. Giles's early English versions ("After Ch'u Yuan," "Fan-piece for Her Imperial Majesty," "Liu Ch'e," and "Ta'si Chi'h") and published them in *Lustra*.

Exactly how the notebooks came into Pound's hands may never be known. Dr. Kenner tells us Mary Fenollosa chose Pound after reading his "In a Station of the Metro" and other poems from *Lustra* in the April, 1913 issue of *Poetry* (Chicago), a theory Pound encouraged, stating that he was "the interpreter her husband would have wished." The rather bohemian Mary Fenollosa would state only that Pound had "pursued" her at a literary gathering in London.

At any rate, Pound and Mary Fenollosa met at the home of the Indian poet and social critic Sarojini Niadu, a friend of Tagore's, in the autumn of 1913. Pound's first mention of the notebooks is in a letter to William Carlos Williams dated 19 December 1913, in which he says only, "I've all old Fenollosa's treasured manuscripts." He also states, "Dorothy [Shakespeare Pound, his wife] is studying Chinese." On 30 April of the following year, he writes to Amy Lowell (who had yet to begin her collaborative translations of Chinese poetry with Florence Ayscough), "I am on my head with Fenollosa notes." And while Pound would spend the next sixty years theorizing and explicating Chinese poetry, history, and philosophy according to his own peculiar brand of neo-Confucianism, about the notebooks and the making of the poems collected in *Cathay,* he was remarkably reticent. The Noel Stock biography barely mentions this episode, perhaps the single most important event in the poet's development.

It is particularly ironic to note Fenollosa's antipathy toward the Confucianists in the light of his widow's having presented his notebooks to the twentieth century's most prominent advocate of Confucianism. Over and over again, one hears the voice of Pound declaring, "As to what I believe, I believe the *Ta Hsueh*" (the *Great Learning*), one of the Confucian Classics. Fenollosa believed the Taoists were responsible for the success of Chinese art in general, and for their greatest contribution—the art produced during the Sung dynasty. Pound, on the other hand, came to hold the Taoists in almost complete contempt, referring to them as "Taosers" and scoffing at their achievements.

Prior to Pound's reshaping of the poems from Fenollosa's notebooks, virtually all the translations from Japanese and Chinese poetry and philosophy had been made by missionaries who understood little or none of the language or who made deliberate decisions to leave out any image or reference to which the true believer might take offense (H. A. Giles's *Gems of Chinese Literature* [1884] and Judith Gautier's *Le Livre de Jade* [1867] are exceptions). This accounts for the erroneous assumption early in this century that the Chinese wrote no erotic poetry and no poetry of invective. In fact, Chinese poetry (and art) is a balancing between the world of social responsibility (Confucianism) and the world of the inner enlightenment (Taoism and Buddhism), and because of Confucian manners, the poets spoke frequently in subtleties, in double entendres, metaphors and conceits. As convention would have it, the classical Chinese poet buries his criticism of the emperor in a euphemism, and, writing an erotic love poem to a "singing girl" (that term is, as well, a euphemism), speaks to an "oriole." The earlier translators either did not know or did not want to know the particulars.

In the early twentieth century, only Pound and Arthur Waley (in his versions published in 1916 and 1919) achieve anything approaching acceptable translation. And although even Waley attacked Pound in a number of lectures, the few poems translated by both show Waley's debt to *il miglior fabbro*.

Pound's "errors" and inventions and "mis-translations" have been so widely documented that even those who know nothing of either the Chinese written character or the Chinese sensibility think nothing of listing them in articles and dissertations. The most accurate, intelligent, and even-handed treatment of *Cathay* is Wai-lim Yip's 1969 volume, *Ezra Pound's Cathay* (Princeton University). There is also an excellent study by the noted Japanese Pound scholar, Sanehide Kodama (*American Poetry and Japanese Culture*, Archon Books, 1984).

What Pound accomplished is phenomenal. He began with the same false assumption as Fenollosa—that is, that Chinese is made up of "ideograms," or little pictures. True, the roots of Chinese writing are pictographic. But does not our *A* come from the Greek *Alpha* which came from the Phoenician drawing of the bull's head? Our *B* from the Greek *Beta*, which is a Phoenician pictograph for the *Beth*, or house; our *D* from the Greek *Delta* from the Phoenician *Daleth*, or door? Are English, Latin, and

Greek "ideogrammic" in nature? Yes, there are "little pictures" in many Chinese characters. There are also many vocables.

But even with his false assumption and his penchant for positively haywire theories regarding etymologies of certain characters, Pound was able, through Fenollosa's notes, to feel his way along and to find the real essence of the poem, even when, in "The River Song," he makes two poems by Li Po into one.

Nor were the notebooks themselves entirely accurate. Fenollosa had speaking ability in Japanese, but he could neither read nor write in Japanese or Chinese. Profs. Mori and Ariga refer to Li T'ai-po by his Japanese name, Rihaku. Hence Pound, working from the notes, slips back and forth from the Chinese names for persons and places to the Japanese, and sometimes, as in "The River Song," has birds singing in transliteration from *both* languages: "the fine birds sing to each other, and listen, / Crying—'Kwan, Kuan' . . ."—the same character repeated in the original, but in translation takes it both ways from the notes: *kwan* transliterated from the Japanese, *kuan* from the Chinese, according to the Wade-Giles system, which was Pound's *modus operandi* as well as that of Fenollosa, Mori, and Ariga. He properly retains the sound of the original, recognizing it as an onomotopoetic language of the birds signalling the arrival of spring.

Pound's feel for the poem is not so surprising when one remembers that he knew poetry in Greek, Latin, French, Spanish, Italian, and Provençal. He also had some German (in which much of the best early work in Chinese literary scholarship was done).

There is a film, made late in Pound's life, in which the old poet begins "explaining" written Chinese. And to illustrate his point, he grasps a calligraphy brush, taking it up in his hand in much the fashion of an Idaho farm boy clutching a pitchfork.

Some of Pound's "mis-translations" are certifiably deliberate, as when, in "Separation on the River Kiang," he leaves the Japanese *Ko-jin* (in the original Chinese *Ku-jen*) as though it was a proper name, but elsewhere properly translates it as "old acquaintances," and as "friend." And *kiang*, incidentally, means "river." The river in the original is the Yangtze. The "Ko-kaku-ro" of the first line is, apparently, a misreading: the place referred to is the Yellow Crane Tower. Also in the first line, the traveler goes *from* the west. This mistake is from the notebooks.

Those who want translation to be literal do not want to read poetry in translation. There is a distinct difference. Pound was the first to place emphasis properly upon the image; he was the first American to use *vers libre* to make the line the unit of composition (a lesson still to be learned by free-versifiers in the U.S. some seventy years later); and he was the first to listen to the sounds of names and to permit those names and sounds to identify and resonate. T.S. Eliot did not overstate the case when he declared, "Ezra Pound has invented Chinese poetry for our time!" As Fenollosa himself once wrote, "The purpose of poetical translation is the poetry, not the verbal definitions in dictionaries."

What Pound accomplished grew out of this ability to read the poem. The footnote to Li T'ai-po's "The Jewel Stairs' Grievance" is a better essay on reading Chinese poetry than almost anything that existed before it:

> The jewelled steps are already quite white with dew,
> It is so late that the dew soaks my gauze stockings,
> And I let down the crystal curtain
> And watch the moon through the clear autumn.

[Note: Jewel stairs, therefore a palace. Grievance, therefore there is something to complain of. Gauze stockings, therefore a court lady, not a servant who complains. Clear autumn, therefore he has no excuse on account of weather. Also she has come early, for the dew has not merely whitened the stairs, but has soaked her stockings. The poem is especially prized because she utters no direct reproach.]

Pound's "gauze stockings" are, in the original, "silk slippers," but he got the point of it right anyhow. The tone and the spirit of the poem are presented beautifully.

Cathay was, as Dr. Kenner points out, a "war book" issued at the outset of World War I. The privations of the old Chinese poets were not inconsistent with the privations suffered by English and American troops invading the continent. Pound had written Thomas Bird Mosher in December, 1914, regarding the manuscript in which he intended to include his own version of the Tiresias episode from the *Odyssey*, several canzoni of Arnaut Daniel, his "Seafarer," and a mere eight poems from the one hundred fifty available in the notebooks. Under such an arrangement, only "Bowmen of Shu" could be considered a war poem. Only in 1915, preparing the manuscript for what would be known as the "khaki-bound" *Cathay* (Elkin Mathews), did he include "South-Folk" and "Lament of the Frontier Guard," the two strongest war poems. But Pound considered

"The River-Merchant's Wife" the supreme accomplishment of *Cathay*, indeed, as he told Mosher, "one of the finest things in all literature."

But why is "The Seafarer" translated from the Anglo-Saxon and placed among Li Po's poems? "Because," Pound says, "the poems are contemporary." Like his Chinese contemporary, the Seafarer himself lived during the eighth century, lived in harsh times and often endured hardship, and learned the truth of "all arrogance of earthen riches."

These songs have survived a thousand years. May they, and Ezra Pound's echoes of them, resonate a thousand years again.

Only One Sky

Outside my office window, three young deer graze peacefully on a meal of newly fallen apples. The first light October frost is just turning the apples red—without frost, apples remain green—and the deer seem to prefer them that way. The buck, a small two-pointer, looks up now and then to keep an eye on the half-dozen human spectators eating their own lunches on a small patch of lawn some sixty yards away. Two kinds of animals, each eating lunch and enjoying same, each interested in the other.

The folks eating on the lawn are from Los Angeles. They are here with Robert Altman's crew to film a remake of Stanley Kramer's classic *The Caine Mutiny,* in what I've known for fifteen years as a musty old gymnasium at Fort Worden on Washington State's Olympic Peninsula. When I asked a member of the crew how anyone could hope to improve on such a classic, he said, "When you translate a novel into film, you've got an almost endless number of options. He won't 'remake' the old classic. He'll address other options."

The lunch-hour picnickers are from the crew. I know they are from L. A. because no one around here pays much attention to deer. But even from here, I can hear our visitors calling to the deer. They talk baby-talk at them: "Here, baby! C'mon, honey!"

Watching this little scenario unfold, I remember a review many years ago in the *New York Times.* The reviewer declared, "Gary Snyder's poems are full of trees!" Poems full of deer or trees or wildlife must sometimes seem odd things indeed in Manhattan or Hollywood. Those for whom relationships with animals has meant only the domesticated varieties or those which are caged cannot understand the subtleties, the implications, the "meaning," in writers like Barry Lopez, Gary Snyder, or Robinson Jeffers. Just as I, in turn, am often baffled by the critical attention given to a James Merrill or a John Ashbery. There is a whole vocabulary of city life known to me only through literature and jazz.

In a country as wide and as various in its possibilities of experience as the United States, there is often—even within the language most of us put to daily use—American English—there is often the need to translate. And for a poet, every poem is a translation into the original: every poem, like every poem in translation, is provisional. And every conclusion is at best marginal as well as excruciatingly temporal. Octavio Paz tell us this: "The history of the different civilizations is the history of their translations."

One cannot help but wonder just how different all our lives might be today had we not, deliberately and with calculated effect, obliterated two hundred languages in the last century—two hundred different ways of knowing that are now lost to North America and the world forever.

The deer continue munching fallen apples, keeping a wary eye on the tourists. Human baby-talk is just so much animal noise to them. And I remember that composing hymns to Krishna, East Indian cultures worked with an octave which was itself built entirely on the sounds of birds and animals, the first note being that of the peacock, the fifth note that of the cuckoo, etc. It follows therefore that in studying, say, the fourteenth-century Bengali poet Vidyápati—who wrote in a regional language, Maithili—one would want to be aware of the tonalities and repetition of certain sounds because, after all, the peacock's cry carries an entirely different emotional consequence than that of the cuckoo. But one also realizes that by the fourteenth century, much of the original octave has faded from consciousness; the music and the language have continued to evolve, just as classical Greek and Latin have informed, have improved, the linguistic gene pool, but are themselves "dead" languages.

Octavio Paz notes, "With a certain regularity, languages suffer from epidemics that for years infect their vocabulary, prosody, syntax, and even their logic." Roland Barthes, Antonio Alatorre, Julien Gracq, Kenneth Rexroth—so many critics have warned us away from those who in the service of structuralism would deny the erotic passion of the text. Paz says that passion "rapidly dispels the pretentious notion that we can construct a 'science of literature,' for the foundations of this would be the quicksands of desire."

Romanticism wreaked havoc in nineteenth-century English verse. Once Byron, Keats, and Shelley had been appointed a triumvirate by the "scholars" who explained them, once their "means" could be reduced to demonstrable theory, their sincere admirers produced what Pound called "emotional slither." Paz calls for a practice of verbal hygiene.

American English is one of the most beautiful and flexible languages in the world. It is capable of both extreme hardness and sweet communion, often—in the hands of a poet—simultaneously. But before the poet can practice verbal hygiene, he or she must establish a practice of emotional hygiene. By clarifying the emotions, one clarifies one's language. Poetry, the preface to the *Kokinshu* says, begins in the heart. Every poem has a *kokoro*, or heart.

And yet so very much recent North American poetry has been the articulation of cultured melancholy, of the elegant ennui and unnameable sadness of the middle class. Most often, we blame the Writing Program or television or the insane policies of corporate publishing. But even that is cowardice. Kay Boyle says this: "Why, after all, should this inability to speak with the heart as well as with the lips be blamed on 'restrictive teaching'? Is it not more of a case of restrictive thinking (induced by restrictive living) causing the muteness, which perhaps no teacher can cure? ... One cannot be sure the students will dare to understand the words another has said. It takes courage to say things differently: Caution and cowardice dictate the use of the cliché."

Ben Belitt, who has taken his lumps as a translator of Neruda, makes a beautifully apropos metaphor when he tells Edwin Honig (in *The Poet's Other Voice*, University of Massachusetts, 1985), "I take my lumps as a translator, hoping as I go that nothing has really been violated and that the proportions of the original have been maintained even though my own dynamics have merged with the poet's. I wear my conscience where it belongs: at the tip of my pen, and not on my sleeve like a medieval garter." Our poetry has been grandly ennobled by translated poetries from throughout the world. It has also suffered a plague of "politically correct" poets wearing their public consciences like medieval garters, poets who devour social platitudes like so many apples in the Garden. The zendos are full of well-intentioned people wearing metaphysical garters and reciting words they do not dare to understand, all in the name of seeking enlightenment.

It is stupid and unthinking to repeat Frost's stupid, unthinking remark, "Poetry is what gets lost in translation." In plain fact, who among us has not been introduced to the world's great literature through translation?

As a child, I was given a "children's" Homer, the *Aeneid,* and *Arabian Nights.* More than mere introductions to great literature, these books brought me something of the character of their original authors. Nearly forty years after that children's Homer, I hear Matthew Arnold say about

translating Homer, "The translator of Homer should above all be penetrated by a sense of four qualities of his author:—that he is eminently
rapid; that he is eminently plain and direct both in the evolution of his
thought and in the expression of it . . . ; and, finally, that he is eminently
noble." Rapid, plain, direct, noble: yes, these are the properties of a readable Homer in English, as any reader of Robert Fitzgerald's Homer will
testify. The great challenge is that of capturing the spirit of the thing, the
soul of the text, rather than wrestling only with its "form and meaning."
In the original, what we find is a form *of* meaning.

What one gets in poetry in translation is what Pound called "gists and
piths," and, on occasion, poetry. An excellent case could be made for
naming Pound's own versions of Li T'ai-po (*Cathay*) the most influential
book of this century in English verse despite the fact that his "errors" have
been widely and repeatedly documented. While most of us parrot the
charges against Pound, few of us ever take time to look closely at his milieu
or pay any attention whatever to what passed as translation both before
and after *Cathay*. Here is the E. Powys Mathers translation of Li T'ai-po's
most famous poem (from *Lotus and Chrysanthemum*, Liveright, 1927):

The Jade Staircase

The jade staircase is bright with dew.

Slowly, this long night, the queen climbs,
Letting her gauze stockings and elaborate robe
Drag in the shining water.

Dazed with the light,
She lowers the crystal blind
Before the door of the pavilion.

It leaps down like a waterfall in sunlight.

While the tiny clashing dies down,
Sad and long dreaming,
She watches between the fragments of jade light
The shining of the Autumn moon.

The first line and the last line are tolerably accurate. Everything between
seems to have come from the Chinese cliché shop, little pseudo-poetic

trinkets and literary bric-a-brac and emotional slither. Mr. Mathers, along with L. Cranmer-Byng whose work infects the same anthology, has the distinction of publishing the worst translations ever to see print.

Most of what falls short in translation may be laid at the feet of theory. It's easy to settle for the ambiguous line or for mere irony. One should remember that in its original Greek, "irony" meant only "dissimulation," a trait Plato characterized as "a glib, under-handed way of taking people in." Socratic irony comes from pretended ignorance. In the Latin, *ironia* denoted a discourse in which meaning was contrary to words stated. Ambiguity can be, like the use of cliché, a cowardly and/or lazy solution to the problems of seeking the soul of the text. Plurisignation is never easily achieved. Our sense of ambiguity comes largely from William Empson's notion that words *connote* at least as much as they *denote*. One workable solution is to combine the poet's feel for that living soul with a scholar's working knowledge of the text.

W. S. Merwin and Sōiku Shigematsu have combined to produce one of the most beautiful books in recent years, *Sun at Midnight, Poems of Musō Soseki* (North Point, 1989). One of these Zen poems ought to be memorized by every translator:

No Gain

Virtue and compassion
    together make up
        each one's integrity
Nothing that comes through the gate
    from outside
        can be the family treasure
Throwing away
    the whole pile
        in your heart
with empty hands
    you come
        bringing salvation

Translation is an act of love, it is a making *of* love, and is its own greatest reward. The self is subsumed, and the poet rises into a state of service in order to honor the original. Musō's poem in English turns the reader's attention inward, toward "reality." Pound may have known zip about classical Chinese syntax, but he got the gist of the stuff all right.

Poetry in translation is most often a first step; it is not a substitute for anything. Its necessity is largely informed by the strictures of time. Kenneth Rexroth told me once, "The greatest tragedy of your age is that it is no longer possible to know the entire poetry of the world in the original." It wasn't possible in his age, either, but it is certainly a tragedy.

The translated poem begins an expanding process that sometimes leads into new languages, new cultures, whole new systems of awareness. Chuang Tzu tells us words exist only to give us a grasp on meaning; once meaning has been grasped, he says, we may get rid of words.

Jonathan Chaves gives us this poem by Yang Wan-li, who wrote some fourteen centuries after Chuang:

> Now, what is poetry?
> If you say it is simply a matter of words,
> I will say a good poet gets rid of words.
> If you say it is simply a matter of meaning,
> I will say a good poet gets rid of meaning.
> "But," you ask, "without words and without meaning,
>   where is the poetry?
> To this I reply: "Get rid of words and get rid of meaning,
>   and there is still poetry."

A translator only begins with the words and their meanings. Beyond that, or through that, the poetry reveals itself. Writing in the third century, Lu Chi says, "The art of letters has saved governments from certain ruin and propagates proper morals. / Through letters there is no road too distant to travel, no idea too confusing to be ordered. / It comes like rain from clouds; it renews the vital spirit." Lu's first line is lifted directly from the conversations of Kung-fu Tze. Each of the following two lines follows the structure of the first, amplifying its meaning by means of repeated patterns of sound as well as by explication and example. It is useful to footnote the last line quoted: "cloud/rain" became a euphemism for sexual congress, the character written differently, but from the same etymological origin.

Beyond the words, understood at some level only as meaning-in-sound, the spirit or heart, the *kokoro,* of the poem continues to establish the rhythm of its experience — "meaning" also "means" the experience of tone and pitch and rhythm. The translator must also "translate" the music in order to have a poem at all. Otherwise, anyone with a dictionary could perform the task.

In Sōiku Shigematsu's brilliant translation of the classic *Zenrin Kushu, A Zen Forest* (Weatherhill, 1981), we can learn these perfect little Zen poems in English:

190

When cold
    say cold;
When hot
    say hot.

200

Sand in the eyes,
    clay in the ears.

462

Three hundred poems
    come to one thing:
"Think no evil!"

653

Blue made
    out of indigo
        is bluer than indigo;
Ice
    from water,
        colder than water.

We see imitations of this sort of thing all the time. It's a literary equivalent of instant Zen, the way a convict, to impress the parole board, will get "born again." But in order to "grasp the meaning" of each tiny poem, one must hold that poem inside oneself, as with kōan study when one learns to sit zazen. With so few syllables, each counts heavily, each should be sounded fully, just as each caesura, each silence of the poem, demands its due measure.

During an evening of parlor poetry games one evening, we were writing invective, much of it imitation Catullus. Someone would pick a title, and each of us would be given five minutes to write a rhymed quatrain or whatever under that title. One title (now altered slightly to protect the identity of the one for whom the poem was written, but retaining the rhyme) prompted the following four-syllable couplet:

To One Who Behaves Despicably

Fuck you.
Bless me.

Some will say it is neither a good poem nor a translation. The parlor game I learned from studying classical Chinese—the game itself is a translation. The invective is stolen (read: translated) from the Latin of Catullus who invented the word *defututa,* meaning fucked-out. But it is not entirely incompatible with the apparently superficial self-indulgences one finds in Chinese and Japanese love poems and drinking songs such as J. P. Seaton's *The Wine of Endless Life* (White Pine, 1985), translated from the Chinese of the Yuan Dynasty. The Chinese poet composes verses celebrating drinking, even drunkenness, but no respectable poet would ever appear drunk at a social function, including the famous wine-and-poetry gatherings. Most of these songs were intended to be slightly shocking.

I like the poem because it shows, on the one hand, good-humored invective. The four notes of the text clang large, then small; large, then small. It's here and gone in four quick gongs of a bell. It reminds me of Ikkyū, who was head master at Daitoku-ji, a huge Zen temple in Kyoto, for nine days. Upon leaving, he composed a poem expressing his disgust with the shallowness of life at the temple and saying that he could be found thereafter in the sake shops and the prostitution quarters. Thumbing one's nose, like raising one's middle finger, is sometimes an appropriate gesture even in a poem. One of the major maladies afflicting contemporary verse is the almost complete absence of humorous invective.

The poem above is coupled with another:

Said the Wise One to the Fool

Fuck me.
Bless you.

As a two-sided poem, it cuts both ways: the initial couplet is high invective; the second is a self-deprecating admonition that is a consequence of indulging in the first. Poetic humor is most often a double-edged sword. When Master Kung tells us, "Governments come and governments go; only the family is forever," his remark is tragic, comic, and pedagogical. Our poetry, so richly informed by various translators' excursions into and importations of other cultures, has begun to sound like it is written in "translatorese" that is the result of academic minds studying the syntax (the structure) of the original without knowing what poetry is or may be in our native culture.

It is commonplace to find poetry translated from the classical Chinese in a kind of word-for-word way which is true to the syntax and the meaning-in-words, but which fails, either partly or completely, to make tolerable poetry in American English. Greg Whincup recently published a selection of fifty-seven Chinese poems, *The Heart of Chinese Poetry* (Doubleday, 1987), which includes a poem by Tu Fu which is almost as well known as Li T'ai-po's "Jewel Stairs' Grievance," a poem usually titled "Night Thoughts While Traveling":

Slender grasses,
A breeze on the riverbank,
The tall mast
Of my boat alone in the night.

Stars hang
All across a vast plain.
The moon leaps
In the Great River's flow.

My writing
Has not made a name for me,
And now, due to age and illness,
I must quit my official post.

Floating on the wind,
What do I resemble?
A solitary gull
Between the heavens and the earth.

Whincup makes a quatrain of each couplet. He is true to the meaning of the words in the original. In his notes on the poem, Whincup tells us that "heaven and earth" mean "the world." Why, then, did he separate the two and place the solitary sand gull between them? Because Tu Fu felt uncomfortable with his lot on earth, nor was he assured a place in heaven. In the first line of the closing couplet, Whincup ignores the repetition of the character "floating" or "drifting," but only at great expense both to the meaning and to the feeling of the line. Whincup gets the words right, but completely misses the powerful emotional meaning of the poem.

In a wonderful scholarly translation of Tu Fu and Li Po together, (*Bright Moon, Perching Bird* by J. P. Seaton and James Cryer, Wesleyan University, 1987) the aforementioned Seaton gives another version:

Slender grass, light breeze on the banks.
Tall mast, a solitary night on board.
A falling star, and the vast plain broader.
Surging moon, on the Great River flows.
Can fame grow from the written word alone?
This officer, both old and sick, must let that be.
Afloat, afloat, just so

. . . .

Heaven, and Earth, and one black gull.

While the inversion of the fourth line rings a hollow note, Seaton comes much closer to the poet's feeling of frustration, especially in the closing couplet. The sixth line says in the original: "office must old sick quit" or "The old and sick should leave office." Both Whincup and, to a lesser degree, Seaton, by inserting Tu Fu himself into the line, create a misappropriate tone—almost as though the poet were whining—that misses the poet's feeling of uncertainty. The occasion of the poem was the death of Tu's patron. The poet, then in his mid-fifties, suddenly had to pack up and leave. The fifth line expresses his feeling of the fleeting qualities of literary success, something the poet himself never knew.

In a brilliant little study of a very famous quatrain frequently mis-translated from the Chinese, *Nineteen Ways of Looking at Wang Wei* (Moyer Bell, 1987), Eliot Weinberger begins by saying, "Poetry is that which is worth translating."

Without giving away the many excellent points Weinberger scores, it is worthwhile to point out that sometimes even the most obvious line of a poem creates problems that get passed on from translator to translator. The last line of Wang Wei's "Deer Park" reads in literal:

Again shine green moss above

The poet is describing rays of sunlight falling in the deep forest. James J. Y. Liu, who has written invaluable books on Chinese poetics, translates the line, "And falls again upon the mossy ground." Rexroth simply ignores the "above" character. Burton Watson has the light "shining over" the moss. Octavio Paz ignores it. In fact, there are a good many more than nineteen versions of this poem to compare, but the only translator I know who approaches the last line with much success is Gary Snyder: "Again shining / on the green moss, above." In his comments to Weinberger, Snyder directs the reader's attention to the most obvious of facts: moss grows in the trees. Had the other translators bothered to look closely at the real and living landscape as the poet had, the line comes almost literally. But it's difficult to see a forest clearly, to understand its most telling details, from the third floor office in the Literature Department.

A hundred years ago, Pinkerton sang in *Madame Butterfly*, "His life is not satisfied unless he makes the flowers of any nation his own treasure." It has been proven to be a prophetic voice. Puccini's libretto is based upon a play by David Belasco initially staged in 1900 at New York's Square Theater.

In his extraordinary study, *American Poetry and Japanese Culture* (Archon, 1984), Sanehide Kodama explores the steady growth of a primary literary relationship that begins, really, in English letters with publication of *Gulliver's Travels* when Swift sends his hero to "Yedo" and "Nangasac" in 1727. Kodama examines several obvious figures: Ezra Pound, Amy Lowell, Kenneth Rexroth, Gary Snyder, and Allen Ginsberg. He also includes lucid observations on the haiku of Richard Wright and on a poem by Richard Wilbur, "Thyme Flowering among Rocks," composed in 17-syllable stanzas of three lines each, counting 5-7-5, the syllabic measure of haiku. *American Poetry and Japanese Culture* ought to be in every poet's personal library. Kodama reminds us of a forgotten poet in his examination of Richard Wright; he presents an accounting of the Pound/Fenollosa notebooks and their consequences that is nonpareil; and his exegesis of Kenneth Rexroth's poetry is a great service to a neglected master and a pleasure to read as we uncover poem after poem brought into English from Japanese classics, but settling into Rexroth's own longer poems of philosophical meditation — they become an integral part of Rexroth's own being.

The real work of the translator/poet transcends even that most honorable of intentions — the bringing into our own language and thus our collective consciousness the classics of other cultures. Poetry demands a wider, fuller, and much more intense response to life. The formalities and idiosyncrasies of Japanese and Chinese poetry, for instance, are relatively unimportant. No one writing in American English is likely to do very much with a rhymed five-syllable quatrain which is the whole foundation of Asian poetry. We North Americans have contributed very little through our haiku-writing. The briefer the form, the more difficult to translate. Our haiku imitators are not much better nor worse than our imitation Romantics. Yet we have a handful of certifiably great haiku from recent years, just as we have a few great Romances.

Jorie Graham told me once about requiring her students to write one hundred haiku each. I don't recall whether she was strict in her definition or whether she allowed "approximate" haiku. It doesn't really matter. Afterward, after much struggle and frustration, she asked them what they had learned from their undertaking. The most common response, she said, was simply, "Humility."

By studying Burton Watson's fairly literal translations of early Chinese poetry, *The Columbia Book of Chinese Poetry* (Columbia University, 1984), we begin to understand the deeply humanistic traditions and the clear perspective on our relationship with Nature afforded by poets like Wang Wei or Su Tung-p'o. And we also see that even a thousand, two thousand years ago, the poet often suffered hardship and exile by insisting upon the necessity of telling people what they already know but do not wish to hear.

In a more civilized culture, Burton Watson would receive the monument he so richly deserves. His translations, while rarely rising into pure poetry themselves, are accurate, readable, and utterly invaluable. As a scholar/ translator, Watson is a national treasure. He has presented us with reliable texts for Chuang Tzu, Han Fei Tzu, Mo Tzu, Hsun Tzu, and the historian Ssu-ma Ch'ien — foundations in Chinese philosophy; he has given us brilliant translations of Su Tung-p'o and Gensei, Han Shan and Lu Yu; he has brought us two large volumes of Japanese literature written in Chinese; and his collaboration with Hiroaki Sato, *Country of Eight Islands* (Doubleday, 1981), is a masterwork anthology of Japanese poetry.

A second volume, *The Columbia Book of Later Chinese Poetry* (Columbia University, 1984, translated and edited by Jonathan Chaves), has just been published. Chaves, like Watson, is not a poet. But like the former, he presents us with excellent, readable texts beginning in the thirteenth century, where Watson leaves off. Chaves's translations of Yang Wan-li, *Heaven My Blanket, Earth My Pillow* (Weatherhill, 1975), and Yuan Hung-tao, *Pilgrim of the Clouds* (Weatherhill, 1978), are superb, as is his study *Mei Yao-ch'en and the Development of Early Sung Poetry* (Columbia University, 1976). This two-volume set is absolutely essential for anyone incapable of deciphering Chinese. While many of our poets satisfy themselves with imitating what they perceive to be the prose descriptive passages of a Chinese or Japanese poem, they generally fail to understand the necessity for those "objectivist" passages. Watson and Chaves, like all great translators, present us with the descriptive passages, but conclude, as all great poetry does, with the essential humane wisdom of the culture.

It's hard to imagine what Gary Snyder's poetry might look like had he not undertaken the intense, lifelong self-discipline which his poems, like all good Chinese poems, reveal. His self-discipline is Ch'an or Zen both in its evidence—the poem—and in its practice. His little poem, "The Uses of Light," from his Pulitzer Prize–winning *Turtle Island* (New Directions, 1974), concludes with a stanza lifted almost literally from the T'ang poet Wang Chih-huan's "View from Heron Lodge."

In another way, we may look at James Wright's great poem, "As I Step Over a Puddle at the End of Winter, I Think of an Ancient Chinese Governor," with its mock-Chinese title, and glimpse a deep personal and humane response to a poem by Po Chu-i written 1100 years earlier. Wright's poem would please Po Chu-i. Wright, by embracing the translation of Po's poem, enters into the intense personal experience of the old poet. Out of his experience with a reflection of the original, he molds his poem. The music of the Chinese is not his *métier;* his music is the music of carefully considered American speech. But the emotions and the fierce intelligence of the poem cannot be entirely detached from the classical Chinese.

Thirty years ago, Kenneth Rexroth observed that what we might learn from Asian poetry in translation is that it "accomplishes in one blow the various programs of the twentieth-century revolutions in poetry—all the manifestos of the imagists and objectivists and so forth have to be fulfilled if you are going to write decent translations of Chinese verse." To which I would add such studies as composition by breath, composition by field, cadenced and open measure along with metrical structure.

In Denise Levertov's "The Poet Li Po Admiring a Waterfall," we find a lovely and sophisticated response not to a particular poem, but to a very generalized yet particular sensibility:

> And listening to its
> Japanese blues, the bass
> of its steady plunging
> tones of dark,
> and within their roaring:
> strands of thin
> foamwhite, airbright
> light inwoven!—all
> falling
> so far
> so deep,
> his two
> acorn-hatted infant
> acolytes fear
> he will long to
> fly like spray
> and fall too, off
> the sloping, pale
> edge of the world,
> entranced!

Most often, the imitation Chinese poem, through the laziness and superficiality of the poet, turns into mawkish sentimentality. James Joyce reminds us, "The sentimentalist is he who would enjoy without incurring a tremendous debt for the thing done." Levertov's poem is full of sentiment and full of acknowledged debt. It doesn't matter that Li Po, T'ang dynasty poet, never heard Japanese music. The poem is American; the experience of the poem is American, the music of that almost breathless experience is American. A conscientious reader is doubly rewarded by an etymology on the final word.

Levertov is not composing an imitation Chinese poem. Rather, she is simply being receptive to that which has been learned from Chinese poetics, adapting or translating the rhythms of perception into a basic line-by-breath which culminates in a four-syllable line from "acolytes fear" on, until the final two-syllable closure. While she makes no particular use of the structure of a Chinese poem, Levertov follows certain of its rhythms of perception and arrives with a poem which is the result of the deep influence of translation rather than the more usual superficial one.

In Robert Bly's best poetry, *Silence in the Snowy Fields* (Wesleyan University, 1962) and *Loving a Woman in Two Worlds* (Harper and Row, 1987), his poems assume their great moral authority in part by embracing classical Chinese and Japanese methods of procedure. Bly, whether consciously or otherwise, has always had a great feel for combining image with statement and grounding the two in metaphor. It is a tactic one encounters again and again in Tu Fu and Li T'ai-po, in tanka and renga, in love poems and in drinking songs. Even as early as "Taking the Hands" in his first book, he writes a poem which could easily pass as a good translation:

Taking the hands of someone you love,
You see they are delicate cages

. . . .

Tiny birds are singing
In the secluded prairies
And in the deep valleys of the hand.

His "Winter Poem" from *Loving a Woman* is composed in four quatrains, the middle quatrains almost forming a parallel:

Winter Poem

The quivering wings of the winter ant
wait for lean winter to end.
I love you in slow, dim-witted ways,
hardly speaking, one or two words only.

What caused us each to live hidden?
A wound, the wind, a word, a parent.
Sometimes we wait in a helpless way,
awkwardly, not whole and not healed.

When we hid the wound, we fell back
from a human to a shelled life.
Now we feel the ant's hard chest,
the carapace, the silent tongue.

This must be the way of the ant,
the winter ant, the way of those
who are wounded and want to live:
to breathe, to sense another, and to wait.

The structure of "Winter Poem" parallels that of a classical Chinese poem in several ways. In Chinese, the poet would use only eight lines composed in four couplets. The middle two couplets would form a double parallelism. Bly's language is far more relaxed, and requires extra syllables, extra lines, extra parts of speech. The Chinese would probably supply no articles, no prepositions, no conjunctions, and the first- and second-person pronouns would be mostly left to the reader to supply. A Chinese poet would admire especially the humility of the first stanza and the intelligence of the final.

In poems such as "Snow Geese" and "Night of First Snow," Bly achieves a moral presence by diminishing his own role in the poem. In the case of the latter, the poem might be even better without the first-person pronoun. Bly finds his responsibilities revealed through the power of simple, accurate description—snow geese, a drunken father and a little boy, a woman and a basket. And by meditations provoked by a winter ant.

A winter ant, a few deer munching October's apples, a weather pattern—almost anything can propel one into the drive to connect. Both the original poem and the "translation" entertain the possibility of becoming true poetry, *traduttore traditore* notwithstanding. Just as now, the deer gone back up the hill, the lunch crowd gone back into the old gymnasium, and John Coltrane is playing "Olé" on tape. The music, now thirty years old, is as fresh and exciting as Bach's concertos. Listening closely, one hears echoes and adaptations of the basic twelve-beat flamenco rhythm which has its roots in the *cante gitano* of the Spanish gypsies; and, behind that, echoes Greek music, of bouzouki and of that great Greek soul music, *rebetika;* and behind that, the sounds and rhythms of early East Indian flute, tamboura, and clay tabla. All of it is in one way or another translation. Coltrane, making his music from inside the heart, explores remnants of older cultures from the world over, then creates an utterly original music that is distinctly Coltrane and entirely American.

Another of Musō's verses from the Merwin/Shigematsu collaboration reminds us:

For Ko Who Has Come Back from China

A brief meeting today
   but it seems to gather up
      a hundred years

We have exchanged
   the compliments of the season —
      that's word-of-mouth Zen

Don't say
   that wisdom and ignorance
      belong to opposing worlds

Look: China and Japan
   but there are not
      two skies

An Answering Music:
American Poets and Chinese Poetry

Writing some seventeen centuries ago, Lu Chi began the Preface to his *Wen Fu,* or *Rhymed Prose on the Art of Writing,* with these words:

> When studying the work of the Masters,
>   I watch the working of their minds.

Lu Chi himself spent a lifetime studying the *Book of Songs, Analects, Chuang Tzu,* and *Lao Tzu.* He had spent ten years "behind bolted doors" studying the Confucian classics. He believed in *tzu-chan,* or "spontaneous origins," in writing, a notion not at odds with the Greek idea of inspiration except that "spontaneous origins" required no Muses per se. Lu Chi also believed in Confucian discipline, and in studying the great literature of the past in order to establish resonances or "answering music" which binds past to present, defining continuity of culture.

   During the many centuries since its composition, Chinese poets have turned to the *Wen Fu* to study the working mind of Lu Chi. In the United States, his influence has grown considerably, especially since mid-century when three versions of the *Wen Fu* were published. Far less known to the general reading public than Li T'ai-po or Tu Fu, Lu Chi has prompted a good deal of "echoing music" from a surprising variety of American poets. This echoing music, echoing not only Lu Chi, but any number of poets from the *Book of Songs* to *Three Hundred Poems of the T'ang,* suggests that classical Chinese poetry in translation has enjoyed a substantial influence on the development of our own poetry, that it has contributed to the shape and the style, even to the process itself, of American verse in this century.

To Lu Chi
(author of the Wen Fu, or Prose Poem
on the Art of Letters, A.D. 302)

Old sir, I think of you in this tardy spring,
Think of you for, maybe, no better reason
Than that the apple branches in the orchard
Bear snow, not blossoms, and that this somehow
Seems oddly Chinese. I too, when I walk
Around the orchard, pretending to be a poet
Walking around the orchard, feel Chinese,
A silken figure on a silken screen
Who tries out with his eye the apple branches,
The last year's shriveled apples capped with snow,
The hungry birds. And then I think of you.

Through many centuries of dust, to which
We both belong, your quiet voice is clear
About the difficulties and delights
Of writing well, which are, it seems, always
The same and generally unfashionable.

Published thirty years ago, Howard Nemerov's verse epistle (*Mirrors and Windows*, 1958) was composed during the heyday of the Beat Generation, but Nemerov is no street-smart pseudo-Buddhist beatnik bawling over the McCarthy hearings; presently poet laureate of the United States, he has most often been praised or attacked as a conservative poet, a poet steeped in the English tradition. Yet Nemerov finds a number of penetrating connections with the work of a devoted Confucian scholar-poet-exile from the fourth century. Nemerov, like Ezra Pound twenty years earlier and like Gary Snyder fifteen years later, responds particularly to a line in the preface to the *Wen Fu:*

When cutting an axe handle with an axe,
    surely the model is at hand.

Snyder's title poem to his 1983 collection of poems, *Axe Handles* (North Point), addresses not only his admiration for Lu Chi, but "corrects"

Pound's version of the *Wen Fu* preface. Snyder opens his book with a translated verse which says,

> How do you shape an axe handle?
> Without an axe it can't be done.

Snyder, arguably the best of the Beat poets, has gone to school on Chinese and Japanese poetry, philosophy, and history, and is himself a brilliant translator of Asian verse. Snyder finds Lu Chi's source in a Confucian anthology compiled nearly a thousand years before the *Wen Fu* and 2500 years before the mid-twentieth century.

At a glance, it would appear that Snyder and Nemerov inhabit opposite corners of the literary universe, yet each is a literary conservationist, and each has been significantly influenced by Chinese poetry in translation. In fact, this century in American verse might well be called the Age of Translation.

Modern poetry began in the nineteenth century with Whitman and Dickinson, the former somewhat indebted to Emerson's studies of Asian philosophy, the latter developing a hard imagistic edge not altogether dissimilar to the poetry Pound and H.D. would develop under the notion of Imagism. But Modernism itself begins with Ezra Pound and the famous notebooks of Ernest Fenollosa which provided the grist for *Cathay,* a thin volume of translations from the Chinese—mostly from Li T'ai-po—published seventy years ago and which has had an enormous impact on American verse. The inventors of Modernism—Pound, T.S. Eliot, William Carlos Williams, H.D., and Amy Lowell—all came under the influence of Fenollosa's notebooks. Eliot, while studying the French Symbolist poets while still at Harvard, read the *Upanishads* and the *Bhagavad Gita,* and also knew the translations of James Legge and, later, Arthur Waley; his famous "objective correlative" could almost be interpreted as a commentary on classical Chinese poetics. Williams's famous dictum, "No ideas but in things," might also be attributed in part to what he learned from Pound's *Cathay.* H.D. is perhaps the most subtly influenced of the major Modernists, but certainly combined many qualities of Chinese prosody, including juxtaposition of images without additional commentary; she remains the quintessential Imagist, even in her longer, more narrative poems. Amy Lowell's poems were generally directly derivative; her collaborations with Florence Ayscough brought her into immediate contact with

Chinese poetry, and their *Fir Flower Tablets,* published in 1921 (Houghton Mifflin), enjoyed several subsequent printings.

During the 1920s and 1930s, American (and Asian, especially Japanese) racism built a long, wide wall between the cultures, a wall which is reflected in American verse written during those years. Despite literary politics, the collaborative translations of Witter Bynner and Kiang Kang-hu, *The Jade Mountain,* was published in 1930 (Alfred A. Knopf). This English version of *Three Hundred Poems of the T'ang* remained in print over several decades and introduced a large number of American poets to Chinese verse in translation. It has become one of the most widely read volumes of poetry in translation in the English language.

In 1938, Stanford University Press published a selection of Henry H. Hart's translations from classical Chinese, *A Garden of Peonies,* and this volume also won over a wide audience and was reprinted several times. Arthur Waley's *170 Chinese Poems,* originally published in 1919, was reprinted in 1941 by Alfred A. Knopf in a beautiful slipcased edition that sold especially well for poetry. And in 1949, Robert Payne edited yet another extraordinarily successful anthology, *The White Pony* (Allen and Unwin, 1949), which also went through many reprintings, remaining available in paperbound editions on both continents until the early 1970s. There were, of course, many, many other volumes translated, including Florence Ayscough's rather prosey two-volume Tu Fu. But few other translations enjoyed the broad readership of these particular anthologies. There probably is not a significant poet publishing in the U.S. today who has not, at one time or another, "gone to school" on Pound's *Cathay;* nor is it likely there are many who have not spent time on the Waley, Bynner, and Payne anthologies. Much of the very personal tone of contemporary poetry is as indebted to these translations as to Whitman and Dickinson; our poets, increasingly disenfranchised by popular culture, found personal examples as well as purely literary ones in Chinese poets.

It was also about this time that Kenneth Rexroth began his now-famous translations of Chinese verse, particularly influenced by Judith Gautier's translations into French. Rexroth had met Witter Bynner during a trip to Taos, New Mexico, in 1925, and had found in Bynner "the first person I had met with whom I could share my own interest. He had a very sensible Chinese informant, and had never fallen victim to the outrageous ideo-graphic theories of Ezra Pound and Amy Lowell. He introduced me to the major Sinologists in French and English. . . ." It was also Bynner who "re-directed" Rexroth's attention away from the ever-popular Li T'ai-po in favor of Tu Fu, whom Rexroth would later call "perhaps the greatest non-epic, non-dramatic poet who ever lived." As a result of "an hour's conversation in a sun-baked patio," Rexroth would spend a significant portion of the next half-century studying Tu Fu—as well as other major Chinese and Japanese poets. More than any other poet writing in English, Rexroth assimilated not only technique, but sensibility itself. In poems such as "The Thin Edge of Your Pride" and "Andrée Rexroth," in "Another Spring" and "The Signature of All Things," he presents poems that read very much like the best Chinese poetry in translation, except that the images themselves are entirely Western; his delicate sense of temporality, his historical sadness, his "ah!" of praise—these qualities have been honed and refined by his study of Chinese classics.

In an essay, "Homage to the Chinese," John Haines remembers years spent along the Tanana River in the Alaskan interior studying Rexroth's *One Hundred Poems from the Chinese* (New Directions, 1956), paying particular attention to the poems of Tu Fu. Through Rexroth, he returned to Payne's *White Pony* and to Pound's *Cathay*. Haines presents the influence of this reading most emphatically: "A few books, read and understood so that they become part of us—that is what matters. I have owned many books since then, but I have seldom read them so well."

While scholars picked apart and illuminated the "errors" of Waley and, especially, Pound, poets were finding new models—Gary Snyder and Philip Whalen, together as undergraduates at Reed College, began to feel that poets like Tu Fu, Po Chu-i, T'ao Ch'ien, and Meng Hao-jan provided role models, examples of personal and social conduct useful to an American poet in the late 1940s and early 1950s; Conrad Aiken was immersed in Shigeyoshi Obata's *The Works of Li Po* (1928) and Waley's *The Poetry and Career of Li Po* (Allen and Unwin, 1950), the result of which, Aiken's own poem, "A Letter from Li Po," published in 1955, remains one of his grandest and most eloquent accomplishments; James Wright's early, more formal poems gave way to the influence of Waley, especially Waley's versions of Po Chu-i which brought Wright to his beautiful poem "As I Step Over a Puddle at the End of Winter, I Think of an Ancient Chinese Governor"; and finally, through Rexroth, Snyder, Whalen, and others, the Beat Movement turned toward Zen, most of the poets reading all the great old Japanese and Chinese masters, especially Han Shan as translated by Gary Snyder, and, after 1962, Burton Watson's brilliant renderings of 100 poems by Cold Mountain. As a translator of Zen, Ch'an, and Confucian classics, Burton Watson has been a primary source for many of our best writers—Watson's is the *Chuang Tzu* everyone reads; Watson brought us *Mo Tzu, Hsun Tzu, Han Fei Tzu,* the *Records of the Historian Ssu Ma Ch'ien,* Lu Yu, Su Tung-p'o, and edited *The Columbia Book of Chinese Poetry,* to name but a few.

In "A Letter from Li Po," Aiken adopts a curious tactic: the poem is composed in the third person. If the "letter" were indeed to be as read as though from Li Po, why the third-person narrative? This eccentricity aside, Aiken's poem is an exercise in literary adulation and camaraderie.

> Fanfare of northwest wind, a bluejay wind
> announces autumn, and the Equinox
> rolls back blue bays to a far afternoon.
> Somewhere beyond the Gorge Li Po is gone,
> looking for friendship or an old love's sleeve
> or writing letters to his children, and to us.
> What was his light? of lamp or moon or sun?

From these opening lines, Aiken constructs a lyric of twenty-odd pages, lifting lines from Li Po's poems in above-mentioned translations and from Herbert Giles's early book, *Chinese Literature.* As many other poets would discover during subsequent decades, Aiken found in Li Po a friend, a companion in poetry.

The consequence is a civilizing process, a broader historical perspective, and a greater sense of compassion. The best translations of classical Chinese poetry are those in which the translator has remained aware of making a *poem* in English. Most often, the "Englishing" has transformed a very formal object into an apparently casually constructed verse form. Rhymed five- and seven-syllable lines have been transformed into irregular unrhymed lines cast in informal, colloquial diction. Whatever the original Chinese has lost in sound and formality, it has gained—in good transla-tion—in clarity of feeling; what it has lost in density—indeed, often almost an impenetrability of compression—it has regained in accessibility and limpidity. The lessons learned from resonance and allusion, from juxtapo-sition of images, and from the interweaving of contrasting threads has not been lost on the poets of North America. These were the qualities which informed Aiken's poem, just as they informed the poetry of Rexroth, Bly, James Wright, and many others.

They discovered a poetry of the present, of presence, and given to the occasion. There was an undertone of confidentiality in Chinese verse, in part the result of a literary class, indeed a purely literary language which automatically excluded all those unfamiliar with its tenets and its nuance. In translation, these poems became far more accessible, in Waley's words, making the old Chinese poets appear more interested in friendship than in romance.

It was, perhaps, the direct treatment of objects, *things,* which attracted William Carlos Williams to Chinese poetry. Between 1958 and 1961, Williams worked over the translations of popular T'ang poems sent to him by David Rafael Wang, a young Chinese-American poet who died mysteriously in 1977. The poems were all drawn from the *Ch'uan T'ang Shih,* or *Complete T'ang Poems,* and nearly all had been previously translated. Nevertheless, Williams wrestled with Wang's versions on and off over the three-year period, only to eventually concede defeat: "I have struggled with the poems but I cannot get a replica of the ancient language." Having listened intently as Wang read the original Chinese aloud, Williams hoped to find a way to present a "replica" of either the tonal patterns or the juxtaposition of images as he (incorrectly) understood how the "ideograms" worked. But he could read no Chinese characters, and the more he struggled, the more baffled he became. "The sound of ancient language is lacking," he wrote, but permitted his name to be attached to the thirty-odd poems collected in *The Cassia Tree* (New Directions, 1989). The poems are expressed in couplet and quatrain for the most part, and achieve a very respectable level, better perhaps than Williams ever realized.

Hayden Carruth's 1959 collection of poems, *The Crow and the Heart* (Macmillan), includes a poem, "The Buddhist Painter Prepares to Paint," a rather formal poem dealing directly with Buddhist philosophy and Chinese aesthetics. Carruth, a wonderfully polyglot literary thief, enriches his verse with some of the widest spheres of influence at mid-century.

Publication in 1965 of Cyril Birch's *Anthology of Chinese Literature* (Grove) introduced a new generation of readers to classical Chinese literature, including Shih-Hsiang Chen's 1952 translation of the *Wen Fu* and Gary Snyder's twenty-four versions of Cold Mountain.

Along San Juan Ridge in the northern Sierra Nevadas, a group of like-minded people developed a significant literary community. The more-or-less official publication was *Kuksu,* an irregular literary journal which regularly published Gary Snyder, Steve Sanfield, Will Staple, Dale Pendell, and others. *Kuksu* represented part of what transpired politically during the late 1960s and 1970s, but its primary methodology was Buddhist-inspired, and its literary root connected the *Shih Ching* to the poets of the T'ang. Behind the journal itself lay the idea of a community founded cooperatively, a community searching for alternative values—alternative economic structure, an alternative to strict inflexible social organization. The model was a combination of Han Shan and Japanese Zen—it incorporated ideas drawn from the Ch'an/Taoist recluse and from the Confucian principle of responsibility. The poetry published in *Kuksu* celebrated the work ethic, daily details, and things-in-themselves; from Snyder's famous poem on family bathing, "The Bath," to an American haiku first glimpsed in the writing of Jack Kerouac and furthered in the pages of *Kuksu,* the literary community on San Juan Ridge joined Eastern religious philosophy and Western ecology, Buddhist economics and Native American mythology, socialist cooperation and capitalist individualism.

Other American poets as diverse as Allen Ginsberg and Frederick Morgan developed approaches to poetry itself which were in part adaptations of Chinese poetics. Ginsberg's poetics are well known; Morgan, founder and co-editor of the rather stately *Hudson Review,* has published two volumes, *A Book of Change* in 1972 (Scribners), and *Poems of the Two Worlds* in 1977 (University of Illinois), which reflect a broad interest in Asian poetry and philosophy. While Ginsberg adopts a more ecstatic, almost Hinayana, tradition, he also adopts the style of the sutra; Morgan's poems reflect a more intellectual influence, especially the reflective qualities of ancient scholar-poets. If Ginsberg's howl is an echo of Li T'ai-po, Morgan's voice hovers about propriety like Po Chu-i.

Publication of Robert Bly's popular *Silence in the Snowy Fields* in 1962 (Wesleyan University) began what could be called a trend in contemporary verse. Choosing a style and a vocabulary neither as rigid as that of the academy nor as idiomatic as Beat slang, a number of poets began writing a poetry rooted in image and implication, of evocation and reflection, the lines based on rhythms of breath and perception. Perhaps the most frequently anthologized of all the poems, "Driving to Town Late to Mail a

Letter" combines description and abstraction so as to juxtapose definite and indefinite image:

> It is a cold and snowy night. The main street is deserted.
> The only things moving are swirls of snow.
> As I lift the mailbox door, I feel its cold iron.
> There is privacy I love in this snowy night.
> Driving around, I will waste more time.

The influence of translation is clearly visible: in Chinese, a poem like this would have none of the passivity of this language, none of the articles or prepositions. But the statements and images might be arranged very much like Bly's—the "telling" images contrasting with the "showing" images. The opening line flirts dangerously with the cliché, "It was a dark and stormy night," but veers quickly away into silence and emptiness. The mystery in Bly's images is evoked by combining concrete tactile information—empty street, snow swirls, and cold iron door—with abstract details—privacy and love—each underscoring the other in a kind of parallelism not completely divorced from that found in Lu Chi's *fu* or in a *chueh-chu* by Li T'ai-po or Tu Fu. Several other poems in the book could well pass for translations from the Chinese, poems such as "A Late Spring Day in My Life," or "Watering the Horse," or, especially, "After Drinking All Night with a Friend, We Go Out in a Boat at Dawn to See Who Can Write the Best Poem." It is illuminating to read *Silence in the Snowy Fields* alongside Kenneth Rexroth's *One Hundred Poems from the Chinese,* published six years earlier.

There was often a conscious effort on the part of the poet to "permit things to speak for themselves." Poetry in the 1960s often sought a more objective, less subjective style. The simple description of landscape and weather implied emotional depth and quality under the hands of a skilled maker. In the hands of poetry workshop imitators, it was reduced to a vocabulary of stones, water, darkness, silence, and polite angst. But our best poets of the time—W. S. Merwin, Denise Levertov, Galway Kinnell, Adrienne Rich, and others—created a more sophisticated and various poetry, a poetry which sought "international style" and universal themes despite a highly localized, even personal, epistemology. Later books by Bly, especially *Jumping Out of Bed* (White Pine, 1987) and *This Tree Will*

Be Here for a Thousand Years (Harper and Row, 1979), bear the indelible handprint of Taoist poetry, especially the poetry of T'ao Ch'ien.

A year after his death in 1962, Robinson Jeffers published *The Beginning and the End* (Random House, 1963), which included a poem, "On an Anthology of Chinese Poems," in which he says,

> These men were better
> Artists than any of ours, and far better observers. They loved landscape
> And put man in his place. But why
> Do their rocks have no weight? They loved rice-wine and peace and
>   friendship,
> Above all they loved landscape and solitude,
> —Like Wordsworth. But Wordsworth's mountains have weight and
>   mass, dull
>   though they may be.
> It is a moral difference perhaps?

Jeffers, with his roots solidly planted in Greek tragedy, with a long life's sensibility founded upon Western logic and Western classics, cannot comprehend the more ethereal reality of weightless Chinese mountains which are found only in an illusory world, a world based upon Buddhist and Taoist mysticism. The young Gary Snyder had already schooled himself in both Buddhism and Jeffers, and had already written from the deep wilderness, "Hard rock wavers / Even the heavy present seems to fail / This bubble of a heart / . . . A clear attentive mind / Has no meaning . . ." and his poems, especially "Piute Creek," presented with his translations from Cold Mountain in *Riprap* (Origin Press, 1959), combine classical Chinese poetics, western North American landscapes, and Buddhist ethics like no other. Jeffers, entering unfamiliar territory, would have learned from Snyder's work how to read the unnamed anthology of Chinese poets.

The decade of the Viet Nam War wrenched poets away from reverie. The "international style" of the late 1960s dissolved as quickly as the social fabric of a nation at war. For Denise Levertov, it was a decade of involvement with Asia—together with Edward C. Dimock, Jr., she translated a book of Bengali songs, *In Praise of Krishna,* published in 1967 (Anchor); she became an anti-war activist; and many of her poems, although reflecting her profound objections to the war, included that which she names "the present, // that which was poised already in the ah! of praise." *Ah* is the first syllable of Sanskrit and is the quintessential seed syllable — mantra — of Buddhism. Others struggled — often self-consciously — to arrive at a poetry which included the expression of outrage and social commitment along with inner harmony or enlightenment. Levertov established a connection which runs far deeper than mere style or aesthetic, one which lies at the root of the very need for poetry, and her "ah!" of cognitive praise universalizes her personal experience. Whether particular volumes of Chinese poetry in translation have directly influenced her writing, perhaps only Levertov knows; but her own poetry, international in every respect from the time of her relocation from England to the United States in 1948, is enriched by her awareness of Asian song.

W. S. Merwin published *Asian Figures* (Atheneum) in 1973. This collection of proverbs, aphorisms, and riddles was drawn from various existing translations from Korean, Chinese, Japanese, Burmese, Philippine, Malayan, and Laotian. Also from 1973, Merwin's *Writings to an Unfinished Accompaniment* (Atheneum) includes poems with such lines as these from "Something I've Not Done" —

Something I've not done
is following me
I haven't done it again and again
so it has many footsteps

and the opening lines from "Tool" —

If it's invented it will be used

and a number of three-line poems (and poems in three-line stanzas) which foreshadow the haiku-like triads used throughout his 1982 book, *Finding the Islands* (North Point). Much of Merwin's poetry of the 1970s had a *kung-an* (or *kōan* in Japanese) quality about it, and the poet has himself become a practitioner of Zen discipline.

Wendell Berry's 1974 chapbook, *An Eastward Look*, offers poems written in the classical Chinese style and based in part upon scroll paintings. His 1977 collection of poems, *Clearing* (Harcourt Brace Jovanovich), begins with an epigram from the *I Ching*.

Charles Wright's 1977 volume of poetry, *China Trace* (Wesleyan University), is indebted to *Cathay*, to Rexroth's *One Hundred Poems from the Chinese* and subsequent translations, among others. The landscapes are American, the volume's epigraphs are from Italo Calvino's *Invisible Cities,* but the poems nevertheless reflect two predominant influences— Chinese poetry and Ezra Pound—two of the latter's most famous lines are slightly recast in a Wright poem the way a Chinese poet will make use of another's lines to establish resonance, context, contrast, homage, or allusion (or almost any combination thereof). *China Trace* is the third volume in a trilogy and is not a "collection" in the usual sense. It must therefore be assumed that the Chinese influence has been carefully considered and is deliberate.

Carolyn Kizer, winner of the Pulitzer Prize for Poetry in 1985, has translated poems from Tzu Yeh, Hsueh T'ao, and Tu Fu, among others. Her 1984 volume, *Mermaids in the Basement* (the title comes from Emily Dickinson) (Copper Canyon Press), contains a number of poems which fall somewhere between translation and imitation, poems which might, in Chinese, be subtitled, "In the Style of So-and-so." Kizer spent a year in China after graduating from Sarah Lawrence College, and her engagement with Chinese poetry has sharpened her own style. She dates her interest in Chinese poetry from the time when her mother read aloud to her from Waley's translations. The young poet was eight. Twenty years before publishing *Mermaids in the Basement,* she published *Knock Upon Silence* (University of Washington, 1968), the title drawn from the *Wen Fu* and quoted in the book's epigraph:

> We wrestle with non-being
> to force it to yield up being;
> we knock upon silence
> for an answering music . . .

For her quotation, Kizer chose the 1952 translation of Achilles Fang. Her "answering music" bears echoes of the high diction of the court and of the acerbic wit of the exile. Her 1988 collection of translations, *Carrying Over* (Copper Canyon Press), gathers her versions of Tu Fu together with versions of the contemporary Chinese poet Shu Ting, along with poems from other languages.

Eleanor Wilner's *Shekhinah* (University of Chicago, 1984) is certainly international in subject matter and range of allusion. One of the finest poems in this brilliant book is "Meditation on the Wen-Fu," a poem likewise of answering music, concluding,

> And, as to the heavenly arrow
> of which Lu Chi speaks—it must have struck
> straight down, deep into stone, into the heart
> of granite. Strange, then,
> what wells up, what pours forth in a flood,
> should be both clear and bright
> as water, heavy and dark as blood;
> that stone be wounded into speech
> and that such wounds should heal us.

Wilner's book explores the idea that what we call "the Past" can indeed be altered, that it is only a collective memory which can be changed by the telling of a story. In this context—a veritable foundation stone of Modernism—Lu Chi becomes her contemporary and his life, like hers, like ours, occurs in the present tense, in the unfolding of the lines of the poem.

Few poets in the past two decades have enjoyed more popularity than Philip Levine; almost none have exceeded him in sphere of influence. In a suite of six poems dedicated to Tu Fu in his recent book, *A Walk with Tom Jefferson* (Alfred A. Knopf, 1988), Levine says,

> Above the bridge lights a rope of stars.
> Alone, late at night, my breath fogging
> the window, I can almost believe
> the sleeping world is the reflection
> of heaven.

But memories invade, as they so often do in Levine's poems, and his attention is turned back to Detroit, to the poet's youth when he and his friends thought they would never die. While the poem probably owes little to any particular poem or translation of Tu Fu, Levine's poem evokes a kind of parallel imagery, almost as though it were a poem Tu Fu *would* write today if he had been born in Detroit in 1928. Levine has expressed his deep respect for Rexroth's work and has surely read Waley—as have virtually all our poets. He finds in Tu Fu, like so many others found, a great kindred spirit, an old friend from very far away. His poem "Winter

Words" resonates with intimate epistemology and place-names from New York, Spain, and Detroit. In another poem, "Another Song," Levine says, "Words go on travelling from voice to voice . . ." As a poet, Levine's primary concerns are identical to those of Tu Fu—social and political corruption, human compassion and endurance, temporality, and the final indomitability of the human spirit.

Colette Inez, in a volume of autobiographical poems, *Family Life* (Story Line, 1988), writes "Reading Tu Fu, I Wait for My Husband." The poem describes Inez's reading of a suite of poems by Tu Fu written in 766 at K'uei-Chou. Soon, she is imagining herself growing "white-haired, waiting for [her] husband." The poem is inspired by Tu Fu, several of its conceits are borrowed from translations of Tu Fu's verses, and even the poem's closing line feels like it might have been lifted from a translation: "We kiss. It is our twentieth autumn in the city." Inez finds in Tu Fu not merely a few quiet lines of verse, but a world of tragedy and comedy and compassion which permeates the poem, the answering music she composes upon a particular occasion. Her particularity is deeply enriched by the particular lucidity of Tu Fu. The irony and the quality of emotional information gathered from the translation informs her own rather mundane experience, elevating the daily detail into the realm of revelation or epiphany. More than providing inspiration, Tu Fu in translation is the wellspring; without the Chinese poem, Inez's poem would have neither context nor image.

Poems from the Hungarian of Miklos Radnoti, from the Spanish of Pablo Neruda or Federico Garcia Lorca, from the Russian of Anna Akhmatova, from the Italian of Cesare Pavese, from the Sioux by way of the ethnologist Francis Densmore, from the Estonian of Jaan Kaplinski or the Japanese of Yosano Akiko or Issa—our poetry has matured greatly in this century, and translation has been a primary influence. But no other poetry of the world has had a greater impact on our poets than that of classical China. Sometimes the influence is subtle and circuitous as with Denise Levertov; sometimes it is direct and immediate as it was with Ezra Pound. But our language and our culture is grandly enriched as a result of our poets' involvement with Chinese masterpieces. Their answering or echoing music does exactly what Lu Chi claimed—it makes our days a little brighter, a little fresher, a little newer. We all become more deeply imbued with a sense of history and humanity, and our own culture, a culture grown wealthy as a result of cross-cultural pollination, is strengthened.

Chinese culture itself provides a perfect example of the ultimate contribution of the translator in the case of Kumarajiva, a Buddhist scholar-monk from the central Asian state of Kucha. Captured by a Chinese military leader and held captive for two decades, he studied the language of his captors. About 401 A.D. Kumarajiva was invited to Ch'ang-an, the capital city. Once there, he set about translating Buddhist texts, most notably the *Lotus Sutra,* translations which altered the course of Chinese history.

Burton Watson has this to say about Kumarajiva: "One cannot help feeling that Kumarajiva's superior degree of understanding is closely related to his general attitude toward translation. For example, when there was some point about Buddhism that he did not fully comprehend, he did not hesitate to set aside his pride and ask for assistance from others who were more versed in the field in question." It was Kumarajiva's translations which first made it possible for disciples to grasp the concept of *shunyata,* or emptiness, the primary teaching of Prajna literature.

As with the ancient monks who studied Kumarajiva, our poets are, to varying degrees, studying modern translations of Chinese verse. It may be fairly said that most of our poets know far more about classical Chinese poetry than about its history, real social conditions, philosophy, and so forth. Thus it may also be fairly said that our poets generally have an extremely limited understanding of the poetry. But our range of understanding has been vastly improved over the past couple of decades thanks to the scholarship of Watson, Stephen Owen, J.P. Seaton, Jonathan Chaves, and others.

Thus, early this morning, reading a translation of *The Blue Cliff Record,* a translation of a book brought into Japanese from the Chinese, and into American English from the Japanese, coming across the expression *mu,* or emptiness, I think back to the Ch'an poets of the T'ang or of the emptiness in certain poems of Tu Fu; and back beyond the T'ang, I think of Kumarajiva in his mid-fifties searching to find a way to bring from the Sanskrit *shunyata* an articulated essence in Chinese. Between my book and Kumarajiva, nearly sixteen centuries and four languages come into play. And one hundred years before Kumarajiva, there is Lu Chi, turning forty, grinding ink to write a *fu* on the Art of Letters, pausing one early sunny morning to listen for an answering music.

The Poetry of Kenneth Rexroth

We have preferred the power that apes greatness—Alexander first of all, and then the Roman conquerors, whom our school history books, in an incomparable vulgarity of soul, teach us to admire. We have conquered in our turn . . . our reason has swept everything away. Alone at last, we build our empire upon a desert. How then could we conceive that higher balance in which nature balanced history, beauty, and goodness, and which brought the music of numbers even into the tragedy of blood? We turn our back on nature, we are ashamed of beauty. Our miserable tragedies have the smell of an office, and their blood is the color of dirty ink.

—Albert Camus

The year was 1948. Camus's relationships with André Breton and Jean-Paul Sartre had just begun to feel the strain that would eventually lead him to disavow all ties with the existentialists. In North America, the official policies of the Cold War were under way: Sen. Joseph McCarthy had recruited young politicos like Robert Kennedy and Richard Nixon to help him "purge the United States Government of Communist infiltrators." And poetry was the province of New Critics. Four years earlier, before the end of the war, Kenneth Rexroth had written in his note on the poems collected in *The Phoenix and the Tortoise* (New Directions, 1944), "If the shorter poems might well be dedicated to [D. H.] Lawrence, 'The Phoenix and the Tortoise' might well be dedicated to Albert Schweitzer, the man who in our time pre-eminently has realized the dream of Leonardo da Vinci. Leonardo died impotent and broken, all his projects half done. He proved that the human will is too small a door for the person to force through into universality. Schweitzer is an outstanding example of a man who found that door which is straight, and smaller than a needle's eye, but through which the universalization of the human soul, the creation of the true person, comes freely, as a guest." Twenty years earlier, Rexroth resolved his own differences with Tzara and Breton in a "cubist" poem, "Fundamental Disagreement with Two Contemporaries," later collected in *The Art of Wordly Wisdom* (Decker, 1949) under the section heading "Interoffice Communications." The exact nature of their disagreement remains for speculation. But one thing is clear: Rexroth believed that the "universalization of the human soul, the creation of the true person," may come freely, but only after enormous struggle to find that "door which is straight, and smaller than a needle's eye." His own search for the door would lead him through the history of philosophy and comparative religion and indeed the whole history of ideas, including his long study of Buddhism, Taoism, and Oriental poetry.

Among the Greek and Latin translations which complete *The Phoenix and the Tortoise* are three poems by the T'ang dynasty poet Tu Fu. Rexroth had become interested in Oriental poetry when he discovered Pound's *Cathay* while still in his teens. While in his twenties, he corresponded with Pound, who introduced Rexroth to James Laughlin, publisher of New Directions and Rexroth's lifelong friend. (One can only speculate as to the nature of the correspondence—Rexroth was deeply involved in the early 1930s with the Wobblies; Pound was immersing himself in the theories of Major Douglas and Social Credit, and actively supporting Mussolini.) In the long title poem, Rexroth incorporates paraphrases and translations of tanka from Gotoku Daiji, *Hyakunin Isshu,* Lady Akazome Emon, the Emperor Sanjo, and many others. By 1948, Rexroth's course and methodology were set. He adopted what has since come to be (inappropriately) labeled the "ideogrammic method" as first used by Ezra Pound. One of the clearest early examples is "When We with Sappho," which begins with a direct translation of the famous Sappho fragment, "about the cool water / the wind sounds . . ." but suddenly becomes an intensely personal love poem that runs nearly four pages beyond the opening lines from Sappho.

William Carlos Williams, reviewing the book in the pages of the *Quarterly Review of Literature* upon publication four years earlier, would say almost nothing about the translations. Rather, he would say, "I know nothing of mysticism. . . . I'm going to try to take out the poetry, appraise it as best I can and leave the mysticism, as far as I can, intact. But first let me say that this is one of the most completely realized arguments I have encountered in a book of verse in my time." Dr. Williams did not qualify his statement; he did not say "a book of verse by a contemporary American poet" — he said, straight-away, "a book of verse . . ." Period.

The long title poem is rich in what Williams called mysticism. It begins with the geologic past of the California Coast Ranges, moving quickly and surely into "the falling light of the Spartan / Heroes of the late Hellenic dusk" while considering various ideas of Aquinas, early Chinese philosophers, the classical Greeks, and far too many other references and accretions to quote from out of context.

In 1948, Rexroth added the finishing strokes to what, surely, must be one of the most beautifully conceived and executed volumes of poetry since Ezra Pound's *Cathay, The Signature of All Things* (New Directions, 1948). Most of the poems and poems-in-translation included in it were composed to be sung, the melodies being composed as part of the poetic process. Among these poems, two elegies stand out: "Delia Rexroth," a poem addressed to the poet's mother who died in 1916 when he was eleven; and "Andrée Rexroth," an elegy for the woman to whom he was married for thirteen years and who died in 1940 following years of struggle with an inherited brain disease which had symptoms similar to epilepsy. There is also a truly remarkable homage, "A Letter to William Carlos Williams," in which he observes, "And you're 'pure', too, / A real classic, though not loud / About it — a whole lot like / The girls of the Anthology. / Not like strident Sappho, who / For all her grandeur, must have / Had endemetriosis, / But like Anyte, who says / Just enough, softly, for all / The thousands of years to remember. . . ." It is a poem which beautifully illuminates the "sacramental relationships" that we come to understand as poetry, and does so at least in part by praising, not Williams's optimism, but its necessity and its profound consequence. Like Williams, Rexroth held on to hope despite all forms of personal and social loss. As we shall see with the later poems, in Rexroth love is the expression of hope and responsibility:

Between Two Wars

Remember that breakfast one November—
Cold black grapes smelling faintly
Of the cork they were packed in,
Hard rolls with hot, white flesh,

And thick, honey sweetened chocolate?
And the parties at night; the gin and the tangos?
The torn hair nets, the lost cuff links?
Where have they all gone to,
The beautiful girls, the abandoned hours?
They said we were lost, mad and immoral,
And interfered with the plans of management.
And today, millions and millions, shut alive
In the coffins of circumstance,
Beat on the buried lids,
Huddle in the cellars of ruins, and quarrel
Over their own fragmented flesh.

"They have hope," Thales said, "who have nothing else." By the age of forty-three, Rexroth had endured the deaths of his mother and first wife; he had roamed the west during the Depression; he had worked as camp cook and roustabout in the Cascades and hiked through most of the Sierras; and, with the "relocation" of thousands upon thousands of Japanese-Americans at the outset of the Second World War, his "disaffili- ation from the American capitalist state" was complete — for the remaining thirty-five years of his life, he would view American letters and history, not as a disaffiliated passive bystander, but as an alienated activist-poet and man of letters. He had written trail-guides for the WPA. He wrote literary journalism "for money or for log-rolling for one's friends," and he endured the collapse of his second marriage. All the while, his poems reflected an enormous sweep of understanding—the many languages he studied and a lifelong study of naturalism and the poetries of pre-literate peoples. He delved into Buddhism and Gnosticism. He translated poems by Neruda and Lorca, Heine, the Chinese classical poets, the Japanese poets, the French of Oscar Milosz and Pierre Reverdy; he studied Bakunin and the Anarchists, the Buddhist and Taoist heretics, the Greeks of the Anthology; he wrote reviews on jazz and composed a libretto for a ballet, "Original Sin," that was performed in San Francisco with the music com- posed and led by John Lewis of the Modern Jazz Quartet.

Rexroth clung tenaciously to his hope for the American left. Mean- while, Dwight Eisenhower warned of the threat to democracy posed by the "military-industrial complex." There was talk of sending U.S. forces into Korea to "police" the northern leftists. While he never, to my knowl- edge, officially declared himself a pacifist, Rexroth remained a conscien- tious objector throughout his life.

He edited an anthology of new young English poets, one of whom, Denise Levertov, he praised and promoted tirelessly although they had never met. He also persuaded New Directions to publish Levertov as he did another passion, William Everson, who would, three years later, don the robes of Dominican Catholicism and publish under the name of Brother Antoninus.

•

By 1958, the American political scenario had changed. Eisenhower had been president for six years. The "police action" in Korea was long since over. Much of the country enjoyed a feeling of well-being. But the San Francisco Renaissance was in full swing. Jack Kerouac's prose had garnered headlines. (Rexroth would later claim in a letter to Morgan Gibson that he'd never read *The Dharma Bums,* and he despised being called "father of the Beats"; but he did not object to being labeled their "Librarian.") There was the now-famous obscenity trial of Allen Ginsberg's "Howl," the result of a reading in November of 1956 at the Six Gallery in San Francisco organized by Kenneth Rexroth. It has often been pointed out that the major model for Ginsberg's poem was not Walt Whitman, but Rexroth's powerful lament upon the death of Dylan Thomas, "Thou Shalt Not Kill" (1953), with its heavy cadences and charged, angry images from a suffering world.

> They are murdering all the young men.
> For half a century now, every day,
> They have hunted them down and killed them.
> They are killing the young men.
> They know ten thousand ways to kill them.
> Every year they invent new ones.
> In the jungles of Africa,
> In the marshes of Asia,
> In the deserts of Asia,
> In the slave pens of Siberia,
> In the slums of Europe,
> In the nightclubs of America,
> The murderers are at work.

. . . .

You killed him,
Benign Lady on the postage stamp.
He was found dead at a Liberal Weekly luncheon.
He was found dead on the cutting room floor.
He was found dead at a *Time* policy conference.
Henry Luce killed him with a telegram to the Pope.
Mademoiselle strangled him with a padded brassiere.
Old Possum sprinkled him with a tea ball.
After the wolves were done, the vaticides
Crawled off with his bowels to their classrooms and quarterlies.

.   .   .   .

The Gulf Stream smells of blood
As it breaks on the sand of Iona
And the blue rocks of Canarvon.
And all the birds of the deep rise up
Over the luxury liners and scream,
"You killed him! You killed him.
In your God damned Brooks Brothers suit,
You son of a bitch."

Rexroth's house had become a weekly meetingplace for pseudo-existentialist poets and free-love advocates, artists and literary hangers-on. Rexroth had married a third time and was the father of two girls. He would later say of those years that, if nothing else, he finally had some readers he didn't know on a first-name basis. He promoted poetry on the airwaves at KPFA, including the surrealist poet Philip Lamantia, the young Gary Snyder and Denise Levertov, his old friend Brother Antoninus, Robert Duncan, and many others. In the early days, these gatherings must have been exciting, but by this time, Snyder and Whalen were leaving for Japan, Duncan was disengaging himself, Brother Antoninus was in his retreat, and Rexroth was about out of patience with the Beatniks who arrived with their imitations of Kerouac. Rexroth considered the late-arriving Beats as mere examples of a veneer, a gastro-pharmaceutical change rather than of a profound spiritual awakening. "An entymologist," he declared, "is not a bug."

•

Rexroth moved to Santa Barbara in 1968 and several years later married Carol Tinker. He taught two classes there under the auspices of the University of California—a poetry-and-music class (which had been designed as a course for a dozen or so students and which, during the protest against American involvement in Viet Nam, drew over 400 students) and a weekly "evening-with-Kenneth" that was modeled largely on the weekly gatherings he'd enjoyed at the old houses on Potrero and Scott streets. For the latter, there were young students of Japanese like John Solt, young poets of almost every persuasion, and some who appeared to be simply literate young people willing to learn from a self-educated man, a scholar out of office.

Everything in those days was colored by American atrocities in Southeast Asia. We would gather at Rexroth's little house in Montecito, twenty or so of us, often with wine and cheese or things for a potluck, and Rexroth, who would install himself in a huge easy chair in one corner of the front room. He read to us in German, French, Japanese, Greek, Latin, Spanish, and so on, one by one, giving us a spontaneous translation of the poem in question along with capsule biographies of the poets under discussion. Of course, everything led to inter-disciplinary considerations. One could hardly be expected to understand Trakl without understanding German expressionism, traditional taboos pertaining to incest, pre–World War I economic conditions, the history of German rebellion against the Catholic church, the peculiarly German approach to Anarchism in Trakl's milieu, and so forth.

What Rexroth understood better than any poet since Ezra Pound (and, indeed, better than the inventor of Modernism himself), is that poetry is not disembodied, it is not something that takes place on the page of a text, but is rather the articulation of human experience as close to perfection as human articulation can be. He resembled Pound in fact in many ways: his appetite for knowledge (not simply information, but *knowledge*) was insatiable; his acceptance of personal responsibility for the course of history, as an active participant in the course of history; his passion, both personal and public. But unlike Pound, Rexroth sought out and enjoyed the company of common working people, ranchers and cobblers and auto mechanics. Unlike Pound, the embodiment of justice, according to Rexroth, could not be separate from the physical and emotional expression of compassion, so much so that the figure of Kuan Shih Yin (in Chinese, "who listens to the world's cries," in Japanese, Kannon) figures prominently in virtually all of his later books. Like his own favorite poet, Tu Fu, Rexroth was a deeply religious poet who included rather than excluded the world's religions. Unlike Tu Fu, he was a poet of erotic love without peer in his lifetime, perhaps without peer in the American language.

Suchness

In the theosophy of light,
The logical universal
Ceases to be anything more
Than the dead body of an angel.
What is substance? Our substance
Is whatever we feed our angel.
The perfect incense for worship
Is camphor, whose flames leave no ashes.

It is a tragedy that Rexroth's death on the anniversary of D-Day in 1982 went almost unnoticed. The newspaper obituaries were brief or non-existent. The major papers noted only the passing of the "father of the Beat Generation." Even the *American Poetry Review*, not once, but twice, called *The Signature of All Things* the "Testament of All Things." But we can't expect editors to remember Jacob Boehme. While Lowell, diminished by the foolish "success" foisted upon him by the academies, was cranking out bad sonnets on various personalities in "history," Rexroth continued working for social justice, equality and partnership among sexes and races and diverse artists, a constant unpaid publicist for young writers and musicians not only from North America, but from all over the world.

The *Selected Poems of Kenneth Rexroth* (New Directions, 1987) contains some of the most beautiful and powerful poetry of the last forty years. The poems of social involvement (for example, "Requiem for the Spanish Dead" and "For Eli Jacobson") are tender and personal, just as the "personal" poems of love and of nature become poems of tremendous social consequence. There are also some poems that are at once funny and profound:

The Advantages of Learning

I am a man with no ambitions
And few friends, wholly incapable

Of making a living, growing no
Younger, fugitive from some just doom.
Lonely, ill-clothed, what does it matter?
At midnight I make myself a jug
Of hot white wine and cardamon seeds.
In a torn grey robe and old beret,
I sit in the cold writing poems,
Drawing nudes on the crooked margins,
Copulating with sixteen year old
Nymphomaniacs of my imagination.

This is the sort of poem that draws heavily from the Greek/Latin poets and from the classical Chinese tradition as well. It achieves tragic proportion through slight self-mockery, and historical balance by implied poetic tradition. It could almost pass as a version of Catullus or of Li Po.

Rexroth also combines the study of science with personal experience as no one before him ever did. Reading Lyell's nineteenth-century study of geology, he composes a poem, "Lyell's Hypothesis Again," (another poem for Marie Rexroth) that looks hard at the "ego, bound by personal / Tragedy and the vast / Impersonal vindictiveness / Of the ruined and ruining world . . ." and concludes:

We have escaped the bitterness
Of love, and love lost, and love
Betrayed. And what might have been,
And what might be, fall equally,
Away with what is, and leave
Only these ideograms
Printed on the immortal
Hydrocarbons of flesh and stone.

He was among the first of our poets to recognize the complex utter interdependence of things, as well as the transparency of our lives and indeed of all the world as we, superficially at least, perceive it.

Anyone interested in Rexroth should also be directed to the later books. Unfortunately, the *Selected Poems* includes but one poem and a fragment from *Natural Numbers* (1964); four small poems from *New Poems* (New Directions, 1974); three short fragments from the major poem *On Flower Wreath Hill* (1976); three fragments from *The Silver Swan* (1978); and but seven of the sixty brief *Love Poems of Marichiko* (1978, translated with Ling Chung). In all probability, this is due to limitations of space. Luckily, there is a Table of Contents. (He habitually interrupted his public readings of *Collected Shorter Poems* with the exclamation, "I've got the only publisher around who's too Goddamned cheap to buy me a Table of Contents!")

The later books are, after all, the culmination of a lifetime's dedication and achievement. Excluded from the *Selected Poems* are some of the most beautiful poems of erotic love ever composed in any language:

Confusion of the Senses (from *New Poems*)

Moonlight fills the laurels
Like music. The moonlit
Air does not move. Your white
Face moves towards my face.
Voluptuous sorrow
Holds us like a cobweb
Like a song, a perfume, the moonlight.
Your hair falls and holds our faces.
Your lips curl into mine.
Your tongue enters my mouth.
A bat flies through the moonlight.
The moonlight fills your eyes
They have neither iris nor pupil
They are only globes of cold fire
Like the deers' eyes that go by us
Through the empty forest.
Your slender body quivers
And smells of seaweed.
We lie together listening
To each other breathing in the moonlight.
Do you hear? We are breathing. We are alive.

We live in an age in which the poetry of mature erotic love is out of fashion. Our poets tend to prefer the cool cerebral play of Stevens to the naked jig of Dr. Williams. (Rexroth once bought a hundred copies of Stevens's *Harmonium* from the publisher's remainder list at fifteen cents per copy.) Rexroth himself read, of course, all the poets, and was especially fond of Yvor Winters, although he often quoted Winters's line, "Emotion in any situation must be as far as possible eliminated," following it with a guffaw.

There is a sweetness, a depth of love, in the later poems that is probably a result of Rexroth's "feminization"—it is surprising to think of it, but during his last years he produced, in collaboration with Ling Chung, the remarkable *Li Ch'ing-chao: Collected Poems* (New Directions, 1979), certainly one of China's greatest poets and a woman who also wrote a deeply personal poetry; and *The Orchid Boat* (McGraw-Hill, 1972, later retitled *Women Poets of China* for its paperback release); and, in collaboration with Ikuko Atsumi, *The Burning Heart* (Seabury, 1977, retitled *Women Poets of Japan* for the paper edition); he edited *Seasons of Sacred Lust* (New Directions, 1975), selected poems of Kazuko Shiraishi; and, in one of the most remarkable of feats, pulled off the invention of "a young woman poet from Japan," Marichiko, whose love poems are both erotically explicit and utterly charming.

VII (from *The Love Poems of Marichiko*)

Making love with you
Is like drinking sea water.
The more I drink
The thirstier I become,
Until nothing can slake my thirst
But to drink the entire sea.

XXV

Your tongue thrums and moves
Into me, and I become
Hollow and blaze with
Whirling light, like the inside
Of a vast expanding pearl.

One might say that he became a female poet in his last years. Those last years seem to have been happy ones. There were trips to Kyoto, some significant literary recognition including a Guggenheim Fellowship and the Copernicus Award for his lifetime's achievement. They were contented, productive years with Carol Tinker; there were also beautiful collaborations in translation. He used his influence at Seabury Press to bring the first volumes of Czeslaw Milosz and Homero Aridjis, among others, to North America.

Perhaps we will eventually have the *Complete Poems*. Such care did Rexroth take with his work that I have seen in his library every edition of his poems clearly penciled with typographical errors corrected, some minor revisions made, and footnotes written into the margins. On a recent visit to his widow, I even came across a small stack of hand-made typewritten errata slips he made upon publication of *In What Hour* (Macmillan, 1940). A *Complete Poems* with generous and accurate notation would make this most accessible of post-Modernist poets available even to the high school and undergraduate readership he loved and deserved.

One can for now only hope that Rexroth will begin to receive his due. Perhaps he can attain in death that which he so richly deserved in life: just recognition as one of the major poets of American letters, a pioneer, a great teacher beyond the scholia, an original mind that has touched so many serious poets in our country (and abroad) in the second half of this century. While many of our more widely popular poets exhibit an incomparable vulgarity of the soul and a dangerous ignorance of history and tradition, while even our critics such as Helen Vendler preach (in the *New York Times Book Review*) that we have nothing to learn from the poets who survived the Holocaust, while our entire culture aspires to a world monoculture that excludes nature and mistrusts true beauty and embraces the musty mini-tragedies of the office, Rexroth points the way back toward an aesthetic that not only encompasses nature and history and beauty, but embraces the three as aspects of the one, the same. As he said of translating the Chinese classical poets while disavowing all affiliation with the beatniks, "You meet a better class of people that way." (As he became disaffiliated from the Establishment, so he disaffiliated himself from the Anti-Establishment Establishment.) He is, as Morgan Gibson asserts in his Twayne study, a poet of intense personal responsibility. This might best be made clear by quoting from Rexroth's famous Introduction to the *Selected Poems of D. H. Lawrence:*

"The ceremonial glory of the sacrament passes from the forefront of consciousness and the period of adjustment to the background of life begins. Every detail of life must be transformed by marriage. This means creative conflict on the most important level.

"Sacramental communion is bound by time. Mass does not last forever. Eventually the communicant must leave the altar and digest the wafer, the Body and Blood must enter his own flesh as it moves through the world and struggles with the devil. The problem lies in the sympathetic nervous system, says Lawrence. And it is not easy for two members of a deranged race, in the Twentieth Century, to learn again how to make those webs mesh as they should."

What he claims for the poetry of Lawrence might, as well, be claimed for his own poems, for "behind the machinery is an intense, direct, personal, mystical apprehension of reality" that is informed by Rexroth's commitment to husbandry, to his own vulnerability in a civilization in collapse.

Bradford Morrow's Introduction to the *Selected* is helpful to the new reader, but a more scholarly approach might better have served this neglected master. Or, better yet, an introduction by a poet. And the notes are utterly inadequate—the note on Yuan Chen's poem, for instance, states, "Possibly an allusion to 'Three Dreams at Chiang-ling' which describes the dreams of a husband for his dead wife, usually understood as referring to the poet and his wife." In plain fact, the poem alluded to is Yuan Chen's "Great Elegy," which begins, "O loveliest daughter of Hsieh, / you married a hapless scholar / and spent your life with a sewing basket / patching his old clothes. . . ." The allusion is perfectly clear in context, for Rexroth, grieving over his wife's death, is reflecting back on their years of poverty and his own (real and imagined) neglect. Other notes are bald, as in the case of the note on Kannon. Hence Morrow's modest disclaimer: "The following notes are intended as a guide to some of the more difficult references . . . and not as a comprehensive commentary."

Publication of the *Selected Poems of Kenneth Rexroth* is just cause to rejoice. Bradford Morrow is to be congratulated for what must have been a painful job—there is so much material to be drawn from. Rexroth has been among our best-known and least-read poets. He was the author of (by my count) some fifty-four books, excluding the second part of the autobiography and an enormous unpublished anthology of poetry of preliterate peoples that surveys the entire globe. His epitaph (drawn from *The Silver Swan*) reads: "The swan sings / In sleep / On the lake of the mind." And so he does, so he does.

Lyric, Miserable Lyric

A critic once suggested that one could pursue a complete curriculum in the humanities simply by reading Kenneth Rexroth's essays and the works to which they refer. I've been doing just that for thirty very rewarding years. Rexroth was a polyglot philosopher/poet with virtually no formal education. The range of his study and understanding is monumental; he is, like Ezra Pound, a lifetime's study.

Rexroth was, like Odysseas Elytis, Pound, Rilke, and Brecht, one of the truly original minds in twentieth-century poetry. Like Pound, he was a great gatherer, a poet of juxtaposition searching for moral accountability in the culture of narcissism; like the Greek Elytis, he was far more interested in the mechanism of mythology than in its beautiful surface; he shared with Rilke a sensuous religiosity, with Brecht a social commitment. Time will prove Rexroth to be one of the three or four poets writing American English in this century who truly matter. But at this writing, he is known in name only; his vast oeuvre—some fifty-four books, including translations from Spanish, French, German, Japanese, Chinese, Latin, and Greek—remains largely unread by the generation of poets now in their thirties and forties.

Bradford Morrow, editing the selected essays, *World Outside the Window* (New Directions, 1987), has served both the poet and the prospective reader very well indeed. He has included several of the best-known of Rexroth's essays ("Poetry, Regeneration, and D. H. Lawrence," "Disengagement: The Art of the Beat Generation," and the brilliant tour-de-force "The Poet as Translator") along with several of the least-read, such as "The Visionary Painting of Morris Graves" and "The Influence of Classical Japanese Poetry on Modern American Poetry." Morrow has also included several excellent previously unpublished pieces.

Rexroth claimed he wrote prose only "for money or log-rolling for one's friends," and many of the later essays were simply dictated, as was the entirety of his marvelous quick study, *American Poetry in the Twentieth Century.* Whatever the case, Rexroth's essays should be preserved in their entirety, but until such time, *World Outside the Window* offers a glimpse into one of the great minds of our age.

"The craft of literature," Rexroth says, "can be said to be in part the manipulation of a structure in time, and so the simplest element of marking time, rhythm, is therefore of basic importance in both poetry and prose. Prosody, which is the science of versification, has for its subject the materials of poetry and is concerned almost entirely with the laws of metre, or rhythm in the narrowest sense." He then observes that of course in the case of organic form, the repetition of metre and sound is not essential to measure. "Since lyric poetry is either the actual text of song or else immediately derived from song, it is regular in structure nearly everywhere in the world. . . ."

There has been much said of late about the resurgence of formal versification. Some, like Diane Wakoski, imply that this literary conservatism is concomitant with political reactionary conservatism throughout the social fabric of the U.S. Others, such as Robert Bly, have implied that organic form is exhausted. And Jonathon Holden has even gone so far as to suggest that the lyric form is a tool for the young, and that one in middle age becomes more drawn to prose.

Lyric poetry is not dead, nor is organic form. In a conversation on this subject with Thomas McGrath, we digressed into a reminiscence of Yvor Winters's comments on prosody and his insistence upon a metred line. He insisted upon formal training in prosody. He despised "organic form," saying Nature was not "irregular." Gazing out his window, McGrath said, "And then I look at that goddamned tree out there and think . . ."

What has "exhausted" organic form in recent years is the super-abundance of merely competent versification. The apprentice poet is told time and again, "Write like you talk." And all too often, he or she does just that. I wonder whether most poetry workshop leaders actually believe Milton spoke in iambic pentameter. We know that natural speech in Chaucer's time approached such a measure, but measure alone does not necessarily include diction. Of those poets we most universally respect for their supreme command of prosody in organic form, poets such as Creeley,

Levertov, Duncan, Kinnell, McGrath, Rich, of how many can it be said there is no discernable difference between the speaking voice and the voice of the poem? And among those masters of metred prosody such as Justice, Wilbur, or Millay?

As Rexroth points out in the same essay ("The Art of Literature"), Greek and Latin poetry was "consciously patterned on the length of syllables (long or short) rather than on their accent; but all the considerations of 'sound' (such as assonance and alliteration) entered into the aesthetically satisfactory structure of a poem. Similarly, both the French and Japanese were content simply to count the syllables in a line—but again, they also looked to all the 'sound' elements."

Over the past couple of years it has become extremely difficult for me to read contemporary poetry. From the effluvia of Amy Clampitt to the Ouija board epic of James Merrill, the poetry being published in New York is of little use to me, either as edification or as entertainment. Perhaps it is an indication of middle age that I turn again and again to old masterpieces for regeneration. But one wants one's contemporaries to inspire and enlighten, just as a musician wants to play with the best possible musicians. One who writes poetry must also share in the failures, successes, and frustrations of one's contemporaries: their failures are also my own. Too often what is most obviously missing is a sense of the line; what one longs for is sound, real and beautiful and true sound as one finds it in the voice of Billie Holiday or the balladry of John Coltrane, sound which is, in itself, meaning.

"Aestheticians of literature like I. A. Richards, Sir C. M. Bowra, Paul Valéry, Suzanne Langer, and Ernst Cassirer have had an influence beyond the narrow confines of literary scholarship and have played in our time something approaching the role of general philosophers," Rexroth says, and to which I would add the names Michel Foucault, Roland Barthes, and others. In fact, the philosophers of language have contributed a great deal to the current decline of the lyric. Thinking over the past year on poetry and music, thinking almost exclusively about the line, I set aside several recent books of poetry to be read together as a means of re-examining the line.

Jorie Graham's *The End of Beauty* (Ecco, 1987) is only her third book, but presents, I think, a turning point. From here, Graham will turn as an artist either to pure lyric or, and more likely, to a prose line. The best poems in her new book are very lyrical indeed, as in "Description":

> Meet me, meet me whisper the waters from the train window and the
>   small skiff adrift
> with its passenger, oarless, being pulled in by
> some destination, delicate, a blossom on the wing of
> the swollen waters.
>
> Will you take him there to the remedy he needs, intelligence,
> current, will you take him singing his song, back in, note by
> note? She has the
> antidote, the girl at the end, the girl who is the end, she has the only cure
>
> which is her waiting and waiting, which is how she will not move or change
> her mind that is
> no mind. Waste
> and empty
> the sea

The long line for melopoesis, the short line for candor. What one finds at the outset is the meaning of sound in the four long *e*'s opening the first line, followed by "waters" and "windows," by "skiff" and "adrift." This is followed by the *p*'s and *b*'s of lines two and three with its *a* and *o* vowels overcoming the long *e* of "being." But Graham is so heady, so consciously arty, that she moves away from the lyric in this book, she begins to approach a philosopher's way of finding meaning rather than that of a musician. "Pietà" opens with a description that is all but impossible to follow:

> —Then the sunshine striking all sides of his body but only
> in pieces, in bits—the torso torn from the back, from the arm
> that falls back, then three
> fingers ripped up by the light into view,
> then the lifted knee taken up, taken back, then the ankle, the back of
> the head—Like an explosion that will not end
> this dismemberment which is her lifting him up, dismemberment
> of flesh into minutes. Are they notes, these parts, what is the
> song, can you hear it, does it sound beautiful and true to the one
> on the other side who hears it all at

Here, too, we find attention to vowels, repetition; here, too, are assonance and alliteration, and formal pacing—a measure. But the meaning is not clarified by the sounds. At the first few readings, I was utterly befuddled: dismemberment into? Torso torn from the back? Later in the same poem, Graham writes:

> the scene dissolves, do you feel it at last, the sinking, where the meaning
> rises, where the meaning evaporates, into history, into the day the
> mind, and the precipitating syllables are free at last
> on the wind, sinking, the proof of god the cry sinking to where it's
>
> just sound, part of one sound, one endless sound—maybe a cry maybe a
>
> countdown, love—

It is a poem to wrestle with and worry through, a poem beginning in noisy, rough prose approximations of prosody and ending in a measure in which sound and meaning become one.

Stephen Berg, in *With Akhmatova at the Black Gates* (University of Illinois, 1972), and more recently with *In It* (Illini, 1986), has written some of the best lyric verse of the past decade. Berg is not so much a balladeer as an old-fashioned bluesman who is poor, streetwise, and often painfully honest. In "The Voice," Berg recalls a childhood situation which itself prompted, even then, a remembrance of his father:

The Voice

Older girls taunted me into one of those
apartment-house basement window wells;
I crouched in that waist-high hole,
hoping they'd go away. Like a bunch of birds
pecking at crumbs they'd flirt and try to kiss me.
After they'd had their fun I'd talk to myself down there,
my Dad's flat, gravely voice was mine,
a twin, bodiless soul
echoing against moist cement walls.
There are quaint streaks of noise inside my head
that are him talking, sometimes cursing the beautiful
mistake of life, sometimes asking how I am—
memory, I guess, but who knows, maybe

it's really him, yearning because he's lonely,
my grouchy old man asking me to a movie,
how the children are, about money,
"How's the poetry business?"—maybe
it is the rich ash of his bones and flesh
learning to speak again.

The language is slightly flat, reflective, and presented in the manner of commonly spoken idiom. But the poem positively resonates with interior rhyme, slant-rhyme, assonance, and alliteration. Consider the variety of *o* sounds in the first three lines; "waist-high hole" is followed by "hoping they'd go away;" consider how "bunch" and "crumb" are followed by "down" and then "twin." In two lines, Berg has "after" followed by "had, dad, flat, gravely." "Echoing" is followed by "moist" and "noise." The *o* sounds carry the musical thread throughout the poem. Rich in meaning, that meaning is carried deeper through its lyricism despite the apparent plain-speaking style.

"The craft of writing," Rexroth says, "involves more than mere rules of prosody. The work's structure must be manipulated to attract the reader." What appeals to me most about Berg is the manner in which he combines a very tough intelligence with a vulnerable soul, the two aspects finding expression in the unity of his singular music. It is a quality I also find in Sharon Olds's poetry, but about halfway through her new book, *The Gold Cell* (Alfred A. Knopf, 1987), I grew so tired of her brutal father and dismal family life—having agonized through two beautifully written volumes on exactly the same matters—that I nearly didn't get to the best of her latest work.

In the first two books, it was her insistence upon precisely drawn images of terror and grief that drew me into her poems—that and a strong sense of a narrative thread that helped to make her books feel of-a-piece as it were. Now I begin to feel that she needs new themes, I grow weary of her miserable childhood, I long for the leap of imagination, for a lyrical exaltation, for a soft song, a tenderness just in the midst of all this unpleasant sexuality and general degradation. It is almost as though her poems had moved out of their initial lyrical self-awareness into a prosaic self-obsession. Then, just as I am about to close the book, I find beautiful poetry in "The Moment the Two Worlds Meet"—

That's the moment I always think of—when the
slick, whole body comes out of me,
when they pull it out, not pull it but steady it
as it pushes forth, not catch it but keep their
hands under it as it pulses out,
they are the first to touch it,
and it shines, it glistens

and each line breaks perfectly with the slight pause I give in the act of pacing, the eye returning and dropping in its own rhythm, following the movement of consonant and vowel, the breath and the heart-beat measuring in the act of experiencing the poem, in the act of making, albeit imprecisely, the sounds which are in final analysis the composition of the poet.

Rexroth notes the radical change in the methods of poetry over the past ninety years. "The disassociation and recombination of ideas of the Cubists, the free association of ideas of the Surrealists, dreams, trance states, the poetry of preliterate people—all have been absorbed into the practice of modern poetry." Probably more than any poet since mid-century, Robert Bly has been a faddist, a programmatic demagogue for this poetry program or that, from "deep-image" to "leaping poetry," from pseudo-surrealism to neo-formalism. For a while, he traveled around banging on his dulcimer; he wore masks to present dramatic personae; and he has written extensively about sound and poetry. Alas, no ear. But in *Loving a Woman in Two Worlds* (Harper and Row, 1987), he has returned to something beautiful and simple and true: the poetry of image. *Res ipsa loquitur:*

The Turtle

Rain lifts the lake level, washing the reeds.
Slowly the milkweed pods open, the yellow lily pads.
Through the mist man and woman see the far shore.
The turtle's head rises out over the water.

This is in a truer sense the "music of not overly excited speech"—the music Mark Strand once said he aspired to. The "meaning" of this poem is not in its music; the "meaning" is hardly in the words at all. Rather, the words frame a meaning which remains unstated. It is a first-rate imitation classical Chinese love song.

The March Buds

They lie on the bed, hearing music.
The perfumed pillow, the lake, a woman's laughter.
Wind blows faintly, touches the March buds.
The young trees sway back and forth.

Robert Bly is sometimes noisy, preposterous, impolite, and self-inflated. But I am grateful for these poems, especially for this quatrain:

What We Provide

Every breath taken in by the man
who loves, and the woman who loves,
goes to fill the water tank
where the spirit horses drink.

—which is a wonderful demonstration of how a brief lyric can be written in flat language without resonance and still perfectly resonate with meaning. Beautiful.

"Throughout literary history," Rexroth says, "many great critics have pointed out that it is artificial to make a distinction between form and content, except for purposes of analytical discussion." The poet is a midwife; the critic is a coroner. The poet, drawing in the breath of one of the muses, inspires, becomes pregnant with meaning, and makes (in the case of lyric poetry) a song. Only after it is sung can we begin to discern the form of content, by which time the poem itself is silent, but, being delineated, continues to contain its meaning within its measure. In a Formalist approach, form helps to determine content: the sonnet or sestina will not accommodate just any kind of poetry. To one who searches for organic form, content determines lineation of form. Neither is better or worse than the other any more than a hammer is superior to a saw. One wants to be in a position to select from the widest possible array the most appropriate tool for the work.

Louise Glück, whose previous books have combined high intelligence and polished versification with what I came to feel was a stinginess of the soul, has written a remarkable new book, *The Triumph of Achilles* (Ecco, 1985). In the eighth and closing section of a wonderful poem, "Marathon," Glück implies something very profound about a poet's form and content:

Song of Invisible Boundaries

Last night I dreamed we were in Venice;
today, we are in Venice. Now, lying here,
I think there are no boundaries to my dreams,
nothing we don't share.
So there is nothing to describe. We're interchangeable
with anyone, in joy
changed to a mute couple.
Then why did we worship clarity,
to speak, in the end, only each other's names,
to speak, as now, not even whole words,
only vowels?
Finally, this is what we craved,
this lying in the bright light without distinction—
we who would leave behind
exact records.

Vowel sounds reverberate throughout the lines, as do rhymes and off-rhymes. The variable line-lengths establish an irregular measure for the breath, and thus for the heart. But beyond these exhumations of lyric structure there is a speaker who is tender, vulnerable, and compassionate in accepting the inescapable obliteration of the Self. There are almost no images. Because there are no images, the poet must rely on pure sound to convey all meaning.

That attribute of the poem which the reader identifies as music is a combination of rhythm and sound. Our poetry most resembles jazz in structure. And do we not have poets who have written the same poem over and over, changing the lines, changing the words, but each poem somehow the same poem? How many different ways could Coltrane play "Lush Life"?

Charles Mingus went through one period in which he believed he must write down every note for each member of the band, and that such a very formal approach would find the sounds he intended. That approach is as formal as any in Beethoven. During another period, Mingus wrote no music at all, not even charts, but shouted directions as a piece progressed. Listening to Mingus's music now, one can barely decipher a difference in result: the genius of Mingus, like the genius of Pound or H.D. or Rexroth, was to make music with an identifiable sound.

If Marvin Bell has an identifiable sound, I have failed to find it. That's one of the things I like most about his *New and Selected Poems* (Atheneum, 1987). All the evidence points toward a recurrent struggle to find new ways to approach the poem, new ways to permit the poem its own organic development. Although most of Bell's poems could be categorized (like most of our poetry in general) as lyric, his approach to language is closer to that of philosopher. In this he would resemble Graham, except that Bell eschews artiness altogether, preferring to search for ideas. His best poems are his most recent. Theirs is a music of plain speech heightened not by sonority, but by the almost imperceptible accretion of mature vision. And a welcoming of an ever-widening sphere of influence upon his work.

Lyric: from the Greek *lyrikos:* "adapted to be sung to the accompaniment of the lyre." For a couple of thousand years, it has invited the poet to speak in a most intimate manner. It is most often direct and it is, customarily, brief. Hence, it is hardly surprising therefore that in the culture of narcissism it predominates. It can, almost, be taught. But perhaps the traditional brevity and intimacy of lyric poetry is also its greatest shortcoming. Bell says it very well in a recent poem written in that peculiarly American "music of not overly excited speech," in the closing section of a poem called "Ten Thousand Questions Answered":

> Nothing is sadder than a book of poetry.
> Before the book is begun, no sadness.
> After the first poem, before the final poem —
> there is no sadness before a thing is finished.
> But afterwards, one grieves for one's failure.
> The answer is to let the poem be too long to finish.

In a recent *New York Times Book Review* article, Brad Leithauser ponders the absurd notion that light verse may be approaching extinction. André Malraux observed that American literature was being produced by non-intellectuals. In fact, most of our poetry which masquerades as lyric is, in truth, light verse in open form. Does anyone believe Allen Ginsberg is not the author of light verse? And what is "light verse" if not the poetry of commonday experience, the verse of poet-as-everyman including the literary everyman? It is the poetry of social taste. *Vers de société*, with its attention to manners and general appeal.

We neatly cubbyhole our poets by "schools" of versification. We aim a lot of darts at a beast called The Writing Program. But writing programs are useful tools—in a civilized culture every educated adult should be expected to write competent verse—only the granting of degrees in poetry-writing is unbelievably silly. The apprentice poet imitates the master-poet. The master-poet picks friends and students and lovers as winners of myriad poetry-writing contests. We are all, as Robert Duncan happily observes, derivative poets.

Form, Duncan says, is significant in so far as it shows control. "Whenever the feeling of control is lost, the feeling of form is lost. The reality of the world and men's [*sic*] habits must be constricted to a realm—a court or salon or a rationale—excluding whatever is feared. . . . Poets, who once had dreams and epiphanies, now admit only to devices and ornaments." At the close of the same essay, "Ideas of the Meaning of Form," Duncan says, "But I can have no recourse to taste. The work of Denise Levertov or Robert Creeley or Larry Eigner belongs not to my appreciations but to my immediate concerns in living. That I might 'like' or 'dislike' a poem of Zukofsky's or Charles Olson's means nothing where I turn to their work as evidence of the real."

"Evidence of the real" is a quality of versification, not a quantity. The music of our poems, drawn from the poems we study, connects us to the past and thus to the present. In Eliot, we find echoes of French versification, Latin, and European "tastes." In Rexroth, we find perfect translations of classical Japanese poetry within the lines of his own poems. In H.D., we find revitalized classics in Modernist idiom. Pope asks, "Pray tell me, sir, whose dog are you?" Can Merrill's Ouija board epic be considered as anything other than light verse on a grand scale? The rhythm, Pound says, is the test of a poet's sincerity.

Just what sort of dog spends a lifetime howling at the moon? And does it "sing a song" in its monosyllables? The poem—that "manipulation of a structure in time"—offers many, many alternatives to the metronome. Pound's great heave "to break the back of the iamb" was not a rejection of lyric modes, but a visionary effort to inform those very modes. And yet fifteen years of teaching in various writing programs of all kinds has taught me that very very few teachers find "meaning" in words beyond their dictionary definitions; consequently, the apprentice writer is immersed in learning "ways of saying" that lie almost entirely outside the scope of meaning-in-sound. Perhaps our poetry workshop leaders ascribe to the hundred monkey theory which, anthropologists tell us, says that a monkey in a community of monkeys may invent a tool which its neighbors learn to use; somewhere in a community of another hundred monkeys, another monkey will simultaneously invent the same tool. This theory may be related to the one which states that if we only had enough monkeys typing, one of them would write *Paradise Lost*. And yet no one believes the latter. In the years since World War II, we have lost a great deal of our poetic tradition: the narrative poem, the epic poem, the poem, the true lyric poem that is chanted or sung, the invocational poem—all are endangered literary species. Still, we continue to put monkeys before the keyboards in hopes one will invent something of use, in hopes one will eventually sing us a classic.

Pound says in the *ABC of Reading* (New Directions), "A classic is classic not because it conforms to certain structural rules, or fits certain definitions (of which its author had quite probably never heard). It is classic because of a certain eternal and irrepressible freshness." Whitman's lists are as much present for their Psalm-like recycling of the music as for the cataloguing of images. Variations on a musical theme refresh the sound, and by doing so assist the memory.

Even so, like the best of a Mingus or a Coltrane, great lyric poetry always leaves us wanting more. Marvin Bell says "To a Friend Who Has Been to the Dentist":

Two teeth lighter? And more to come out!
Like an old, toothless lion,
soon you will have to munch butterflies with your gums.
Don't despair, my friend. You look better than ever.
There's more room in your mouth now for drink and song,
now that those old canine molars have gone to the boneyard.
Are we ever really happy with all we have?

The Justice of Poetry

Poetry that will last a thousand generations comes only as an unappreciated life is passed.

—Tu Fu

The poetry and career of the T'ang poet Tu Fu (712–759 A.D) were marked by several major events: 1) the An Lu-shan Rebellion in the 750s; 2) poverty so severe that his own young son died of starvation; 3) years of wandering in exile in the north country, writing without an audience (his poems were "forgotten" for nearly three hundred years); and 4) a commitment to and belief in poetry unmatched by any writer of his time. Kenneth Rexroth has called Tu Fu "the greatest non-epic, non-dramatic poet who ever lived."

Certainly exile, poverty, and anonymity are often the earmarks of a poet's life. We remember that Dante was a prominent member of the city council in Florence from 1295 until his own exile in 1301; he served immediately after a time of crisis, the struggle for power between the *magnates*, or wealthy and powerful, and the *popolo,* or working class traders and shopkeepers. As the *Guelphs*, the wealthy merchant-class of Florence, regained power, Dante wrote *Le dolci rime d'amor* denouncing the "long-standing possession of wealth combined with pleasing manners," objecting strongly to the inherent hypocrisy. He also spoke out against the absolute power of the Pope, and, in late 1301, went into exile; in March, 1302, he was sentenced, in absentia, to death. He would never return to Florence. About this time, he wrote his great lyric "*Tre Donne*" ("Three Ladies"), in which he says, referring to those in power, "*ma far mi poterian di pace dono. / Pero nol fan che non san quel che sono.*" ("They could make me a gift of peace. But because they do not understand me, they don't.") And Dante sees the three women, grandmother, mother,

175

and daughter, as the embodiment of three kinds of Justice: divine, human, and written Law. When Dante makes Love acknowledge such a hierarchy, he presents us with a Justice that becomes attainable through its metaphysics, a Love that is no longer divorced from Justice.

Two examples, then, of the consequences of the search for Justice through poetry. I have chosen these two examples, one from the East and one from the West, in order to frame a few remarks regarding the poetry (there is no "career") and achievement of Thomas McGrath, who, in our time, exemplifies both the poet's struggle for Justice through Love, and the importance of commitment and responsibility.

Since any reasonably literate reader ought to have a working knowledge of Dante, I shall draw a number of parallels between McGrath and Tu Fu, concentrating on certain traditional attitudes toward poetry among the classical Chinese poets, and return to Dante later.

In his earliest full-length book (*First Manifesto* was more a chapbook than a full-blown volume of poetry, and *The Dialectics of Love* was but a third of Alan Swallow's *Three Young Poets*), *To Walk a Crooked Mile* (Swallow, 1947), McGrath opens with "The Seekers," a poem written in Pueblo, Colorado, in 1940. Although a decidedly "new world" poem ("Our grandfathers were strangers . . ."), its thrust, especially in the closing stanza, expresses ideas the classical Chinese poet would readily embrace:

> Every direction has its attendant devil,
> And their safaris weren't conducted on the bosses' time,
> For what they were hunting is certainly never tame
> And, for the poor, is usually illegal.
> Maybe with maps made going would be faster,
> But the maps made for tourists in their private cars
> Have no names for brotherhood or justice, and in any case
> We'll have to walk because we're going farther.

The poem was written a year after McGrath's graduation from the University of North Dakota, a year which would, under normal conditions, have been spent enjoying his Rhodes scholarship. But he would not visit Oxford until the end of World War II. This war has been to McGrath as the An Lu-shan Rebellion was to Tu Fu: it signalled not only a world in chaos culminating in the invention of the Atomic Bomb, but simultaneously the end of a three-decade struggle for unionization and social organization for the oppressed, and the birth of the Cold War and all its attendant reactionary realpolitik. The war against Nazism was father and midwife to the Cold War. Every direction had its attendant devil.

And for the poor, for whom Justice has always been illegal, for the poor whose sons are cannon fodder and whose dreams "are never fancy"? Tu Fu said, "I am happiest among the best people I have found anywhere—poor woodcutters and fishermen." Like Tu Fu, McGrath cannot, by virtue of his erudition, be Common Man, but chooses to be among the common people, to serve as advocate and, when necessary, agent provocateur.

"Maybe," McGrath says, "with maps made going would be faster." But there is no map for Justice. The maps are made "for tourists" rather than for those for whom the going itself is everything. We go on foot because "we are going farther," that is, we are going into the realm of ideas, we are entering pure process, the Tao. For McGrath, as for Tu Fu, the means is the end, and the end is a beginning.

It is also useful to note the vast difference in McGrath's use of irony from that of most scholar/poets. McGrath grounds the severe irony of the last line in an idea that is both accessible and useful—it points the way toward a fully conscious awareness of being. It addresses Dante's notion (and Tu Fu's) of metaphysical "justice" found within one's self. "If thee does not turn to the inner light, where will thee turn?" Asked once about the use and appropriateness of irony, Charles Olson declared, "I don't get the 'iron' in it." Then he sat down and wrote, "I have had to learn the simplest things / last. Which made for difficulties." McGrath begins with a very complex simplicity, one which indeed rimes with that of Tu Fu. Rather than searching his intellect for an ironic closure made entirely of artifice, McGrath seeks limpidity which permits the truth of the poem to find its own resonance—a purely organic irony pointing the way toward the unending journey of the spirit.

Several poems later in the same book, there is a poem called "The Tourists." I shall quote only from its repeated refrain:

Get off the highway, Brother, they are the tourists,
Marveling sweetly along.

.   .   .   .

The place they seek, Brother, they cannot remember,
Marveling sweetly along.

. . . .

They cannot stop, Brother. Their hearts are too empty,
Marveling sweetly along.

. . . .

It is himself, Brother, that each one is looking for,
Marveling sweetly along.

. . . .

Be careful, Brother, that you are not one of them,
Marveling sweetly along.

The poet sends a warning about the "dead faces" and "crazy eyes" of the passing populace with its "forlorn" voice. He says they will not stop "for love or for labor, for right or for wrong."

Tu Fu has a poem with a similar warning, albeit quite different circumstances. Visiting the site of the former Ts'ui family estate, he remembers the poet/painter Wang Wei, who accepted a government position only to find the consequences devastating to the family.

At the Thatched Hall of the Ts'ui Family

It is autumn at the grass hut on Jade Peak.
The air is cool and clear.
Temple bells and chimes echo from the canyons.
Fishermen and woodsmen wind over sunset trails.
We fill our plates with chestnuts gathered in the valley
and rice grown in the village.
For what, Wang Wei?
Bamboo and pine, silent, locked behind a gate.

Just as McGrath, addressing his everyman as "brother," with all its confidentiality of diction, warns against infatuation with superficial travel, Tu Fu recalls the Buddhist/Taoist Wang Wei in his home village with its working class nobility and implications represented by temple bells and wind chimes and cool, clear air. There is calm in the village, and great dignity. There is plenty to eat. Still, Wang Wei wanted power. His government position forced him to leave behind the very source, according to Tu Fu, of his humility, of his greatness. For Tu Fu, as for McGrath, the common workaday experience is the true source of spiritual awakening, the source of the very concept of Justice.

Later, in *To Walk a Crooked Mile,* we come across a "Postcard" from Amchitka in the Aleutians where McGrath spent two years during the war. Remembering the midwestern summers and girls, he contrasts those images with the very real images of military movement, the "Nameless figures" which move "over the clamor / The yammer of trucks, in the dark ..." The poem reminds a reader of Chinese of Tu Fu's best-known anti-war poem, "Song of the War Wagons," with its opening image of clanging wagons and crying horses in the dust.

Next in McGrath comes a poem, "Emblems of Exile," which is so sturdy, so compassionate, and so truly felt that Tu Fu might have written it. McGrath opens the first stanza with the image of a hunchback "with a halo of pigeons / Expelled from towers by the bells of noon ..." and, in the second stanza, to "the beggar in the empty street / On whom the hysteria of midnight falls ..." This "prince of loneliness" calls "the hours of conscience" until, in the morning, the "supplicants" bribe him into silence. Calling them "symbols of bereavement," the poet intimates a death much larger than that of a more customary bereavement, and closes his poem with

And if I assume the beggar's or the hunchback's shape
It is that I lack your grace which blessed my heart
Before the war, before the long exile
Which the beggarman mind accepts but cannot reconcile.

The mind of the poor, of the oppressed, accepts the conditions of exile, but the heart is incapable of reconciling either the injustice of the situation or the absurd logic which creates that situation in the first place. The pointed difference between acceptance of a situation and reconciliation with outrageous conditions is one of the most recurrent themes in all of Chinese poetry.

After the Harvest

The rice is cut and clouds glisten in the fields.
Facing Stone Gate, the river is low.
Winds shriek, ripping leaves from shrubs and trees.
At dawn, the pigs and chickens scatter.
Out of the distance, I hear the first sounds of battle.
The woodcutter's song is over. Soon he will leave the village.
Homeless and old, I long for a word from the homeland.
A wanderer, I place my trust in the world.

—Tu Fu

Like Tu Fu, McGrath has spoken often of the (to use Tu Fu's term) "essential goodness" of the poor and the oppressed. Besides the themes I have provided above (and the parallels between the two poets, the shared themes and attitudes, are all but inexhaustible), there are stylistic similarities in abundance. McGrath has written some of the most accomplished formal verses of mid-century, just as Tu Fu revitalized forms during his own time; McGrath and Tu share a common interest in inventing forms and exploring the organic line; each is very much concerned with sound and rhythm and harmony; each writes long poems, short poems, lyrics, polemics, homages, praises, and invective (although Tu Fu wrote very little of the latter). Tu Fu writes praises for flowers, rice, or wine; McGrath writes praises for bread or for beer. McGrath's *Open Songs* and *Letters to Tomasito* are perfect counterparts to Tu Fu's short Taoist poems (or, for that matter, to the haiku's predecessor, the tanka in Japanese). And McGrath writes new lyrics to an old song (as he did for Cisco Houston to the tune "Matty Grove") just as the *tz'u* poets of the T'ang and Sung wrote new lyrics for their old tunes.

Nearly all poets attempt, at one time or another, to write an ars poetica. Most often, the result is self-inflation and/or leaden seriousness. But both McGrath and Tu Fu find enormous good humor in the situation of the poet. McGrath begins his "You Can Start the Poetry Now, Or: News from Crazy Horse" with a drunken poet on stage, probably in some tavern, mumbling into a microphone "—I guess all I'm trying to say is I saw Crazy Horse die for a split level swimming pool in a tree-house owned by a Pawnee-Warner Brothers psychiatrist about three hundred feet above—" when someone in the audience, not knowing whether this unrhymed diatribe is the poem or the introduction to a poem, calls out, first softly, "You can start the poetry now." But the poet continues to mumble along, and the demand to "start the poetry now" grows louder and louder. It is a beautifully funny assessment of a bad poetry reading, and it teaches the young poet a great deal without harangues or insults to poetry itself; it also says a lot about those who have never learned how to listen to a public reading.

And another well-known poem is McGrath's "Ars Poetica: Or: Who Lives in the Ivory Tower?" with its references to roundelays and sestinas, Hedy Lamarr, Gable, Louella Parsons, and the "to hell with the Bard of Avalon and to hell with Eliot Auden." And of course, the poem's famous closing line: "Your feet are muddy, you son-of-a-bitch, get out of our ivory tower."

Tu Fu approaches the poem about writing from another equally humorous and practical angle, by addressing the necessary arguments of like-minded poets in his "To Li Po on a Spring Day" —

> There's no one quite like you, Li Po,
> you live in my imagination.
> You sing as sweet as Yui,
> and still retain Pao's nobility.
> Under spring skies north of Wei,
> you wander into the sunset
> toward the village of Chiang-tung.
> Tell me, will we ever again
> buy another keg of wine
> and argue over prosody and rhyme?

Tu is less ironic in his references to past masters, preferring to hold them up as standards which he finds Li Po has met. But the spirit of the poem finds a counterpart in McGrath's drunken mumbler who, no doubt, is as earnest as any poet. And while Tu makes clear that what he really misses is the drinking and arguing—traditional camaraderie among poets of all tongues—he manages to draw a smile from the reader while simultaneously revivifying the need for a dialectic. Tu's homage to Li Po might also recall McGrath's wonderful satire, "Driving Towards Boston I Run Across One of Robert Bly's Old Poems." McGrath, like Tu Fu, joins criticism to humor, caustic argument with good cheer.

But neither is a poet whom Plato would admit into the Republic. Plato has Socrates tell Glaucon, "We must remain firm in our conviction that hymns to the gods and praises of famous men are the only poetry which ought to be admitted into our State. For if you go beyond this and allow the honeyed muse to enter, either in epic or lyric verse, not law and the reason of mankind, which by common consent have ever been deemed best, but pleasure and pain will become the rulers in our State. . . ." Socrates goes on to warn Glaucon about the "mob of sages circumventing Zeus," and the "subtle thinkers" who quarrel with philosophy and who are, after all, "mere beggars" in the State. Plato, embarrassed by the emotional truth of the poet who is "drawling out his sorrows in long oration, or weeping, or smiting his breast," admits only the singer of praises for famous men and gods, in short, the platitudinizers of the powerful, into his State. And Plato speaks for every State.

For Tu Fu, the result was a decade and more of wandering through Shensi, Kansu, and Szechuan—the Chinese equivalent of the Badlands—a beggar in a feudal time. He had criticized the ruling class. He had been an advocate, a voice of compassion, a deeply religious poet with no formal religion. He fought a daily war with bitterness, only to write some of the most humane poetry in all history.

Five-hundred-odd years later, Dante, writing in exile, would proclaim, "Let the eyes that weep and the mouths that wail be those of mankind whom it concerns." And still later, in the *Convivio,* states, "I have gone through nearly all the regions to which the tongue [Italian] reaches, a wanderer, a beggar showing against my will the wounds which fortune makes, and which are often unjustly held against the one who bears those wounds. . . . I have appeared to the eyes of many who had perhaps imagined me, through fame, to be otherwise." And, in exile, Dante wrote that masterpiece of precision, thirty-three cantos each, of Hell, Purgatory, and Paradise. In Dante, Love and Justice become inseparable. We remember, if only by reputation, that Dante survived his Hell and entered Paradise; but we should not forget that Paradise lasts but a day, and Hell is at least seven times longer.

And six-hundred-odd years after that, Thomas McGrath finds himself on the West Coast, in the mid-century, where "things are happening," and the Army–McCarthy hearings have ended, his old friends can't get themselves into print, Dalton Trumbo and others are growing famous on the Blacklist, and Eisenhower is giving speeches warning about the "Military-Industrial Complex," and some Black folk down South are talking civil rights. He sits down one day and writes:

—"From here it is necessary to ship all bodies east."

It is a line he had carried around for years without finding a way to begin what he hoped would be a poem long enough to invest several years in writing. This time, he wrote it down. And then he wrote

> I am in Los Angeles, at 2714 March Street,
> Writing, rolling east with the earth, drifting toward Scorpio,
> > > thinking,
> Hoping toward laughter and indifference.

The rest we know, or ought to know, in the name of poetry and justice. McGrath invests a quarter-century in his poem. He writes his Christmas poem all during the war in Viet Nam. He writes it while the Freedom Riders ride. He writes on through the funerals of the Kennedys and King. He writes while Nixon tells us lies.

And he continues to write little songs, formalist verses, neo-Nerudean polemics, drinking songs, Taoist poems, elegies, and praises—many of his best poems. And because, to quote William Irwin Thompson, "One instinctively suspects people who meet in drawing rooms to praise the peasant over tea and cakes," McGrath returns to the "cold, black North" where he was born, writing in a kind of self-imposed exile, in compassionate, passionate "laughter and indifference."

Poetry and exile—how very often they combine. One remembers Neruda in the Orient, innumerable Chinese sages, the Modernists, the Romantics, Tu Fu, Dante, and McGrath; one recalls Rilke's homelessness, Rexroth's self-exile in Santa Barbara and his teaching for what amounted almost to Teaching Assistant-ship wages at "Surf Board Tech" (University of California, Santa Barbara), the exile of Ritsos and Seferis, and the murder of Garcia Lorca when he refused to leave Spain. One becomes resigned to the circumstances without accepting the injustice; the struggle with the self is greater than the struggle with the State. No poet wants to inhabit Plato's Republic; but neither does one wish for the life of exile and/or poverty. To write is to speak. To speak implies the necessity of audience.

Several years ago, McGrath was questioned by a student about "the writing program" at Moorehead—what would be expected, and what a graduate of the program might look forward to. "The first thing I tell my students," McGrath replied, "is that most of my former students drive right down the road and get a job in the beet-packing plant." His remark says as much about what a poet's responsibilities are as it does about the general situation of poetry in our country. Such is the justice of poetry — for McGrath, for Dante, for Tu Fu . . .

It might have been different. I doubt McGrath ever courted the New York publishing scene. It certainly never courted him. But if it were otherwise, it wouldn't be McGrath. As with Tu Fu, his end lies in his means. The truth of the poem is in the voice, not printed on the paper a "publisher" buys and sells. Poetry contains silence, but is not silent. Nor is Justice. Nor, often, love.

Praise for the achievement of Thomas McGrath is long overdue. And it is only now beginning. But, lest we run headstrong through these parallels with Dante and with Tu Fu, let me close by quoting a quatrain from Senzaki, one which would, I'm sure, please Tu Fu and Dante both, one which serves as epigraph to one of the greatest long poems of our century:

> In the moonlight,
> The shadow of the bamboo
> Is sweeping the great stairs;
> But the dust is not stirred.

Contrary to the beliefs of traditionalists and free versifiers alike, the lyric is the most difficult poetry to write. Any flaw in the rhythm or tone, any false note or forced emotion results in an audible warp — hearing the false note, the listener loses a few words, captivated not by the poem itself, but by the flaw.

McGrath writes some of the finest cadenced poetry of the twentieth century. At his best, he is metrically irregular, the lines lifting and falling with vowel and consonant reverberating through the rhythms of a carefully speaking voice. He also composes in a quantitative line, writes parodies, variations of haiku, and perfect little Imagist poems. Now Orphic, now extremely personal, there is almost no subject unsuitable for a McGrath poem. His virtuosity is staggering. Some of the poems are, as Kenneth Rexroth said of Lawrence's, nobly disheveled; some are semiprecious stones; a few are jewels.

Throughout these poems, everywhere evident, is Thomas McGrath's great good humor, an astonished observer awed by beauty and sadness and *joie de vivre* — camaraderie found only in the hope for justice and in his fierce commitment to compassion and common good.

Here and Now

In the spring of 1989, we will note the three hundredth anniversary of Matsuo Bashō's nine-month, 1500 mile walking tour of northern and western Japan. The journal of that journey, the *Oku no hosomichi,* or *Back Roads to Far Towns* in Cid Corman's translation (Grossman, 1968), is one of the most distinguished and enduring books of these past three centuries, and the most endearing of Bashō's diaries.

Bashō was a wanderer. His curiosity was at once modest and boundless, his ability to present the universal in a single detail unparalleled. He visited villages and mountain temples and walked the isolated trails with his protégé Sora, noting the plants and birds and weather patterns, and observing rites. He was a wanderer who roamed a Japan that never really existed, a Japan that is born today, even in translation, as it was there born in the beautiful slow dance of his brush three hundred years ago: a spirit world that is the opposite of the material world we live in.

But it is January, 1986. And this is North America. And the only thing that has exceeded the growth of human suffering which accompanies the overpopulation of the earth is our insane obsession with multiplying our capacity to deliver death. I live just forty minutes by car from one of the most hideous products of mankind—the Trident nuclear submarine base at Bangor.

When I'm troubled, I like to take a short walk out a dirt road from my house, winding down through an old clear-cut and out to a point on a bluff which looks out over the Strait of Juan de Fuca. I first walked that road twelve years ago. The clear-cut then was mostly dirt clods and Cat-tracks, a few scarred remnants of salal, here and there a blackberry vine or a few mangled spines of fern. It's dense now with life. The alders form a natural canopy. Everything is green.

I watch the fishing boats and shipping lanes. Sometimes I see a submarine and know it is all that is evil in men. At the point where I sit on
my stump, there is a tall black lightning-struck ruin of a tree where an
eagle nests every summer. Benjamin Franklin thought the eagle a ridiculous
symbol for a nation. He much preferred the wild turkey. Now both approach extinction.

A thousand years before Bashō's last attack of wanderlust, a middle-
aged Chinese gentleman named Tu Fu began a journey of several years'
exile from the city, living in abject poverty in thatched huts in the mountains. While the An Lu-shan Rebellion raged, he wrote some of the most
humane poetry in the world. And the spirit of his enormous humanity lies
in his ability to permit a place to speak through him, always with a long
note of compassion:

Moon, Rain, Riverbank

Rain roared through, and now the autumn night is clear.
The water wears a patina of gold
and carries a bright jade star.
Heavenly River runs clear and pure, as gently as before.
Sunset buries the mountains in shadow.
A mirror floats in the deep green void,
its light reflecting the cold, wet dusk,
dew glistening, freezing on the flowers.

The "place" of the poem is unimportant. It doesn't exist as a reference. The
poem is its own place in the same way a poem is its own occasion. This
could be any river in any green mountain range in any rainy season in
the world. Its particularities arise out of the increasingly focused attention to details, moving, line-by-line, to a sharper attention to smaller detail
until, in the last line, the "truth of the experience" is realized. And suddenly
we understand that what we are seeing we are seeing only in mirror-image.
That the material world we live in is no more or less real than that same
world turned upside down in a mirror of water. That being "awake" is a
dream.

Was that Chuang Tzu lifting his chalk-white wings from a blossoming
scrotchbroom that afternoon in August? Can a butterfly become a man
in its dreams?

Perched on my favorite stump, I look out at Protection Island, and beyond—the huge empty ocean and blank sky. I listen to the gulls and ravens all year, to summer birds and winter birds, to nighthawks and early morning finches, to birds that mourn, and to birds that celebrate. And I think about how a few small drops of dew freezing on a few dying blossoms over a thousand years ago still speak.

I made a conscious choice to live in the shadow economy of my nation— in a specific location, in a particular fashion. As a poet, I am interested only in poetry that is aware of the need to radically alter the policies and priorities of those who rule. I am not interested in the poetry of wit or in pseudo-nature poetry that insists upon personification. It is disheartening to observe on a daily basis the degradation of a singularly materialistic culture. It is sad to know that so many lives pass silently by without having ever glimpsed another world.

But to participate in the continuity of humanity is to remain bound not only to a sense of "place" (whether as a wanderer or as a resident), but to the "other world" as well. Tu Fu is greater than Ronald Reagan because he finds justice—the "other" justice—in freezing dew. He finds it in every-day detail, in natural convergence and daily and seasonal cycles. The "poetic" justice of Tu can save us from ourselves. The "justice" of Ronald Reagan may well kill us all, but it can never *save* a single one of us.

.

Bashō, happy to be wandering again, came to a temple at Pine Mountain Point, and wrote, "Everywhere between pines graves, bringing home the fact that even vows of 'wing and wing, branch and branch, forever merging' must also come to such, sadness increasing, and at Shiogama Beach a bell sounded evening."

There is nothing to save.

Here, alone on my stump taking notes in the falling mist of the new year, I look far into the west, remembering far east. Bashō concluded his journey at Kyoto; in many ways, mine began there.

Hours of sitting, aching back, trying to get my spine straight. Sometimes I thought my knees would break. I struggled with my first few words of Japanese, drank tea, and ate white rice. It was all a dream, but it was beautiful in its time.

Here, a few miles from Port Townsend Bay, I built a house of cedar and fir. The years between were ten years of wandering: from school to school, mountain range to range, river to river. The journals from those years I burned—no use to anyone (except their negative capability), even me. But without those years of wandering, who would I be? What I wrote was not good writing. For all my years of struggle to gain facility with language, all my thinking was unclear.

It seems, looking back over twenty years, like someone else's life, like a long foreign film I somehow got swept up in.

The Zen hermit monk Ryōkan (1758–1831), late in his sixties, met and fell in love with a nun less than half his own age.

> I wondered and wondered
> just when she would come.
> Now we are together.
> What need have I for thinking?

I suppose Ryōkan's love poem expresses most of what I feel about this life in this place. With enormous uncertainty, and through all the trials and tribulations imposed by poverty and frustration, I built a small house, most of it alone, but with the generous help of friends as well. I knew somehow that the *doing* of it mattered. I thought about how good it would be never to have to face a landlord or a monthly interest payment, and about how that economic freedom would translate into hours of studytime.

The average U.S. citizen of the male persuasion spends about 5000 minutes per year looking at his own face in the mirror while scraping hair from his face. I spend about 7000 minutes per year sitting and breathing and leaving things alone. As a nation, we spend almost twice as much money per year on women's hairdos as on medical research.

Building the house, buying it board by board, spending weeks in motels while visiting public schools and prisons to pay for those boards, I thought about very practical matters such as shaving or getting a hairdo, and what those things mean at their most basic level. It is one thing to value a hairdo over medical research. It is quite another not to be aware of having made that choice.

There is almost no astonishment in Ryōkan's poem. An old man, he comes to a love he believed in all along, indeed a love he long anticipated. And, having found it at last, finds perfect ease. Although he "wondered and wondered" when or whether he would find it, he did not seek it. He must have wanted it, but he did not wish to be ruled by desire.

And now they are together. He does not wish to possess her, nor to be himself possessed by her. He was himself, Ryōkan. She was Teishin. They were together for a time and it was good.

The land I paid for, the lumber I bought and nailed . . . this land is not mine. This house my partner suffered and sacrificed to see through to completion . . . while it is "our house" and in the legal sense our land, it is ridiculous to say "I own this land." What passes for love is often pathetic, our claims for things most often enervating and degrading. Another Zen poet, Ikkyū (1394–1481), put it this way:

What is it in the heart?
The sound of a pine breeze
there in the painting.

And Dōgen spoke of "enlightenment in the voice of bamboo, heart-radiance in the peach blossom." The Chinese painter Chin Nung said that if one paints the branch well, one hears the sound of the wind.

It is easy to be good; it is impossible to love the devil. We know what is right, but we are not often brave enough to ask ourselves that question, not, at least, at its most basic and meaningful level. The one who listens to a wind in the trees hears a thunderous silence between breezes. There is no truth in words. But when words are used with care, truth may be glimpsed through their framing. Just as the Japanese term *mono no aware* refers to the poignant temporality in the beauty of things. The words are only a pointer. To one who has turned away from death, to one who refuses to see death (as to see life also) in the face (or spirit) of things, the words are almost useless. To the modern Japanese writer Ryunosuke Akutagawa (1892–1927) as he contemplated suicide, it meant that nature would appear to him "more beautiful than it has ever been before."

No potential suicide, I am nonetheless astonished each day to find another day. I work each day at perfecting a kind of heretical Zen discipline. All Zen discipline is heretical. I do not ask myself what certain Zenbos would say about my practice. "If you meet the Bodhidharma, kill him!" Confucius says it this way in *Chuang Tzu,* translated by Burton Watson (Columbia University, 1968): "Not to know, not to be able to do—from these things mankind can never escape. And yet there are those who struggle to escape from the inescapable—can you help but pity them? Perfect speech is the abandonment of speech; perfect action is the abandonment of action. To be limited to understanding only what is understood— this is shallow indeed!"

.

Lightning!
From the darkness, passing,
the night heron's cry

Bashō wrote this poem perhaps a month before his death. I cannot remember this poem without thinking of the great blue herons that used to nest in Kah Tai Lagoon where we now have a Safeway "superstore" that gives us "everything we want and a little bit more."

Bashō's words are not as simple as they at first appear. Robert Aitken, in his excellent study of Bashō (*A Zen Wave*, Weatherhill, 1978), points out how Bashō used a Chinese character (*goi*) in naming the night heron rather than the more common Japanese phonetic, *kana*. By making use of the Chinese character, Bashō draws an allusion to the five degrees of interfusion of the universal with the particular. Bashō's apparent simplicity is, upon closer inspection, an expression of deepest experience.

How noble—
The one who is not enlightened
At a flash of lightning!

Another way to understand this poem is to see it through the following observation of Confucius (again via Burton Watson's *Chuang Tzu*): "When you're betting for tiles in an archery contest, you shoot with skill. When you're betting for fancy belt buckles, you worry about your aim. And when you're betting for real gold, you're a nervous wreck. Your skill is the same in all three cases—but because one prize means more to you than another, you let outside considerations weigh on your mind. He who looks too hard at the outside gets clumsy on the inside."

The one waiting for the lightning flash may never hear the thunder in the silence.

Another old Zenbo I've lived with for many years is the Rinzai monk Hakuin. A contemporary of Thomas Jefferson, he used to go to the Soto meditation halls and poke the other monks as they sat in zazen. "Get up!" he would tell them, "and go do something useful! The work is part of the kōan."

For me, the work has most often *been* the kōan. I interrupt that work at times to go out into America and poke a few sleepers to see whether they (or I) can be awakened. It would be easy to spend a life in cloisters. It would be easy to practice inaction, especially here where the trees meet the sea and the winds and clouds all sing. But, to quote Ryōkan once again, "When I consider the sadness of the world's people, / Their sadness is mine."

The best response I can make to the arrogant, banal evil of the Trident nuclear submarine base lies in the simple gesture of nailing one board to another, then adding another, and then another. The hours pile up, the sun and moon slide by, the days grow into weeks and then the weeks into months, and I am still amazed to find that we remain, against all odds, alive.

Looking east, I see the sun high over the Cascade Range. Beyond the mountains, the huge noisy sprawl of the United States. In the past decade, thirty thousand women have died in the U.S.A. at the hands of their "lovers." We will not build them a monument of the sort we built to honor the fifty thousand men we sent to die in Viet Nam. We do not "value" their deaths as we define, as a nation, that which is heroic. We say we are an honorable nation where human life is respected. We say everyone gets a vote. We place our faith in a Great American Dream in which we can truly believe. And then we construct an Auschwitz, a Treblinka, a final solution. And if even the mention of an Auschwitz sounds like hyperbole, one must remember that we shall send our Auschwitz out over the world where it will kill not only soldiers, not only Jews or Blacks or Latinos or less-than-human things like Communists, but where it will incinerate every living thing.

We have written our history in blood. And unless we understand how that came to be, we shall write our future in human suffering as well. The government of the United States of America broke *each* of the first 389 treaties it signed with Native American nations. Is this land where I sit making notes for an essay not their land? And will it not become the land of future generations if we manage, somehow, not to bring on armageddon? Don't we belong to the land?

We cannot lie about the land the way we lie and pretend to ethics. Land is neither good nor bad, but is land. In the course of a decent life, the land yields sustenance, a livelihood, and feeds also the spirit by yielding a sense of place, of order, and layers of mythology—a personal mythology, a family mythology, then that of community, etc.—which keep us in touch with ourselves, with one another, and with the continuities of history.

The Navajo have a custom whereby one gives away something of one's own to another with whom one has just become friends. The gift is accompanied by a semi-public declaration of friendship. The first time I witnessed it, I was slightly uncomfortable throughout. I was relieved I wasn't the recipient. Over many years, it kept creeping back into my mind—I was a boy watching a man take off his bracelet and give it to another man and speak a kind of vow. When I was small I wondered whether it was like getting married. It wasn't until many years later that I realized that what embarrassed me so was the fact that I didn't have any real friend.

Making a peaceful world begins in making peace with one's self. Since the self is not detached from one's environment, one must make peace with the environment as well. *Husbandry* and *wyfdom* speak of land and sea, of proper care and the self's sense of proportion, of silence and of "making waves." The etymology speaks of keeping boundaries. Love that is founded on the notion of possessiveness and exclusivity is not love. The poem which objectifies one's lover is not a love poem. We cannot evade responsibility for the deaths we permit each day by pretending the victims are other than ordinary people who are most often born hungry and suffer all their lives and die. We cannot "save life" by serving as merchants of death any more than we can contribute to love by objectifying our lovers.

.

If there is a hope for our culture, if we are to avoid self-annihilation, that hope lies in self-discipline, in cultivation, and in rejuvenation. To make the world young again (re-juvenation), it must become more feminized, for the most "feminine" attributes are those we most desperately need: fluidity and interior abundance and communion, all in direct opposition to masculine rigidity and possessiveness and violence. And if honor and dignity and responsibility do not begin in the self, in the home, in the community, where will they begin?

One searches for a balance between the receptive and the responsive. These attributes apply to everything from the use of language to loveplay, from right work to proper inactivity, from economics to philosophy.

Because I was among the last of the generations born before The Bomb, I am among the last to have enjoyed a childhood that entertained a belief in "the future." But public education soon brought me (and all subsequent generations) face-to-face with the realities of a world in which "technological achievements" lead directly into final and irrefutable disaster, and in which even the vehicle of "higher learning" itself, the university, has, to paraphrase Sen. William Fulbright, betrayed a sacred public trust by becoming dependent on government-subsidized research and thereby becoming no more than employment agencies for the technocracy of death.

One must therefore, if one is to live life without killing, live in the shadow economies of industrialized nations, avoiding even traditional "Marxist" tactics as defined in the 1960s by the New Left, since that same New Left makes every use of violence (in fact mirrors the violence) of the Old Right. It is perfectly common to see those who protest American-supported atrocities in Central America address their legitimate grievances with the same violent rhetoric one hears issued from the White House. Hannah Arendt divides the world into those who hear the time-bomb ticking and those who do not. The "one of letters" who both supports and is dependent on the acadamies (and this includes myself), which are themselves dependent upon the business of violence, may make no legitimate claim to living a life of non-violence.

Where I live is irretrievably bound up in how I live; and the "where" and "how" of a life define the life itself. When Marx borrowed Hegel's notion of the seed of rebirth (revolution) being found in every society just as it is found in every living organism, he was exercising an optimism that is not often available to those born into a Nuclear Age. And yet the seed remains, just as surely as the final solution remains, forty minutes down the road, ticking, ticking . . .

•

While we enjoy the creature comforts made possible by the suffering of those who came before us, we also inhabit the hells they created. The "one of letters" should be aware that a mid-sized paper mill fouls as much potable water in a single day as does the entire population of France, and that it costs us more to dispose of the four billion tons of waste we create each year than we spend on schools and hospitals combined. We have delivered 300,000 tons of non-biodegradable DDT into the world's water-table, enough to destroy the plankton (our primary source of oxygen for the entire planet) in 100,000-million cubic meters of water *forever*.

The Buddhist precept of "right livelihood" means "not killing." Nearly four hundred million automobiles pour lead into the air each day, and each automobile "consumes" as much oxygen as thirty humans. It costs about the same to construct a six-lane freeway as it would to provide an electric train for the same route, and the train will deliver thirty times the number of passengers with only a fraction of the waste and pollution and only a fraction of the number of accidental deaths. But we have chosen our privacy over the quality of life for future generations. Partly, presumably, because we have little faith that there will *be* future generations.

We must come to the startling realization that a nation is nothing but an enormous commercial enterprise poisoned by patriotism, as Jerôme Deshusses made clear in his astonishing study *The Eighth Night of Creation* (Dial, 1982), and that a purely materialistic economics rooted in the idea of a "balance of trade" means that each country, in order to prosper, must export more than it imports, and that "the prosperity of one half of the world depends directly on the deficit [and suffering] of the other half. . . ."

But it is impossible to live without producing waste. It is impossible to live without "technology." Right livelihood, right thinking, and right action are therefore founded in questioning the most basic assumptions about life in a technocratic state. Pseudo-science is not a suitable substitute for religion any more than the accumulation of "goods" is a substitute for being conscious.

Driving past the Hanford Nuclear Site, driving through the "Red Zone," driving down Hood Canal past the Trident nuclear submarine base as I head for my prison writing classes, I cannot help but think that our proclivity for technologizing and institutionalizing violence is nothing more than a feeble attempt to remove the human element from our incessant struggle to satisfy an obsessive and insatiable greed. And all the while, we continue to stockpile death, lying ourselves into believing we are other than the merchants of death, and that we build these weapons as a "deterrent" to war, knowing full well that humanity has made use of *every* weapon ever invented, no matter how unspeakably terrible the consequences.

And later, having returned past the same evil reminders, I walk out through the woods into the clear-cut, and I note each month's developments, how the whole process of reforestation relieves the wounds and scars we give the world. And I believe that it is not too late. It *is* late. But it may not be too late to begin a new life, one with its roots in human dignity, one with its roots in compassionate action and compassionate economics. And I remember the face of my friend who leads the struggle locally against domestic violence, how she looked at me and asked, "How can you spend so much time with those batterers, those sick, violent men?" And I remember particular faces from my prison writing classes, how certain of these men pay and pay with the memory of their cruelties, and how they begin to learn that cruelty is only a sick man's reaction to fear. And if I who have lived by violence cannot love them and remain unafraid, who will show them that fear is nothing and that our most precious commodity is hope, and that without hope there can be no love in the world?

I do not hope to change the world. I do not hope to save us from ourselves. I do not even dare to hope that my poems will be of any use to other generations. Poetry does not exist in materialistic culture because poetry is a commerce of the spirit.

During my journey through this world, I hope to live a fruitful life, a life of non-violence, a life of charity. I want to know that I have made choices, and I want those choices to be realistic. When I think of Bashō's travels three years from now (if we have a life three years from now), I will remember that he inhabited the real world, and that he, too, felt that sense of *mono no aware*, and set out on his journey with compassion in his heart. In three years I will be forty-six years old and turning forty-seven, the same age as Matsuo Bashō when he began his last, greatest journey. And I will hope against odds that my own greatest journey will still remain ahead. And if there is to be a journey for the soul, and if the journey of a thousand miles indeed begins with a single step, I begin mine here. Now.

Bashō's Ghost

The moon and sun are travelers through eternity. Even the years wander on. Whether drifting through life on a boat or climbing toward old age leading a horse, each day is a journey, and the journey itself is home.

—Bashō, *Oku no hosomichi*

Bashō rose long before dawn, but even at such an early hour, he knew the day would grow rosy bright. It was spring, 1689. In Ueno and Yanaka, cherry trees were in full blossom, and hundreds of families would soon be strolling under their branches, lovers walking and speaking softly or not at all. But it wasn't cherry blossoms that occupied his mind. He had long dreamed of crossing the Shirakawa Barrier into the heart of northern Honshu, the country called Oku lying immediately to the north of the city of Sendai. He had patched his old cotton trousers and repaired his straw hat. He placed his old thatched-roof hut in another's care and moved several hundred feet down the road to the home of his disciple-patron, Mr. Sampu, making final preparations before embarkation.

On the morning of May 16, dawn rose through a shimmering mist, Fujiyama faintly visible on the horizon. It was the beginning of the Genroku period, a time of relative peace under the Tokugawa shogunate. But travel is always dangerous. A devotee as well as a traveling companion, Bashō's friend, Sora, would shave his head and don the robes of a Zen monk, a tactic which often proved helpful at well-guarded checkpoints. Bashō had done so himself on previous journeys. Because of poor health, Bashō carried extra nightwear in his pack along with his cotton robe or *yukata*, a raincoat, calligraphy supplies, and of course *hanamuke*, departure gifts from well-wishers, gifts he found impossible to leave behind.

Bashō himself would leave behind a number of gifts upon his death some five years later, among them a journal composed after this journey, his health again in decline, a journal made up in part of fiction or fancy. But during the spring and summer of 1689, he walked and watched. And from early 1690 into 1694, Bashō wrote and revised his "travel diary," which is not a diary at all. *Oku* means "within" and "farthest" or "dead-end" place; *hosomichi* means "path" or "narrow road." The *no* indicates a possessive. *Oku no hosomichi:* the narrow road within; the narrow way through the interior. Bashō draws *Oku* from the place of that name located between Miyagino and Matsushima, but it is a name which inspires plurisignation.

The *Oku no hosomichi* is not simply a travel journal. Its form, *haibun,* combines short prose passages with *haiku.* But the heart and soul of this little book, its *kokoro,* cannot be found simply by defining form. Bashō completely redefined haiku, he transformed haibun. But these accomplishments grew out of arduous studies in poetry, Buddhism, history, Taoism, Confucianism, Shintoism, and some very important Zen training.

Bashō was a student of Saigyō, a Buddhist monk/poet who lived five hundred years earlier (1118–1190); Saigyō is the most prominent poet of the imperial anthology *Shin-kokinshu.* Like Saigyō before him, Bashō believed in co-dependent origination, a Buddhist idea holding that all things are fully inter-dependent, even at point of origin; that no thing is or can be completely self-originating. Bashō said of Saigyō, "He was obedient to and at one with nature and the four seasons." The *Samanta-bhadra-bodhisattva-sutra* says, "Of one thing it is said, 'This is good,' and of another it is said, 'This is bad,' but there is nothing inherent in either to make them 'good' or 'bad.' The 'self' is empty of independent existence."

Bashō, dreaming of the full moon as it rises over boats at Shiogama Beach, is not looking outside himself; rather he is seeking that which is most clearly meaningful within, and locating the "meaning" within the context of juxtaposed images, images which are interpenetrating and inter-dependent. The images arise naturally out of the *kokoro* or *shin*—the heart/soul/mind.

Two hundred years before Bashō, Komparu Zenchiku wrote, "The Wheel of Emptiness is the highest level of art of the Noh—the performance is *mushin.*" The art of artlessness, the act of composition achieved without "sensibility" or style—this directness of emotion expressed without ornament set the standards of the day.

At the time of the compiling of the *Man'yoshu,* the first imperial anthology, compiled in the late eighth century, the Japanese critical vocabulary emphasized two aspects of the poem: *kokoro,* which included sincerity, conviction, or "heart"; and "craft" in a most particular way. The *Man'yoshu* poets were admired for their "masculinity," that is, for uncluttered, direct, and often severe expression of emotion. Their sincerity (*makoto*) was a quality to be revered. The poets of the *Man'yoshu* are the foundation upon which all Japanese poetry has been built.

One of the first *karon,* or literary criticism, in Japanese is that of Fujiwara Hamanari (733–799), author of *Kakyo-hyoshiki,* an essay listing seven "diseases of poetry," such as having the first and second lines end on the same syllable, or having the last syllable of the third and last lines differ. There were various dissertations on "poem-diseases," all largely modeled on the original Chinese of Shen Yo (441–513). The idea of studying craft in poetry must have caught on quickly because by 885 the first *uta-awase,* or poetry-writing contests, were being held.

At the time of the compilation of the *Man'yoshu,* very little poetry was being written in Chinese; Hitomaro and Yakamochi, the great eighth-century poets of the *Man'yoshu,* wrote without many allusions to Confucian and Buddhist classics, their poems drawing inspiration from the landscape and experience which is uniquely Japanese. Another court anthology contemporary with the *Man'yoshu,* the *Kaifuso,* represents the introduction of poetry written in Chinese, despite a few samples in the *Man'yoshu.* Through the influence of the monk Kukai, also called Kobo Daishi (774–835), the study of Chinese became the norm for what amounted to a Buddhist aristocracy. As founder of the Shingon, or "True Word," sect in Japan, Kukai followed a tradition of secret oral teachings passed on from Master to Disciple, and had himself spent two years studying in China under Hui Kuo (764–805). The later influence of Sugawara no Michizane established Chinese as the language of scholarly poets, so much so that upon his death, Michizane was enshrined as a god of literature and calligraphy. His followers found Japanese forms too restrictive for their multilayered poetry. Every good poet was a teacher of poetry in one way or another, many taking on disciples. Michizane's influence was profound. He advocated both rigorous scholarship and genuine sincerity in composition, his own verses substantially influenced by the T'ang poet Po Chu-i. The form was *shih,* lyric verse composed in five- or seven-character lines written in Chinese, but unlike the poems of most earlier Japanese poets, Michizane's poems were deceptively simple, and like the poetry of Po Chu-i, strengthened by a combination of poignancy and conviction. Poetry written in Chinese was called *kanshi,* and Michizane established it as a major force.

In his *kana* (phonetic alphabet) preface to the *Kokinshu* in the tenth century, Ki no Tsurayuki, author of the famous *Tosa Diary,* lists "six types" (*rikugi*) of poetry:

1. *soe-uta:* suggestive or indirect expression of feeling
2. *kazoe-uta:* clear, direct expression of feeling
3. *nazurae-uta:* parabolic expression
4. *tatoe-uta:* expression which conceals powerful emotion
5. *tadagoto-uta:* refinement of a traditional expression
6. *iwai-uta:* poem expressing congratulations or praise

Tsurayuki's list owes something to Lu Chi's "catalogue of genres" in his third-century Chinese *Art of Writing* (*Wen Fu*), which is itself indebted to various treatises on the classic Confucian poetry anthology, *Shih Ching,* or *Classic of Poetry.* Much of the penchant for cataloguing and classifying types of poetry is the result of the Confucian classic, *Ta Hsueh,* or *Great Learning,* in which Master Kung-fu Tze says "All wisdom is rooted in learning to call things by the right name," and that when "things are properly identified, they fall into natural categories, and understanding [and, consequently, *action*] becomes orderly." Lu Chi, the dedicated student of Confucius, reminds us that the art of letters has saved governments from certain ruin. He finds within the study of writing itself a way to set his own life in order. Studying Chinese, the Japanese literati picked up Lu Chi's habit of discussing poetry in terms of form and content. And from the fifth-century Chinese scholar Liu Hsieh, drew the term *amari no kokoro,* a translation of Liu's original *yu wei,* or "after-taste." As a critical term, it would be used and re-shaped, and used again, still a part of literary evaluation in the late twentieth century. Narihira says of a poem in the *Kokinshu,* "*Kokoro amarite—kotoba tarazu,*" or "Plenty of heart; not enough words." Kuronushi says, "*Kokoro okashikute, sama iyashi,*" or "Interesting *kokoro,* but a rather common form." The poet strives for a quality called *amari no kokoro,* meaning that the heart/soul of the poem must reach far beyond the words themselves.

For Bashō, this most often meant a resonance found in nature. When he invokes the call of the little mountain bird, *kakkodori,* the name of the bird (a cuckoo) invokes its lonely cry. Things are as they are. Insight permits him to perceive a natural poignancy in the beauty of temporal things, a word identifying a bird-call—*mono no aware. Aware* originally meant simply emotion initiated by engagement of the senses. In its own way, this phraše is Japan's equivalent of William Carlos Williams's dictum, "No ideas but in things," equally misappropriated, misapplied, and misunderstood. In *The World of the Shining Prince* (Alfred A. Knopf, 1964), Ivan Morris's study of *The Tale of Genji,* Morris says of *aware,* "In its widest sense it was an interjection or adjective referring to the emotional quality inherent in objects, people, nature, and art, and by extension it applied to a person's internal response to emotional aspects of the external world . . . in Murasaki's time [ca. 1000 A.D.] *aware* still retained its early catholic range, its most characteristic use in *The Tale of Genji* is to suggest the pathos inherent in the beauty of the outer world, a beauty that is inexorably fated to disappear together with the observer. Buddhist doctrines about the evanescence of all living things naturally influenced this particular content of the word, but the stress in *aware* was always on direct emotional experience rather than on religious understanding. *Aware* never entirely lost its simple interjectional sense of 'Ah!'"

As a more purely critical term in later centuries, *aware* identified a particular quality of elegant sadness, a poignant temporality, a quality found in abundance, for instance, in the novels of Kawabata Yasunari. In failing health, Bashō found plenty of resonance in temporal life.

Tsurayuki, whose own diary would provide a model for Bashō seven hundred years later, would ruminate on the art of letters during his sojourn through Tosa Province in the south of Shikoku Island in 936. In his preface to the *Kokinshu,* Tsurayuki lists several sources for inspiration in poetry, all melancholy in one way or another: "Looking at falling blossoms on a spring morning; sighing over snows and waves which reflect the passing years; remembering a fall from fortune into loneliness." Tsurayuki's proclivity for melancholy perhaps explains the general tone of the *Kokinshu.* This, too, is *mono no aware.*

At the time of the *Man'yoshu,* Zen was being brought to Japan via a steady stream of Japanese scholars returning from China. Along with Zen equations and conversations, they also brought with them Chinese poetics, which included a Confucian faith in the power of the right word rightly used. The attitude is paradoxical: the Zen poet believes the real poetry lies somewhere beyond the words themselves, but, like a good Confucian, believes simultaneously that only the perfect word perfectly placed has the power to reveal the "meaning" or experience of the poem.

Ki no Tsurayuki's co-compiler of the *Kokinshu,* Mibu no Tadamine

(868–965), introduced another new term to the Japanese critical canon
by praising a quality in certain poems which he called *yugen*, a word
borrowed from Chinese Buddhist writing and which was used to identify
"depth of meaning," a character made by combining the character for
"dim" or "dark" with the character identifying a deep, reddish-black
color. But Tadamine uses *yugen* to mean "aesthetic feeling *not explicitly
expressed*." He wanted to identify subtleties and implications by adopting
the term. Over the course of the next hundred or so years, the term would
also be adopted by Zennists to define "ghostly qualities" as in ink paintings. But the term's origin lies within seventh-century Chinese Buddhist
literary terminology. As an aesthetic concept it was to be esteemed
throughout the medieval period. An excellent study of Buddhism and
literary arts in medieval Japan, William R. LaFleur's *The Karma of Words*
(University of California, 1983), devotes an entire chapter to *yugen*.

It was also the compilation of the *Kokinshu* which institutionalized the
makura-kotoba, or "pillow word," in Japanese poetics. Although such
devices appear in the *Man'yoshu*, they appear with far less frequency,
indicating that they were not widely understood. But by the time of the
Kokinshu, most everyone was aware that "clouds and rain" might mean
sexual congress as well as weather patterns. The *makura-kotoba* often
permitted a poet to speak in double entendres or to disguise emotions; it
was both "polite" and metaphoric. Along with the "pillow word," the
apprentice poet also learned how to make use of the *kake-kotoba*, or
"pivot word," which would later become central to the composition of
haiku. It is a play on different meanings of a word which links two phrases.
It is virtually *never* translatable. Consequently, when we read haiku in
translation, it is usually severely "dumbed down," to borrow Willis Hawley's phrase. The pivot word creates deliberate ambiguity, often implying
polysignation. The pillow word and the pivot word would later become
subjects to be re-assessed and discussed and re-examined time and again.

As this critical vocabulary developed, poets learned new ways to discuss
the *kajitsu*, or formal aspects of a poem. The *ka* is the "beautiful surface
of the poem," and the *jitsu* is the "substantial core."

Studying the "beautiful surface" of the poem along with its interior
structure, Fujiwara no Kinto (966–1041) composed his *Nine Steps of
Waka* in order to establish standards based almost solely upon critical
fashion. Certain rhymes were taboo at a poem's closure. Certain vowel
sounds should be repeated at particular intervals. Rather than a general
and moral and emotional discourse such as Lu Chi's, or those of Tsurayuki

and Tadamine, Kinto relies upon reasoned study of the architecture of the poem for his aesthetic. His critical vocabulary is that of the poem's structure. His anthology, *Shuishu,* has never enjoyed either the popularity or the controversy of the *Kokinshu* and *Shin-kokinshu.*

Zen demolishes much of this kind of literary criticism by pointing out that, seen from the core, the surface is very deep; inasmuch as cause leads to effect, effect in turn produces cause. A poem's "depth" cannot be created by packing the poem with allusions and implications—hermetics alone. Still, "surface" and "core" may be useful terms for establishing a necessary dialectic; they provide frames for reference.

As this critical vocabulary came into use, it was balanced by a vocabulary of the emotions. A contemporary of Saigyō, Fujiwara Sadaie, also called Teika (1162–1241), attacked structural criticism as hopelessly inadequate. "Every poem," he said, "must have *kokoro.* A poem without *kokoro* is not—cannot be—a true poem; it is only an intellectual exercise." Thus, by combining a vocabulary for the apparatus of poetry with a vocabulary for the emotional states of poetry, Teika believed, a poem could then be examined and judged. His insistence upon the true poem's *kokoro* returns the experience of the poem to human dimensions.

Another term in use at the time, *kokai,* expressed a feeling of regret after a poem, a consequence of the poet having failed to think sufficiently deeply prior to its composition. It was a criticism not often applied to Bashō, nor to other poets working in the Zen tradition. Bashō sought a natural spontaneity, a poetry which would indulge no regrets of any kind. Zen discipline is built in part around the idea of truth articulated in spontaneous response. A "correct" response to a Zen *kōan,* for instance, need not be rational or logical. Bashō sought a poetry which was a natural outgrowth of being Bashō, of living in this world, of making the journey itself one's home. Two hundred years earlier, the Zen monk Ikkyū Sōjun wrote, *"Ame furaba fure, kaze fukaba fuke."* ("If it rains, let it rain; if it blows, let it blow.") Bashō spent many years attempting to learn how to listen as things speak for themselves. No regrets. He refused to be anthropocentric. Seeing the beautiful islands off the coast of Matsushima, he wrote:

Matsushima ya
ah Matsushima ya
Matsushima ya

It is the sort of poem which can be done once, and once only. But it is quintessentially Bashō, both playful and inspired, yet with a bit of *mono no aware,* a trace of the pathos of beautiful mortality. Simple as it is, the poem implies co-dependent origination, physical landscape, and a breathless—almost speechless—reverence.

Just as Bashō learned from Ikkyū, he learned from Ikkyū's friend, Rikyu, that each tea ceremony is the only tea ceremony. Therefore, each poem is the only poem. Each moment is the only moment in which one can be fully aware. Standing on the shore, he saw dozens of tiny islands carved by tides, wind-twisted pines rising at sharp angles. *Matsu* means "pine"; *shima* is "island." *Ya* indicates subject, but also works simultaneously as an exclamation. It functions as a *kireji,* or "cutting word." The township on the mainland is itself called Matsushima. Bashō entered Matsushima by boat in June, 1689, so taken by its beauty that he declared it to have been made by Oyamazumi, god of the mountains.

Bashō walked and dreamed along the beach at Ojima beneath the moon of Matsushima. From his pack, he withdrew a poem written by a friend and former teacher, Sodo, an acknowledged haiku master. The poem describes Matsushima and is written in Chinese. And another, a poem in Japanese about Matsugaura-shima composed by an Edo doctor, Hara Anteki. The poems, Bashō says, are his companions during a sleepless night.

Two days later, he visited the elegant temple Zuiganji, founded thirty-two generations earlier by Makabe no Heishiro upon his return from a decade of studies in China. Bashō would wonder whether it might be the gates of "Buddha-land." But Bashō was no flowerchild wandering in Lotus Land. His journey is a pilgrimage; it is a journey into the interior of the self as much as a travelogue; it is a vision quest which concludes in *insight.* But there *is* no conclusion. The journey itself is home. The means is the end just as it is the beginning.

Bashō visited temples only in part because he was himself a Zennist. Temples often provided rooms for wayfarers, and the food, if simple, was good. The conversation was of a kind only the literate enjoy. Bashō, among the most literate of his time, seems to be everywhere in the presence of history. The *Oku no hosomichi* overflows with place-names, famous scenes, literary Chinese and Buddhist allusions, echoes called *honkadori,* borrowed or quoted lines, and paraphrases. But he didn't stay at temples during his famous journey; he rarely stayed at inns; he was generally and generously entertained by local *haikai* poets and put up by wealthy families. He enjoyed his celebrity and its benefits.

His literary and spiritual lineage included Kamo no Chomei (1154–1216), *Shin-kokinshu* poet, author of the *Mumyōsho,* a kind of manual of writing, and of the *Hojōki,* an account of Chomei's years in a "ten foot square hut" following a series of calamities in Kyoto. Like Chomei, Bashō was deeply versed in Chinese and Japanese literature, philosophy, and history; and like Chomei, he enjoyed talking with working people everywhere.

After "abandoning the world," Chomei moved to the mountains on the outskirts of Kyoto. But his was not the life of the Zen ascetic. He made very regular trips to town if for no other reason than to listen to the people he met there. Reading the *Hojōki,* it is easy to forget that Chomei served as a kind of journalist, a deeply compassionate witness to the incredible suffering of people during his lifetime. Chomei's world was shaken to the core when winds spread a great fire through Kyoto, leveling a third of the capital city in 1177. In 1181, a famine began which lasted two years. Those and other calamities informed Chomei's deep sense of compassion. Just as a disciple of Sakyamuni, Vimalakirti, served as a model for Chomei's retreat, Bashō found in Chomei a model for compassionate engagement with others. Chomei had written, "Trivial things spoken along the way enliven the faith of my awakened heart."

Chomei's interest in people in general was a trait Bashō shared. And unlike Saigyō, Kamo no Chomei could not separate his life from his art. Bashō enjoyed the possibility of making a living from the writing of haiku, and therefore his art and life were indeed one. He also felt a deep connection to history. He speaks as though all eternity were only yesterday, each memory vivid, the historical figures themselves almost contemporary; he speaks confidentially, expecting his reader to be versed in details so that his own brief journal may serve to call up enormous resonances, ghosts at every turn. But Bashō doesn't "pack" his lines with references. His subjects and his knowledge flow freely, almost casually, through his writing.

Chomei bears witness to countless thousands of deaths after a great fire swept Kyoto, and says, "They die in the morning and are born in the evening like bubbles on water." Bashō walks across the plain where a great battle once raged. Only empty fields remain. The landscape reminds him of a poem by Tu Fu (712–770) in which the T'ang poet surveyed a similar scene and wrote,

> The whole country devastated,
> only mountains and rivers remain.
> In springtime, at the ruined castle,
> the grass is always green.

For Bashō, the grass blowing in the breeze seems especially poignant, so much so that his eyes well into tears. If Tu Fu, both as a poet and as a man, is a fit model—to be emulated rather than copied—Bashō is reminded of how little we have learned from all our interminable warfare and bloodshed. The wind blows. The grasses bend. Bashō moistens his brush months later and writes, remembering,

Natsugusa ya	Summer grasses—
tsuwamono domo ga	after great soldiers'
yume no ato	imperial dreams.

His echo of Tu Fu underscores the profound irony. For Bashō, the journey into the interior of the way of poetry had been long and arduous. His simple "summer grasses" haiku carried within it the sort of resonance he sought. The grasses with their plethora of associations, the ghosts of Hidehira, Yoritomo, and Yoshitsune, an allusion drawn from a famous Noh drama—Bashō framed his verse with rich and complex historical, literary, and philosophical associations. The poem implies that the grasses are the *only consequence* of the warriors' dreams, that the grasses are all that remains, a Buddhist parallel to the Bible's "dust into dust," the accompanying prose drawing the reader into a vast network of allusion.

The haiku itself is spare, clean, swift as a boning knife. The melopoeia combines *a, o,* and *u* sounds: *tsu, gu* in line 1; *tsu* and *yu* in lines 2 and 3; the *tsu* sound is very quick, almost to the point of silence. The *a* sound punctuates the whole poem: *na, sa, ya* among the five syllables of line 1; *wa* and *ga* among the seven syllables of line 2, the four remaining being *mono* and *domo;* and a semiconcluding *a* before *to.* Among the seventeen syllables are six *a* syllables, six *o* syllables, and four *u* syllables.

The Western reader, accustomed to being conscious of reading translation and having fallen into the slothful and unrewarding habit of reading poetry silently, often misses Bashō's ear by neglecting the *Romaji,* or "Romanized" Japanese so frequently printed with the poems. Onomatopoeia, rhyme, and slant rhyme are Bashō's favorite tools, and he uses them like no one else in Japanese literature. He wrote from within the body; his poems are full of breath and sound as well as images and allusions.

What Bashō read, he read deeply and attentively. As a poet, he had blossomed slowly, ever-changing, constantly learning. The poetry of his twenties and thirties is competent and generally undistinguished. It is the learned poetry of received ideas composed by a good mind. It lacks breadth and depth of vision. But his interest in Chinese poetry continued to grow. He studied Tu Fu (To Ho in Japanese) assiduously during his twenties and thirties, and he read Li T'ai-po (Rihaku in Japanese). Along with the Chinese poets, he traveled with a copy of *Chuang Tzu.* He seems to have struggled with Zen discipline and Chinese poetry and philosophy all during his thirties, and the result was a poetry at first clearly derivative, but later becoming more his own as he grew into his studies. Upon entering his forties, Bashō's verse changed. He learned to be comfortable with his teachers and with his own scholarship. His Zen practice had steadied his vision. Fewer aspirations stood in his way.

Born in 1644 in Ueno, Iga Province, approximately thirty miles southeast from Kyoto, the son of Matsuo Yozaemon, a low-ranking samurai, Bashō had at least one elder brother and four sisters. As a young man, he served in the household of a higher-ranking local samurai, Todo Shinshichiro, becoming a companion to his son, Yoshitada, whose "haiku name" was Sengin. Bashō often joined his master in composing the linked verses called *haikai,* but was still known by his samurai name, Matsuo Munefusa, despite having taken his first haiku name, Sobo. Bashō also had a common-law wife at this time, Jutei, who later became a nun. And although there is little verifiable information on these years, Bashō seems to have experimented a good deal. He would later say upon reflection, "I at one time coveted an official post," and "There was a time when I became fascinated with the ways of homosexual love."

Whether because of a complicated love-life or whether as a result of the death of his friend and master, Sengin, Bashō apparently simply wandered off sometime around 1667, leaving behind his samurai name and position. It was not unique for a man like Bashō to leave samurai society. Many who did so became monks. Some early biographies claim he went to Kyoto to study philosophy, poetry, and calligraphy. He re-emerged in 1672 as editor and commentator on a volume of haikai, *The Seashell Game* (*Kai Oi*). With contributions from about thirty poets, *The Seashell Game* shows Bashō to be witty, deeply knowledgeable, and rather light-hearted. It was well-enough received to encourage him to move to Edo (present-day Tokyo).

While it is not clear whether he made his living in Edo working as a haiku poet and teacher, Bashō does tell us that those first years in the growing city were not easy ones. He would later recall that he was torn between the desire to become a great poet and the desire to simply give up verse altogether. But his verse was, in many ways, his life. He continued to study and to write. And he continued to attract students, a number of whom were, like himself, drop-outs from samurai or *bushido* society who also rejected the vulgar values of the class below the samurai, the *chonin*, or urban merchant class. Bashō believed literature provided an alternative set of values which he called *fuga no michi*, "the way of elegance." He claimed that his life was stitched together by "the single thread of art" which permitted him to follow "no religious law" and no popular customs.

Robert Aitken's study of Bashō, *A Zen Wave* (Weatherhill, 1978), draws many parallels between Bashō's attitude and Zen poetics. But it is mistaken to think Bashō retreated into Buddhism. He admired the Zen mind; the "Buddhism" attached to Zen was, to him, almost superfluous. And he did, during his years in Edo, study Zen under the priest Butchō (1642–1715), apparently even to the point of considering the monastic life, but whether to escape from decadent culture or as a philosophical passion remains unclear. Despite his ability to attract students, he seems to have spent much of the time in a state of perpetual despondency, loneliness everywhere crowding in on him. No doubt this state of mind was compounded as a result of chronically poor health, but Bashō was also engaging true *sabishi*, a spiritual "loneliness" which served haikai culture in much the same way *mu*, or "nothingness," served Zen. Achieving true spiritual poverty, true inner emptiness, everything becomes our own. This is a path leading directly toward selflessness, toward *kensho*, or "enlightenment."

In the winter of 1680, his students built him a small hut where he could establish a permanent home. In the spring, someone planted a banana (or *bashō*) tree in the yard, giving the hut, "Bashō-an," its name, and the poet a new *nom de plume*. Bashō-an burned to the ground when a fire swept through the neighborhood in the winter of 1682. Friends and disciples built a new Bashō-an during the winter of 1683. His disciples were also beginning to earn names of their own. Bashō wrote of one, Kikaku, that his poems contained the "spiritual broth" of Tu Fu. But his followers were also time-consuming. And there were suddenly disciples *of* his disciples, literally hundreds of "Bashō group" poets springing up. More and more projects were offered for his possible participation. He longed for quietude.

During 1684 and early 1685, the poet traveled to Kyoto, Nara, and his old home in Ueno, and composed *Journey of a Weather-beaten Skeleton,* the first of his travel journals and one notable for its constant pathos. His mother had died in Ueno. The trip was a long eight months, arduous and extremely dangerous. The forty-year-old poet had spent thirty years in Iga and a decade in Edo before beginning the wanderer's life for which he became so famous. Donald Keene has said this first travel journal reads as though it were translated from Chinese, allusions and parallels drawn from Ch'an (Zen) literature in nearly every line. Bashō was struggling to achieve a resonance between the fleeting moment and the eternal, between the instant of awareness and the vast endless Void of Zen.

In 1687, he traveled with his friend, Sora, and a Zen monk to Kashima Shrine, fifty miles east of Edo, where, among other things, Bashō visited his Zen master, Butchō, who had retired there. His record of this trip, *A Visit to Kashima Shrine,* is very brief, as is his *Visit to Sarashina Village,* each the result of a short "moon-viewing" journey to a rustic setting. At Kashima, they were greeted by a rainstorm, but at Sarashina, Bashō watched the moon rise through the trees, offered a toast with his companions, and was given a cup by the innkeeper, a cup which caught his attention: "The innkeeper brought us cups that were larger than usual, with crude lacquer designs. . . . I was fascinated with those cups . . . and it was because of the locale."

Bashō, after flirting with dense Chinese diction, was turning toward *sabi,* an elegant simplicity tinged with the flavor of loneliness. *Sabi* comes from the more pure "loneliness" of *sabishi.* It was an idea which fit perfectly with his notion of *fuga no michi,* "the way of elegance," together with his rejection of bourgeois society. Elegant simplicity. Visiting the rustic village of Sarashina to view the moon, the poet is given a cup by an innkeeper, and he examines it closely by moonlight and lamplight, his imagination held captive by the working hands of some villager. His idea of *sabi* has about it elements of *yugen, mono no aware,* and plenty of *kokoro.* His poetry, so indebted to Japanese and Chinese classics, could be simplified; he could find a poetry which would leave the reader with a sense of *sabi.* Perhaps he had followed classical Chinese rhetorical conventions a bit too closely. He wanted to make images which positively radiated with reality. He turned the sake cup in his hand, and as he did so, his mind turned.

During his years of Zen training, he had spoken of striving to achieve the "religious flavor" of the poetry of Han Shan (Kanzan in Japanese, Cold Mountain in English); he had wanted to "clothe in Japanese language" the poetry of Po Chu-i. But in *A Visit to Kashima Shrine,* he chose a far simpler syntax, writing almost exclusively in *kana,* the Japanese phonetic alphabet, rather than in *kanji,* or Chinese written characters.

In late 1687, Bashō had made another journey, visiting Ise, Nagoya, Iga, Yoshino, and Nara, traveling with a disciple who had been exiled. The writing from this journey would not be published until 1709, more than ten years after the poet's death. Scholars date completion of the *Manuscript in My Knapsack (Oi no kobumi)* at about 1691, the same time the poet was writing *Oku no hosomichi.* He says in the *Knapsack* manuscript that "Nobody has succeeded in making any improvement in travel diaries since Ki no Tsurayuki, Chomei, and the nun Abutsu . . . the rest have merely imitated." Clearly, he was searching for a style which could reinvigorate an ancient form. He must have felt that he had gained a powerful knowledge which only a simple style could accommodate. He also said in the *Knapsack* manuscript, "Saigyō's waka, Sogi's renga, / Sesshu's sumi, Rikyu's tea, — / the spirit which moves them is one spirit."

Whether he had arrived at his mature style by that early morning in late March, 1689, he was eager to begin his journey north to Sendai and on to Hiraizumi, where the Fujiwara clan had flourished and perished. He would then push west, cross the mountains, turn south down the west coast of Honshu, then turn east again toward Ise, the vast majority of the trip made on foot. He left behind the idiosyncrasies and frivolities of the Teitoku and Danrin schools of haikai. He left perhaps as many as sixty students of the Bashō School who, in turn, were acquiring students of their own.

When his disciple Kikaku over-praised a Bashō image of a cold fish on a fish-monger's shelf, saying he had attained "mystery and depth," Bashō replied that what he most valued was the poem's "ordinariness." He had come almost full circle from the densely allusive Chinese style into a truly elegant simplicity which was in no way frivolous. He had elevated the haikai from word-play into lyric poetry, from a game played by poetasters into a spiritual dimension. "Abide by rules, " Bashō said, "then throw them out!—only *then* may you achieve true freedom." Bashō's freedom expressed itself by redefining haiku as a complete thing, a full lyric form capable of handling complex data and emotional depth and spiritual seriousness while still retaining some element of playfulness.

Kung-fu Tze says, "Only the one who attains perfect sincerity under Heaven may discover one's 'true nature.' One who accomplishes this participates fully in the transformation of Heaven and Earth, and being fully human, becomes with them a third thing." Knowing this, Bashō tells his students, "Do not simply follow the footsteps of the Ancients; seek what they sought." In order to avoid simply filling the ancient footsteps of his predecessors, Bashō studies them assiduously, attentively. And when he has had his fill of ancient poets and students and the infinite dialectic that is literature and art, when his heart is filled with wanderlust, he chooses a traveling companion, fills a small pack with essentials—and, of course, a few *hanamuke*—and walks off into the dawn, into history, into the geography of the soul which makes the journey home.

AFTERWORD

Some Days:
The Years at Copper Canyon Press

The first printed book, *The Diamond Sutra,* was the final teaching of the Buddha, a commentary on the *Prajnaparamita,* or "Perfection of Wisdom." The year was 868 A.D., seven hundred years prior to Gutenberg's re-invention of movable type in the West. The text, *Vajrachedika,* or "Diamond-cutter," came from the Sanskrit, translated into Chinese in the fifth century. Our word diamond is itself derived from the Sanskrit *dyu,* meaning "luminous one," symbolizing the brilliance of knowing at its deepest level. The second syllable arrives via the Greek *adamas,* "the indomitable." The diamond, Greeks believed, exerted enormous physical and spiritual influence over humanity. And the *vajra* of *Vajrachedika* is the "diamond sceptre" of Indra, symbolizing the highest spiritual power used to ward off evil. A holder of such powers is called Vajrasempa, or "diamond-souled." The Buddhist practice of Vajrayana recognizes the direct connection between the spiritual and immediate life experience. Vajrayana is the path of "direct energy."

The monks who undertook the printing of *The Diamond Sutra* did so only in part to spread its teaching; the work itself was *vajrayana,* a link between spiritual and immediate daily life. In Zen, the word and the deed are one. Ever since the time of the Oracle Bones, long before Confucius, the Chinese believed, as did the rest of the world, that words held magic powers. *Vajra-yana* unites "means and end" irrefutably.

We were first drawn to study the art of the printed book by purely practical considerations: because our lives are centered in and by books, we undertook the study of their elemental nomenclature. At this writing, it has been fifteen years almost to the day since we hauled a huge old proofing press up three flights of tenement steps in Denver and installed it in our kitchen. That single event began a course of study which rapidly became a way of life, uniting the spiritual search with our daily physical world.

The tradition of the printed book is, among the general populace, one of the least understood of all contributions to culture. The printer's art has been a struggle to achieve invisibility, to accomplish the impossible. It is not enough to attend to the innumerable details of a single book, from letter-forms to margins, from cover design to its integration with text design, from leading between lines of type to overall shape and feel of the book. Some of these considerations are purely practical, having to do with readability or with attracting the eye of the potential buyer. Other considerations include visual or aesthetic concerns, permanence of colors, durability, and appropriate use of materials.

The printed book is not divorced from spiritual economics. By studying the traditions of the book, one comes to understand the necessity of maintaining links between the physical experience of the book itself and its spiritual life.

In 1972, Stephen Berg published a small volume of poems from the Aztec, *Nothing in the Word* (Mushinsha), which included this poem:

> is the word of god with us
> on earth
> it is in the book of your heart
> it is your song

The poem reminded us of our real work during the first days of the press. It also reminds one that the tenth-century Japanese classic anthology, the *Kokinshu,* says in its introduction, "Poetry begins in the heart." The Chinese character *hsin* (in Japanese *kokoro*) means both heart and mind. When we first met the Chinese calligrapher Yim Tse, he presented us with a scroll which reads, "Great things begin in the heart." Of course, the earliest Chinese books were scrolls, and the educated mind was expected to know "about five cartloads" and have them on hand. A good writer was expected to produce a five-foot shelf: ten thousand poems from Po Chu-i, over thirty thousand from Shotetsu! Our work is informed by this spirit of plenitude, and characterized by our choosing quality over quantity, means over ends. "One who obtains has little," Lao Tzu says. "One who scatters has much."

In 1973, as we completed production of our first book, we worked full time at menial jobs. Printing and studies were relegated to late nights and weekends. But we published our first three books in tiny editions, and our fourth in a reasonably large one. We had begun to fill our shelf and committed our lives to learning.

In the spring of 1974, we moved to Port Townsend, Washington, to become press-in-residence with the arts organization Centrum, moving our printing equipment into a large building at the back corner of a small Army fort built at the turn of the century and which had since become a state park. From these quarters, we've seen more than a hundred volumes of poetry through production.

Neither of us makes a living at the press. But we make a life here. In the fifteen years we've served as editors and publishers, private contributions to the press could almost be counted on the fingers of one hand. But they are doubly valued because they have come from people who believe as we do in the value and use of poetry. We have no fund-raisers on payroll, no full-time marketing director, no advertising department as such. Nor have we dreamed of an ever-expanding publishing empire. In recent years, we have not sought growth except for the size of our editions. Rather, we commit ourselves to doing well with few hands, to paraphrase Wendell Berry, that which is usually done poorly by many. We publish poetry because we learn from poetry that which cannot be learned in prose. We draw a portion of our livelihood from the press and supplement that with outside income from occasional employment.

Necessity dictated a life of labor-intensive economics rather than the customary capital-intensive structure of corporate publishing. We have remained generalists rather than becoming specialists. Poetry is recognized as Art, but is generally poorly supported. An October, 1987, story in the *Seattle Times* is typical: The Corporate Council for the Arts, a Seattle foundation created in 1976 by the regional business community, announced grants totaling $1.36 million. *None* of this money recognized writers or publishers of serious literature. The same newspaper published a feature article, "The State of the Arts," on Sunday, January 8, 1989, in which literature was not even mentioned.

Yet, through a combination of personal commitment and generous grants from the National Endowment for the Arts, we persist.

In 1984, Mary Jane Knecht joined the press as office manager, and in 1986, we joined Consortium in order to establish a coast-to-coast network of books sales representatives and to streamline distribution. The "business" of publishing and selling books is an uneasy ally with the business of the soul, but the work is indeed one work. "One lamp lights a hundred thousand lamps, and the darkness is made bright, and the brightness never ends."

Some days we read an article in *Publishers Weekly* about how somebody made millions of dollars on some insta-book by a celebrity, and we wonder why we publish poetry at all. Other days, we read proofs for a new book and are humbled by the force and beauty of its truth. Some days we realize just how very little we knew about publishing or printing when we began and it staggers us to think that we have not only survived, but have managed somehow to make an actual contribution to poetry and to the tradition of the printed book. It is possible in these United States to earn one's livelihood by writing prose. But no poet in the country lives on royalties alone.

It is miraculous, isn't it, that poetry can exist in this world at all? Somehow a rhythm or a sound reaches or arises from the innermost core of a poet's being, and a line or phrase begins to form; and then another line, and yet another. Weeks, months, years later, the poet is still repeating lines, listening, re-visioning the experience in order to experience the poem. Finally, the day comes when the poet feels confident with the work and it goes into the mail.

Some days go by, filled with bits of anxiety, with fear and elation, with hopes or dreams or doubts.

One day, the poet receives a package. It is a small, pliable brown bag stapled at the end. It really doesn't look like much. It is several years since that first impulse toward song. Inside the bag, a couple of "advance" copies of a paperbound book. Inside each copy of each book, small black squiggles on the page tell the literate reader not only what to say, but how to say it in a particular rhythm in order to understand, through the saying of the words, more than the words themselves say.

Some days go by. Eventually, copies of the book move from a warehouse to shelves in nooks and crannies of bookstores where more days pass. Poetry is not news that makes news. One day, someone buys a copy and takes it away and becomes bemused, enchanted, entranced. This reader tells someone else, who then also buys a copy. Thousands of copies get into people's hands in exactly this way, and it is miraculous.

But the poetry is not in the book. Our love is in the book right beside the love and anger of the poet. But only the words of the poem are printed there. The poetry is right where it always was, shining and indomitable like a diamond in the heart.

Index

Design by John D. Berry. Text set in Sabon by Meriden-Stinehour Press, Lunenburg, Vermont. Composition of additional front matter for this edition by John D. Berry Design. *Printed by McNaughton & Gunn.*